Young Children as Artists

From the moment a child is born, they interact with the sensory world, looking at colours, feeling textures; constructing mental and physical images of what they see and experience. Within all early years settings and into primary school, the aim for the practitioner is to provide as many opportunities as possible to stimulate, excite and ignite the visual and tactile imagination of the young children they teach.

Young Children as Artists considers how art can be managed, understood and relished as an essential ingredient towards the creative potential of each unique young child. The book focuses, on how to enjoy, celebrate and extend what a young child can do in art and show how engaged adults and the wider school community can become confident participants in the process of early years art making.

Full of practical advice, on how to design, develop, resource and extend art and design environments within the early years setting, the book covers:

- Developing skills for positive and participative adult interaction and engagement
- Understanding and analysing child involvement in art
- Planning for opportunities and responding to observation and schema in art and design
- Practical suggestions for activities and resources (inside and out)
- Ideas to explore sensory development and awareness
- Ways to manage and savour the art transition into KS1
- Ways to encourage parental participation and their understanding of the art process with their children
- Opportunities to engage with practising artists

This book will help to invigorate the art experiences offered in your early years setting by considering what is accessible, individual, inspiring and meaningful for young children and how you can best support their formative paths of enquiry.

Suzy Tutchell is Senior Lecturer in Education (Early Years and Art) at the University of Winchester. She has extensive experience of documenting and promoting creative learning through the Early Years Foundation Stage, and continuing and extending learning through creativity, curiosity and imagination into KS1 and 2.

Young Children as Artists

Art and Design in the Early Years and Key Stage 1

Suzy Tutchell

Routledge
Taylor & Francis Group
LONDON AND NEW YORK

First published 2014
by Routledge
2 Park Square, Milton Park, Abingdon, Oxon, OX14 4RN

and by Routledge
711 Third Avenue, New York, NY 10017

Routledge is an imprint of the Taylor & Francis Group, an informa business

British Library Cataloguing in Publication Data
A catalogue record for this book is available from the British Library

Library of Congress Cataloging in Publication Data
Tutchell, Suzy, author.
Young children as artists: art and design in the early years and key stage 1/
Suzy Tutchell. – First edition.
pages cm
1. Art – Study and teaching (Early childhood). 2. Creative ability in children.
I. Title.
LB1139.5.A78T87 2014
372.5 – dc23

ISBN: 978-0-415-51725-6 (hbk)
ISBN: 978-0-415-51727-0 (pbk)
ISBN: 978-0-203-12373-7 (ebk)

Typeset in Celeste and Gill Sans
by Florence Production Ltd, Stoodleigh, Devon, UK

MIX
Paper from responsible sources
FSC
www.fsc.org
FSC® C013056

Printed and bound in Great Britain by
TJ International Ltd, Padstow, Cornwall

For two young artists, Maia and Joel

Contents

Illustrations

Plates

Figures

Illustrations

Tables

Acknowledgements

My thanks go to those inspiring minds who contributed to the book:

- Helena Nilsson and the children at Wildflowers Kindergarten
- Staff and children at Grandpont Nursery School, Oxford
- Jo Sloley, Jo Price and the EYFS children at St Ebbe's Primary School, Oxford
- Sandra Sherlock, registered childminder, Kingston-upon-Thames
- Hazelwood Infant School, Southampton
- The Lawns Nursery School, Windsor
- Maidenhead Nursery School, Maidenhead
- South Ascot Village Nursery School, Ascot
- Cookham Nursery School, Cookham
- Old Town First School and Nursery, Poole
- Open Sesame artists: Clare Halstead, Jenny Staff, Jane Gordon, Anne Colvin, Alex Sutton-Vane, Rebecca Parrant, Rosie Heafford, Lauren van Niekerk
- Open Sesame practitioners and settings:
  - Madelaine Dailey, Stepping Stones Nursery, Bognor Regis
  - Chris O'Dwyer, Our Lady Queen of Heaven Pre-school, Crawley
  - Lisa Smith, Colgate Pre-school, Colgate, Horsham
  - Maddie Dalley, The A House Pre-school, Shoreham
  - Faye Robinson, Beach House Day Nursery, Hassocks
  - Anne Shrieves, Woodstock Day Nursery, Worthing
  - Caroline Taub, The Ark Nursery, Bolney
  - Laura Griffiths, Lancing Children and Family Centre Nursery, Lancing

To the artists, Bob and Roberta Smith, for permission to use their wonderfully powerful image to help open the book.

A big thank you to Zoe for her WRAP support!

I am grateful to my critical friend Sian who managed to help reinvigorate me with her supportive and constructive comments.

Thank you to both Vicky and Maria for their wonderfully inspiring contributions to the book.

To my parents for their never-ending ability and commitment to seeing the joy and humour of young children in their roles as teachers, parents and grandparents.

And finally to Steve for his endless patience, interest, positivity and encouragement.

Introduction

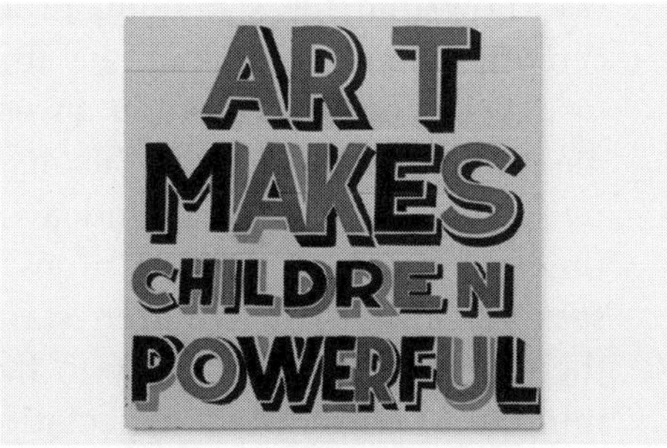

Figure 0.1 Bob and Roberta Smith, *Art Makes Children Powerful*, 2012: Signwriter's Paint on Board, 60 x 60 cm, 23⅝ x 23⅝ in. (Courtesy of the Artist and Hales Gallery, London; copyright of the artist.)

Art releases the imaginative spirit within an individual – it makes visible and real the creative discovery that defines ideologies, thoughts and understandings in the most wonderful, iconoclastic and exciting way. Art permits the individual to play with extraordinary ideas and form magical connotations of these concepts. To a child, art serves as a visually and haptically rich platform from which to improvise with the unknown and known delights of exploring, making, creating and transforming. Their initial art-making experiences are absolutely and totally owned by them and this is one very powerful fact.

Art allows children to share their inner worlds in ways that cannot be as easily communicated through other forms. It makes available to children a richness of opportunity to investigate ideas and feelings in relation to an external world of things seen and an internal world of things imagined. Art is about the child and their ways of looking, seeing and feeling, which can be translated, particularly for the pre-verbal child, through making and creating – a language which is about their hands, eyes and minds. Art motivates a young child's embodied imagination where they are able to transcend and interpret a space that can tell themselves about themselves.

Young children's sensorimotor skills, combined with their developing sensory awareness, cast moments of great power in the making experience as they continue to discover aspects of their emerging and expressively alert characters. Their ability to work as 'artists' is unselfconscious and dynamic. They capture the essence of what it means to create visual art – bringing new imaginative ideas into existence through their playful endeavours.

Introduction

> Watching children at play allows us to marvel at young children's flexibility of thinking and their unselfconscious ability to flick from one mode of representation to another. These are capabilities that many artists spend their lives trying to recapture.
>
> (Anning and Ring, 2004: 3)

What a privilege it is, as teaching adults, to have the opportunity in our everyday working lives to witness such young creativity. Kudryavtsev (2011) passionately describes children as 'personifications of divine creativity that an adult creator should look up to'. Recognition of this privilege should drive us to do the right thing by the child and hold on to the very magic that is art education. The 'magic of art' (Allen-Harris, 2008) should follow the child throughout their primary school experience, into the lives of their secondary selves. Unfortunately, we know that the schooling process in relation to the maturation of children can often deprecate the innate abilities of children to use their imaginations and to develop creative thought through art. The opportunities of the 'worthwhile meat of art' (Wilson and Wilson, 1977) become less frequent, the children often more sedentary in their endeavours, and prescribed art activities dictated by timetable pressures are, at times, more visible. The very worst scenario of this sees generations of children start out life excited about art – where they see themselves as artists – only to fade as the school years progress, as a result of inhibition, prescriptive expectation, routinal hindrances and a lack of freedom to express.

This book is largely focussed on savouring, understanding, sharing and supporting young children and their art. Our definition of 'young children' relates to the 0–7 age group, purposefully floundering the current educational system which compartmentalises a five- to seven-year-old into a key stage that does not always recognise them as 'young' and is led by expectations that often relate to target setting. Let us be aware of the fact that six or seven years of age hardly amounts to many years of existence in our world. The golden age of young childhood is still very much alive in Key Stage 1 and something to be cherished as opposed to rushing them through it. We may not be able to change for the forseeable future the current imposed system that is embedded, but we can serve our children with the nurture and nourishment that their artistic selves deserve. So, throughout the book, 'young children' is inclusive of the early stages of Key Stage 1 (KS1) in order to emphasise the continual right and heritage of a young child to their artistic journey.

A historical perspective

Since the introduction of the Early Years Foundation Stage (EYFS) and Birth to Three Matters over ten years ago, the subsequent subsumed format as shaped by the EYFS in 2008, and most recently the implementation of the newly revised EYFS in 2012, there has been a huge shift in understanding and practice for those involved in early years education. Attitudes towards children learning through play and the consideration of a balanced child-initiated and adult-led day has changed and the majority of practitioners working in the early years and KS1 have welcomed a more 'creative' emphasis within the curriculum.

If we take a moment to refer to the current EYFS (2012), the guiding phrases afford an understanding of the expressive arts and design process and one that is active and alive for all young children, and relevant to extending the art experience beyond the confines of the EYFS years of schooling. The EYFS' aptly chosen words in relation to Expressive Arts and Design – *play, explore, original, thoughts, feelings, critical* and *imaginative* (see Figure 0.1) – retain the key features of young children engaged in expressive arts and design learning. They are features that will be referred to throughout the book in a variety of themes and issues and so consistent links can be found in relation to the guidance.

Definitions of the guidance's statements are drawn out in a critical manner, in order for us to truly scrutinise what they actually mean in practice. It is important, throughout the reading of this book, to keep in mind that guidance of this sort is there to retain a consistency for us all, but not to dictate or designate a linear approach that we all adhere to in our teaching and facilitating approaches. Curriculums can have an overpowering effect on practitioners; we can allow them to employ us and we become subservient to their guidance. Instead a prescribed curriculum should represent a set of principles, which we work with but which we also then define in our own ways, so that children, rather than us or a set of printed words, have the freedom, space and time to negotiate their own creative rules and regulations.

Box 0.1 Guiding phrases for expressive arts and design from the EYFS

Expressive arts and design involves enabling children to explore and play with a wide range of media and materials, as well as providing opportunities and encouragement for sharing their thoughts, ideas and feelings through a variety of activities in art.

Exploring and using media and materials: children safely use and explore a variety of materials, tools and techniques, experimenting with colour, design, texture, form and function.

Being imaginative: children use what they have learnt about media and materials in original ways, thinking about uses and purposes. They represent their own ideas, thoughts and feelings through design and technology, art, music, dance, role-play and stories.

(British Association for Early Education, 2012)

Focus: visual and tactile art

It is important to establish from the outset that our focus is on visual and tactile art in response to young children's artistic creativity. Creativity is a wonderfully rich field of learning but one that links to many modes and areas of learning, not just the arts. The creative soul is predisposed to learn in an active and enquiring way within different aspects of engagement and so similar skillscapes will be generic to a creative mind working in maths, in literacy, in physical development. Sharp (2004) summarises three possible aspects of creativity and psychological processes:

> *Personality traits*, such as self-confidence, being able to tolerate ambiguity, curiosity and motivation.
>
> *Emotional processes*, such as emotional fantasy in play, pleasure in challenge, involvement in tasks and tolerance of anxiety.
>
> *Cognitive abilities*, such as divergent thinking, ability to 'transform' thinking (for example, by being able to reorder information or shift thinking 'sets'), sensitivity to problems, breadth of knowledge and judgement.
>
> (Sharp, 2004: 7)

In support of the distinction of what constitutes creativity in learning, the Robinson Report (1999) argued that, whilst there are strong links between the expressive arts and creativity, viewing creativity as solely or mainly the province of the arts is unhelpful because it can lead to a denial of the role of creativity in other areas, such as science and mathematics.

For the purpose of clarity, our creativity focus is on visual and tactile arts in relation to the development of expressive arts and design. We do not attempt, during the book, to consider in detail other aspects that are of equal importance in response to this area of learning, such as dance, drama and music. We know, as creative human beings ourselves, that all these areas are interconnected, and aptitudes and approaches in learning can be broadly applied across the spectrum of the arts. We are reminded here of Anna Craft's theories on little 'c' creativity: '[Little 'c' creativity] acknowledges the potential for developing creativity in a potentially infinite range of contexts and drawing on a potentially infinite span of human abilities' (Craft, 2002: 67).

However, we remain focussed with the area of 'art' in our study of young children and any reference to other disciplines will be as part of this interconnectedness. We do not attempt to define creativity but we use it to help us to consider the aspects of young children as they engage in the art-making process.

Barriers

Despite years of seminal research papers, inspiring projects and substantial evidence, the fact remains that there still exists practice which fails to recognise and embrace what creative and critical thinking in relation to art and design really means for a young child: what it signifies about their learning journey and development and, very importantly, the role for the adult within this journey. Visual art educators are keenly aware of the significant contribution art can make to the growth and development of young children as it provides unique opportunities for personal expression and creativity. However, while it is acknowledged that art contributes to the development of the whole child, the link between thought and practice is often tenuous.

Many students and qualified early years practitioners can still have a latent fear of art relating back to their own school days of the 'I can't draw' syndrome. Lessons steeped in adult expectation of representational drawing and formulaic techniques can deter, quite understandably, the majority of learners. This fear can be passed down through generations and has the power to influence, hinder and subsequently alter the art and design experiences we offer our young children. Fewer opportunities to experiment and a tendency to override and overpower children's raw creative talents through template-driven and adult-directed art activities are commonly seen flaws. Knowing ourselves as professional art educators can be both challenging but also exceedingly rewarding as we celebrate the role we can potentially play in children's creative lives in helping to foster a generation of children who are confident to form new and imaginative thoughts.

This book seeks to allay fears and open up the possibilities and potentials of art as one of the most exciting areas of exploration in the early years learning environment. It will attempt to rejuvenate our adult conceptions and memories of art, so that we can view the learning experience through the eyes of the young children we work with. The content and messages in the book aim to invigorate the art in our early years settings by considering what is accessible, individual, inspiring and meaningful and how we, as the adults, interact, support and participate to extend and nurture these formative paths of enquiry. "What counts is that the very young child produces entirely from imagination. . . . It is a thing quite in itself, quite shut off and isolated, following its own laws and not the laws of the grown-up people" (Franz Cizek cited in Kelly, D., D., 2004).

About the book

From the moment a child is born, they interact with the sensory world, looking at colours, feeling textures and making mental and physical images of what they see and experience. Within all our early years settings and into KS1, our aim, as practitioners, is to provide stimuli and opportunities to stimulate, excite and ignite the visual and tactile imagination of our young children. This book will consider how art can be managed, understood and relished as an essential ingredient towards the creative potential of each unique young child. The focus throughout the book will be to enjoy, celebrate and extend what a young child can do in art and how we, as engaged adults and the wider school community, can become confident participants in the process of early years/KS1 art making.

The following aspects are examined in detail in separate chapters as well as continued threads of thought throughout the book:

- recognising and analysing child involvement in art;
- developing skills for positive and participative adult interaction and engagement;
- planning for opportunities and responding to observation and schema art and design;
- consideration of environment, activities and resources (inside and out);
- exploring sensory development and awareness;
- managing and savouring the art transition into KS1;
- encouraging and sustaining parental participation and understanding of the art process with their children.

In Chapter 1, we focus on the unique and distinctive nature of young children in their endeavours and journeys as artists. We will consider what happens during these journeys and how children's individual characters unfold as they experiment, explore and make 'micro-discoveries' as artists. The chapter considers the 'competent child' who is in charge of their *own research base* (as children are from birth). By examining children's journeys of *personal interpretation and idiosyncratic quests* for learning, we will, in this opening chapter, consider and celebrate the essence and significance of young children's *curiosity and imagination* and how play in art enhances valuable moments of awe, wonder and excitement.

The message of the unique artist is continued into Chapter 2 when we examine the individual child in more detail, with an emphasis on **schematic art experiences**. We consider how the roots of these schema can, whether distinctively singular or multi-modal in character, influence the young artist's activities and his or her developing knowledge and understanding. The physical human dynamics associated with artistic endeavour are considered and examined as *somatically driven experiences*; key to the individual's growing conception in art.

Chapter 3 continues our exploration of young artists with a closer examination of the sensory world that is their domain. We consider the active relationship of *infant brains and sensory awareness.* The triangulation of mind, body and sensory modalities is a focus throughout the chapter, and we have the opportunity, as adults, to step into a child's world and experience, mnemonically, the excitingly expressive universe he or she resides in. We consider the importance of sensory explorations enriching the *embryonic understanding of aesthetic awareness* and the importance of young language development and articulation as part of this dynamic.

In Chapter 4 we return to the *playful narrative of artmaking*, where mistakes and storymaking are of the essence. The chapter offers a brief insight into the involvement levels of young children engaged in art experiences, again, to promote the *importance of process* and the powerful learning it incubates. Having regarded the vitality of process, we consider *quality-driven moments* in artistic endeavours, affording thoughts and suggestions as to how to engage children in reflective thinking.

In Chapter 5, we look in more depth at our role as adults working with young artists: supporting, extending and analysing their learning experiences. We examine the valuable opportunities for *cooperative and shared art moments* between adult and child. We consider the value of experiential learning paradigms, which also negotiate an element of structure in order to achieve the most beneficial and rewarding balance of intervention and non-intervention (Duffy, 1998), with regard to a child's extension and progression. We will focus on how to encourage, appraise and support an advocacy of *working alongside children* so that we continually strive to value their own interpretations and self-assessment as a tool to meet individual needs and to plan for the next steps.

Chapter 6 will examine how we can incorporate a richer and more genuinely responsive approach to *environment provision,* where resources and practice challenge and extend the young artists we work with. This chapter will include ideas regarding artists' studio spaces within the setting, in order to promote longevity of pieces of work, again in response to valuing the *process* of making. Our consideration of environment relates throughout the chapter to both inside and outside spaces, placing importance on the latter not just as an open natural space to be physically explored but as an exterior tool which lends itself to a variety of *art invitations and possibilities.*

In Chapter 7, we consider how to continue the visual art journey as young children progress through the education system into a new curriculum and classroom, with new structures, routines and expectations, and how to cherish and nurture young artists *beyond the early years classroom* and into KS1. This chapter will consider possible links and partnerships as part of a whole-school approach to art where *inter-phase art activities* are owned and collaborated on by all the children involved.

As an additional response to a whole-school community approach to art we consider our families in Chapter 8 and the potential for *positive parental participation* where understanding of the visual and tactile creative process is key. Our discussions will focus on how to nurture and secure lively links between the home and the setting and, in doing so, ensure a *valued and combined approach* in relation to the child's young creative spirit. This chapter is dedicated to fostering a constant atmosphere of support for children's art, enjoyed and promoted by the firm network of family–child–setting.

In Chapter 9, we consider the positive aspects of artists working in settings and the *longevity* of such projects. We focus on specific examples of *artist-in-residency* initiatives, which range from artists working in nursery settings to children working with museums and outreach projects. Our consideration, which will continue to be debated beyond the reading of this book, is how to retain the positivity of visits and special occasions so that longevity of achievement and success is continued and the legacy of new ideas and artistic confidence is sustained.

Conclusion

Artists, which many of us are, and educators of art understand the unique contribution art can make to the quality of our life experiences and, also, to our sense of well-being. By making art, we are able to interpret and respond in visible form and thereby achieve deep personal involvement and satisfaction from the experience. As art educators, we are acutely aware of the significant benefits art brings to children's overall development, not just in terms of creativity and individual expression but also less apparent gains such as critical thinking, creative problem-solving and cross-cultural communication. In art, young children learn ways of experiencing, developing, representing and understanding ideas, emotions, values and cultural beliefs. They learn to take risks, be imaginative, explore alternative solutions, engage in art criticism, develop, practise and refine techniques, share opinions and challenge definitions in art. Some of this, it could be argued, is only collectively possible in the visual arts, as it asks the individual to engage in his or her own unique way and continue to do so for a lifetime of experiences.

Children are rather amazing as they have a capacity to create art in a way that is abstract to the adult perception. Whether it is abstract as such to them is another question altogether, as by defining it in such terms we assume it has an identity that may not have been the intention of the child creator. But they do have a knack and a tendency to see, in contemporary design speak, 'outside the box'. Their ability to wildly create, uninhibited by expectation and stringent rules, affords them the title of contemporary artists. They are the artists of the here and now and their art is, therefore, of today. Prentice's (1999: 156) description of contemporary artists draws a very similar parallel to the surprising and unpredictable inventions of young children in their eclectic use of materials: 'Contemporary artists break boundaries; they push forward the frontiers of art. They use materials in ways that challenge ideas about the "appropriateness" of media and art.'

The wonderful thing about art is that it liberates the individual from boundaries and such freedom enables the search for and location of amazing discoveries. Liberally fused art spaces enable children to imagine and bring into existence something intangible and other-worldly, which is then often, though sometimes in transient mode, reconstituted in works of art.

Child Art
I want to paint sunshine,
Moonbeams and stars.
I want to paint hedgehogs
And rainbows in jars.
I want to paint laughter,
Clouds filled with rain,
Music and songbirds
Again and again.
I don't want to paint Monets,
Miros or tones
Textures and shadings,
Peppers and bones.
I want to paint paintings
Of things that I see,
Grandmas and cuddles
Belonging to me.
(Peter Dixon, 2004)

Peter Abbs wrote that the purpose of education is 'to engender a quest in the search of what is not known, of what may never be known, of what is emotionally alluring' (Abbs, 2003: 15). His words offer an allegiance to our lifetime adventures as artists – continuing quests and searches that began in childhood. The 'allure' of art is one to be felt early in childhood; the need to make a mark on a steamed-up window or sculpt castles out of sand. Such a desire does not disappear with the demise of childhood. If we remember what it is to be the young artist, we begin to thoroughly enjoy that experience too, and that is what forms the content of this book.

CHAPTER 1

Curiosity and the sparkly thinker

> 'Nothing there!' said Peter, and they all trooped out again – all except Lucy. She stayed behind because she thought it would be worthwhile trying the door of the wardrobe, even though she felt almost sure that it would be locked.
>
> (C. S. Lewis, 1998: 12)

Introduction

Children can be astounding to work with as we watch them discover the wonders of life and within this first chapter we look at how curiosity and involvement are richly combined in the journey of a young artist. We will consider a general view of the young child's innate and overwhelming desire to find out and become immersed in curiosity-driven play. This play is what allows them to discover, think and refine and it is this sequence that forms their artistic character. It is important, initially, to establish what drives the young child to exist in an exploratory moment.

Absorption of the moment

The image of the absorbed child whose tongue sticks out as they carefully draw a line or whose jaw is set whilst their fingers deftly work a pair of scissors is very familiar to us all as adults who work with young children. Both these external indicators inform us as to the intensity of involvement that has, at that particular moment, consumed the child. Fully submerged engagement such as this is an unselfconscious indulgence in the unequivocally challenged moment of exploration; a state which young children frequently experience.

We, as busy adults in our world of chores, timescales and deadlines, can easily forget how wonderful it can feel to switch off from all external pressures or expectations and indulge in 'the moment'. As we grow older, we only occasionally remember to lose ourselves in a sensory-based or investigative experience. For young children, however, it is central to their world of discovery and hence understanding of their existence. Their ability to be consumed in what they are researching, to be totally absorbed in study, where no distraction is powerful enough to shift concentration, allows them to make sense of their world and also to make new and exciting discoveries.

Being curious

We first need to contemplate and value what it is that sparks a child's interest. Interest comes from the sense of being curious and as Keith Gentle (1985) so rightly stated a few decades ago: 'All children are born curious . . . they have a natural curiosity and like to touch and hold things, to manipulate them and include them in their play' (Gentle, 1985: 53). Curiosity feeds the hungry and expectant mind and explorations follow repast and so quests are sustained. Curiosity is the search engine inside a child that enables the stratification of understanding. This busy and intensive cognitive laboratory develops the ability to rationalise, realise and form opinions as suggested in Figure 1.1.

Curiosity motivates learning; a child is captured in a moment of 'wanting to know' and so they are motivated to find out and consequently learn something new. A good early years setting should always have a sense of 'curiosity' about it – interesting materials, strange artefacts, unusual books, for example. Contained within these props are motivational qualities that spark the imagination. EYFS guidance reminds us of this as outlined in the two following statements:

> Provide stimulating resources which are accessible and open-ended so they can be used, moved and combined in a variety of ways.
>
> Children will become more deeply involved when you provide something that is new and unusual for them to explore, especially when it is linked to their interests.

Let us magnify and examine a curiosity-driven moment. Have in your mind two children as they unwrap a mysterious parcel found in the classroom. This unknown and unwrapped object is like a jewel to a magpie for the children. The parcel's presence provokes powerful motivational forces – seeing it, approaching it, prodding it, pulling at the string, tearing it open and looking inside to see what it contains . . . Once it is opened, they will probe further and explore its contents. Their eagerness has vigour, determination and, importantly, excited

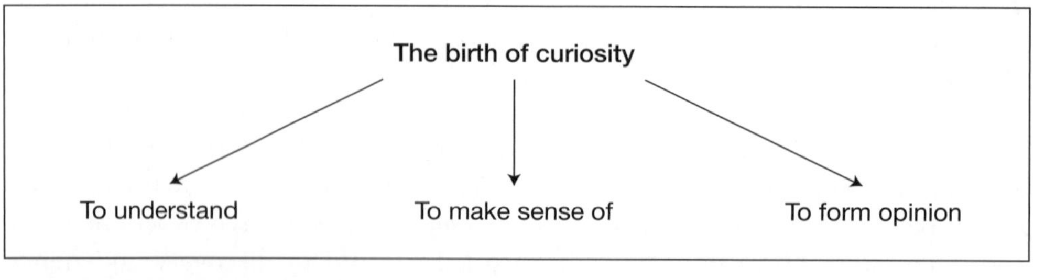

Figure 1.1 The birth of curiosity

interest. There is no doubt that, in this moment, curiosity was the trigger for engagement and a conduit for learning in action.

Curiosity-based play

> Within us all there exists a powerful tug-of-war between a desire to satisfy curiosity, to explore the unknown, and a need to adhere to that which is familiar, comfortable and safe. For an artist, the challenge of the new, the magnetism of the unfamiliar, is stronger than the need to reinforce the status quo.
>
> (Prentice, 1994: 127)

Children often engage in two types of curiosity-based play – ludic: playing in a more open-ended, ad-hoc way, and epistemic: exploring to find out – knowledge acquisition. It is arguable that the former will lead to the latter but perhaps this is not always the case as if it was it would undermine the delicious unknown of the ludic explorer. A mission to 'understand' is not always part of the agenda. As we get older, our curiosity tends to dwell in the epistemic camp, as we want to know and understand a situation, a problem or a new experience with more clarity.

> Epistemic curiosity states are aroused by novel questions, complex ideas, ambiguous statements, and unsolved problems, all of which may point to a 'gap' in one's knowledge, and reveal a discrepancy between that which one knows and desires to know.
>
> (Litman *et al.*, 2005: 559)

It could be argued that human maturation brings with it fewer opportunities and self-induced limitations to exploring with a carefree spirit. We are less open to ludic curiosity and play as it may unbalance our status quo and send us off on other tangents, which can be time-consuming. Children, it seems, veer between the two but their ability to indulge and wallow in ludic curiosity leads to great and surprising adventures, as the child in Figure 1.2 discovered.

Marion Dowling (2005) once referred to young children as 'sparkly thinkers', defining the image of a young child very much alive and buzzing with ideas. If we value and listen to these energised young bodies – what they are doing, what inspires them to be curious in their thoughts and where these 'sparkles' travel – we realise how exceedingly unpredictable they are. Whether it is that our paths of enquiry become more linear, logical and predictable as we get older is debateable, but adults have moved away from the often surprising tangents that young children take. It is wise not to underestimate the value of 'surprise' both as a learner and as a teacher – it is something intangible and unique that we cannot plan for but can maximise when it happens. We will consider the element of surprise in learning and motivation in more detail in Chapter 3.

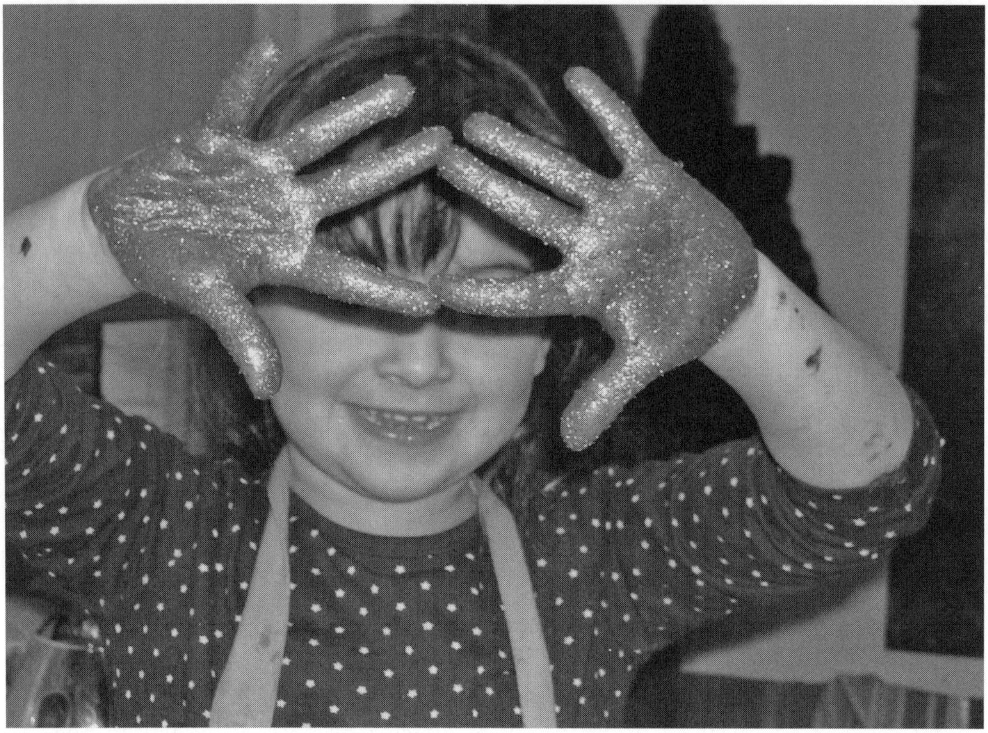

Figure 1.2 Sparkly investigations

Curiosity and personal transcendence

If we return our thoughts to the 'sparkly' element of young children, we need to understand and relive what it might be like to encounter their sense of adventure. The unknown is a phenomenon and there is an almost 'magical' aspect to children's ability to pore over and work out. Dowling (2005) talks of young children's experiences of 'transcendence', where their great adventures and explorations enable them to reach out to the limits of their world as part of growing up. The magical spirituality of childhood is something that is inexplicable and not easy to describe in words.

This living enchantment is so very personal and often fleeting, but it does very much exist in young children's engagement with the world. As previously stated, we adults can miss a momentary phenomenon, for reasons mostly to do with our busy lives. The joy of spending time with young children is that they can remind us of a beautiful spider web that has rain droplets hanging from it on the walk home from nursery, that the moon is out at the same time as the sun, that there is a ladybird crawling up a brick wall . . . someone wise once referred to these as 'beads of happiness'.

Children are very successful at collecting such beads all through the day – existing in their esoteric and individual encounters. It is a testament to their age that they allow themselves to be distracted by beauty, fun, interest and phenomena. Spiritual curiosity such as this throws into the ring all the whys, whats, wheres and what fors, and requires the young mind and brain to think, consider and ask questions.

In Figure 1.3, we witness India, who found a woodworm in the thick, peeling bark of a tree. She had been brushing her hands against the rough surface and suddenly squealed as her hands and eyes met to find a worm. Her discovery was non-verbal in its description of the experience, her hands told the story of the two haptic experiences – hard bark and soft wiggly worm. Her experience had a secret sense of discovery and her absorption in the moment was intense.

Let us contemplate that feeling of absorbed concentration, where curiosity has ignited involvement. As writers, we know the experience of being so absorbed in an idea that we lose all track of time; as readers, we know the joy of reading a novel that is so gripping that we cannot put it down; as internet users, we know that the myriad of connections can take us to ideas and concepts so fascinating that time ebbs away. As artists, colour, shape, form and line can become so all-consuming in their infinite possibilities that dawn turns to dusk.

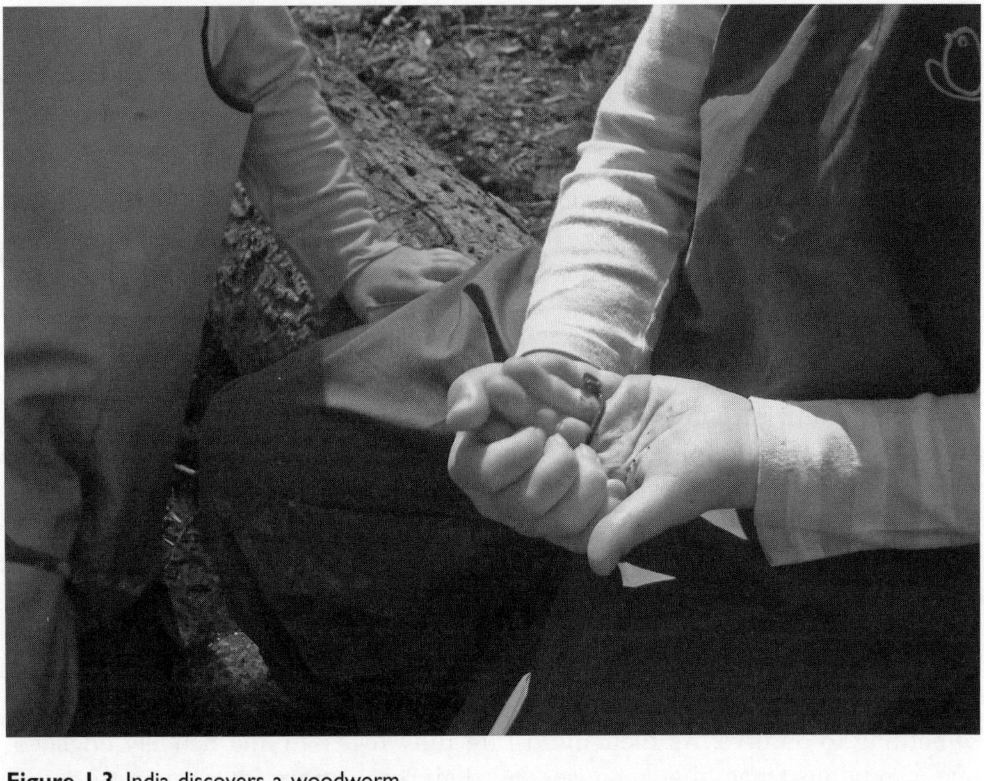

Figure 1.3 India discovers a woodworm

Young children as artists

'Beads' – leading to creativity

Allow yourself to take a journey back in time to remember a 'bead':

- a wonderful moment of play;
- a captured experience of wonder;
- a moment of curiosity and excitement.

If you can do this, consider the emotions involved in those experiences and the glorious memories attached to discovery, exploration and a whole world alive with mysteries to be solved. They are emotions associated with familiar sensations such as butterflies in the stomach, lumps in the throat and tingles down the spine. We are all familiar with such human responses and recognise them but they are perhaps less prominent in our everyday lives as adults. They are, however, essential and necessary in the holistic development of children if we want to treasure what makes them the 'children' of their 'todays'.

The task of nourishing young children's spirituality is one of releasing, not constricting, children's understanding and imagination. We can think about this as the internalisation of a young child's learning, as it brims over with natural fascination. Their unpredictability is what makes them so alive. Hart's (2003) studies on the spirituality of young children and their insights emphasises an infant's ability to surpass the ideas held by adults, because they have a natural sensitivity that allows them to hear their inner wisdom. Listening to intuition means noticing those subtle cues that we often tell children not to pay attention to – a gut feeling, a vague discomfort, a fleeting idea.

Eisner (2002) refers to these early explorations as 'micro-discoveries'. Discoveries are uncovered and also, very importantly, contain an element of surprise, as previously mentioned. Sue Palmer (2008) takes this idea further and forms a scientific character portrayal of a young scientist, who uncovers quandaries and answers through a combination of various factors including the information to hand and, very importantly, their individual learning patterns.

We also need to note here how very serious all these explorations are to children. We often smile when observing a child at investigative play – we view it from an adult viewpoint and we see them 'playing' at life. But micro-discoveries are complex and committed in their unfurling lives. The psychoanalyst Adam Phillips (2009) talks about the seriousness of young children's curiosity-driven quests when he says, '[c]hildren are just working it out, that's all they're doing, in the most extraordinary ways . . . it's much, much more urgent and integral and essential to their lives, it's what they do'.

Somatic Involvement of the curious child

Children's involvement and concentration in a moment of learning is quite something to observe. As their minds are fully focussed and actively engaged, one can almost see the synapses of their brain forming, separating and multiplying. These precious moments in time when they have the space and time to occupy their investigative needs are essential to children's brain development and intellectual growth.

Children invest both thinking and physical understanding as they make sense of a situation. Their whole body involvement and idiosyncratic behaviours cohabit a state of immersion that is described as their developing somatic knowledge. Their bodies are energised, both physically and mentally, as they are consumed in the learning and the micro-eureka moments: 'The infant quickly learns to detect and exploit the expressive characteristics of his or her body actions and it is upon these expressive actions that the first use of visual media is based' (Matthews, 1999: 157).

The journey is very personal to the child and follows a particular self-designated path – this route cannot be predetermined by someone else. Perhaps because young children are in general, by rule of growth, smaller and more inclined to be happily haphazard in the coordination of their body parts, they are able to give themselves wholeheartedly to an immersed creative moment without anxiety. As we grow and often become more self-conscious, full physical involvement tends to be more controlled, with less haptic possibilities. We go along a more linear route of physical enquiry and compartmentalise what we know and how we use it in our movement.

As our bodies and minds mature, we are inclined to engage less with the quality of a somatic experience. But that experience exists in the integrity of the young child's ability to combine mental and physical participation; not separating body from the mind. This is an unconscious act but one that Cavazzoni (2012) refers to as children understanding the 'beauty of life'. Their active ability to fully immerse, engage and 'throw caution to the wind' is testament to how they hold hands with the world around them.

Playing with art

> I begin with an idea and then it becomes something else.
>
> (Pablo Picasso)

As children come into contact with the objects and fascinations of life, they spend a lot of physical time and energy playing with and exploring them. The exploration is driven, as we have discussed, by the power of curiosity and the desire to know. What we need to confirm in our minds is the very necessary and delightful link between playing and art. As children physically and mentally explore a material, they become acquainted with its properties and possibilities. Spooning a dollop of gloopy paint onto a surface, prodding a giant lump of clay, sharpening a point on a colourful pencil, are all acts of investigative play which allow the child to find out and define their own relationships with these materials through playful actions.

> Play, like art, provides opportunities for imaginative leaps to occur, encouraging inventive ways of handling ideas and materials beyond the constraints of convention. Familiar objects can be placed in unfamiliar settings as a result of which they are perceived in different ways: a device exploited by the surrealists to disturb and amuse.
>
> (Prentice, 1994: 127)

Such intimate and life-experience-affirming moments confirm the very intense quality of play and its arena which house the dynamic meeting between the child's inner life (emotions and thoughts) and its external world (Ring, 2006).

Playing with art is not simply confined to the realms of childhood, it is something we all do and artists often refer to this in their work. Paul Klee once said, '[a] line is a dot that went for a walk'. As the dot is animated by the drawer's playful actions, it starts to transform into something. These very transformations are the conduit for artistic development and discovery. As one 'thing' becomes 'another', a very important process has taken place and play was the conduit.

Play in art allows for opportunities to find out and explore and not to just do and finish. Paintings are often produced on a prolific scale in early years settings. These paintings are often created on a vertical easel, put on a drying rack and then either taken home or put away somewhere. Of course, there is no denying the home-taking element is of high importance in the child's ownership stakes. And home-taking ensures artwork is shared with the family, establishing further links between home and school. However, the proliferation is far more a consequence of the process-driven playing than it is of the end product.

The numerous images produced and marks made with paint at an easel are episodes of art-playing owned by the child protagonist. They document a child's development, enhanced by the materials that have engaged them. The movement and quality of the materials are revealed during interaction: a clear action of cause and effect. Their busy art endeavours flow and can be prolific in production, providing evidence which can serve as documentation for the children to see and consider. Here is a perfect moment of living and active research.

The research will not necessarily be of a verbal nature; looking, touching and collating will be the language of their research. Their non-verbal observations will consider and peruse the artistic transformations that have taken place. What is powerful here is the fact that those changes came about because of them – they were the protagonists and their investigations led them on their own art-based adventure where high levels of curiosity were at play.

This kind of play is an action that has no defined end, it is something that happens when we want to explore. Purpose, however, can still be very apparent as the young child embarks on a playful journey that may be to do with curiosity about a particular material in the art area. The embarkation and continuation of play is being actively defined by the child. He or she is not passively reflecting a given reality or following a set of rules and a prescribed pattern of events.

Individually owned curiosity entices the child and causes physical actions of enquiry that belong, in their entirety, to him or her. The enquiry will always have some sort of purpose otherwise it would not have happened in the first place. But that purpose need not be finite and so the play continues. Here we can see the important stratification of art play; ideas and understandings assembling and coagulating. These strata, rich in creative knowledge, allow the child to use their play experiences as firm foundations for understanding themselves as artists. Cox (2005) refers to this work in progress, this continued enquiry as a young child's 'central source of data'. They know that by soaking the clay with more and more water, they can squidge and squeeze the sticky slip between their fingers and create weird and wonderful landscapes.

In our example of clay manipulation, the process is explored through playing with possibilities; the children utilise their idiosyncratic tendencies to subvert 'reality' and, in effect, create new realities (Cox, 2005). The layering of idiosyncratic ideas as well as newly found knowledge builds the children's confidence as sculptural artists. Their discoveries are a part of the intricate web of growing sensory awareness that is unique to them. As they play, they develop their mastery of how to use and be discerning of their senses. So both time and practice conjoin to develop the emerging young artist, who is proud and confident of what she/he finds out and takes ownership of.

Encouraging confident artists

Playing in art will help to promote and maintain a positive and self-affirming message to all children – that they can play, find out, discover and add to their artistic repertoires with each new adventure. Self-confidence is often at the heart of the 'I can't draw' lament. It is very present in a teacher education classroom of art as student teachers arrive to take part in an art lesson with looks of dread and fear on their faces. That old feeling of 'I can't draw' returns before they get the chance to play again. Without fail, as they start to play with materials and engage in possibilities, smiles of confidence emerge and very creative souls are uncovered.

Pedagogues in Reggio Emilia often talk about 'the competent child' who enters the world sufficiently qualified in their ability to understand what lies in wait. Their competencies to invest in the world, to get to know the world and to use their own innate abilities actively exist at the very beginning of their adventures as human beings. Such thinking is supported by Dowling (2005), as she defines the three aspects of developing confidence in a young child:

1 Becoming aware of oneself – self-concept;
2 Developing a view of oneself – self-esteem;
3 Understanding one's own strengths and weaknesses – self-knowledge.

Concepts of self and the confident development of self, as discussed, are intrinsically caught up in the web of playing and finding oneself. The discovery of 'self' in art play is incredibly powerful and one that will remain. It is rooted in children's ability to self-realise and to build strong layers of self-confidence. They are also discovering what it is that is of interest to them – their own enquiring path of self-knowledge.

Research and imagination

As a child becomes transfixed by a situation, event or moment of discovery, they are following their line of enquiry and putting a lot of time and energy into their research. They are able to build on what they need and find out a little bit more – this may be through verbal questioning, or discussion with a friend or with themselves. It may be a form of research that requires more resources, further foraging in order to find the answer and make sense.

Research is steeped in the child's huge imagination.

> Imagination, that form of thinking that engenders images of the possible, also has a critically important cognitive function to perform aside from the creation of possible worlds. Imagination also enables us to try things out – again in the mind's eye – without the consequences we might encounter if we had to act upon them empirically. It provides a safety net for experiment and rehearsal.
>
> (Eisner, 2002: 5)

Imagination is a rich source of content, which continues to increase in volume as the quest for knowledge continues and progresses. Children need to make use of their imagination in order to keep filling this container of knowledge. It is what makes up their interior landscape and makes them unique. No one child has the same landscape, which is why they are so very exciting to observe and listen to – the jumble of ideas that their imaginations stimulate can lead to weird and wonderful creations and artworks.

The 'roots' of these imaginations convey a solid and growing image of the very important beginnings where young children flower from using both their imagination and their curiosity. Their creative work in art is rooted in personal experiences and existences and so the imagination that grows from this is owned and nurtured by the child. Their roots give them confidence to venture forth and continue their foraging in the big, wide, exciting world. But what are these roots and how do they form and grow as children develop their artistic characters and preferences? We consider this in more detail in Chapter 2, with our examination of schematic art behaviours.

We can consider these 'roots' in three emerging and significant ways: those of imaging, imagining and using the imagination (Craft, 2005):

1. *Imaging*: Moments of remembered imagery, prompted by olfactory, auditory, gustatory and visual experience. This is a highly private process often hard to put into words, especially for non-verbally confident young children, but extremely powerful to the mind and memory.
2. *Imagining*: To form a mental image or concept of – beginning to understand what it is.
3. *Being imaginative*: The thinker forms new thoughts, discovers new truths and builds up new worlds where they go beyond the obvious and with originality of thought and unusual interpretations.

It is important to consider these three aspects of creative endeavour in order to fully contemplate the different participatory skills forming as the artist emerges. As the three stages converge in their own sequential pattern (defined chronology is not of consequence here), the creative ownership of the curiosity-driven moment takes place. Consider this pattern of experience with the following two examples: we will focus our attention on Ben and Daniel, who interact and experiment in their own individual worlds where aesthetic understanding and appreciation are key to their engagement.

In Figure 1.4 Ben headed straight for the huge shard of ice – he saw it glinting in the sun from some distance as he scaled the frozen mud ridges on the forest path and quickened his pace in his excitement to extricate the ice glass from its puddle. Pulling the ice from the mud absorbed Ben's whole body as he had to balance on either side of the mud ridge and pull with some strength in order to carefully hold the fragile shard on the edges so that he did not disturb the beautiful translucent surface. He watched as the sun shone onto and through the material, casting rays beyond where he stood. He also watched as sparkling droplets ran from the melting ice – this caused a juggling act full of decision-making and problem-solving in how he could steadily hold the shard without it shattering. His careful manipulation took a different route and temperament as he threw the sheet onto the ground with great force, with, it seemed, the intention to see it dramatically shatter into as many pieces as possible.

In Figure 1.5, Daniel (on the left) became absorbed in the layering of coloured sand. He was predominantly interested in mixing colours and filling up the egg cups (see Figure 1.6) in order to achieve an even top layer. As his friends explored with him, uninvited, they also sifted through colours and layers, but Daniel was not perturbed by their lines of enquiry. He was interested but remained loyal to his own research. He followed this intently for some minutes and in doing so also made a slow humming noise, which echoed the concentration in his body. His investigation followed a new path, as he was keen to see the actual colours in the layers, and so sought the help of an adult co-explorer. A long, glass vase was found and presented a wholly satisfying result in his aesthetic adventure as the layers emerged through his careful manipulation and their distinct steps of colour were awarded with a clear sense of satisfaction in Daniel's broad smile. He had been fully engaged with his experimenting and was clearly energised by his discoveries.

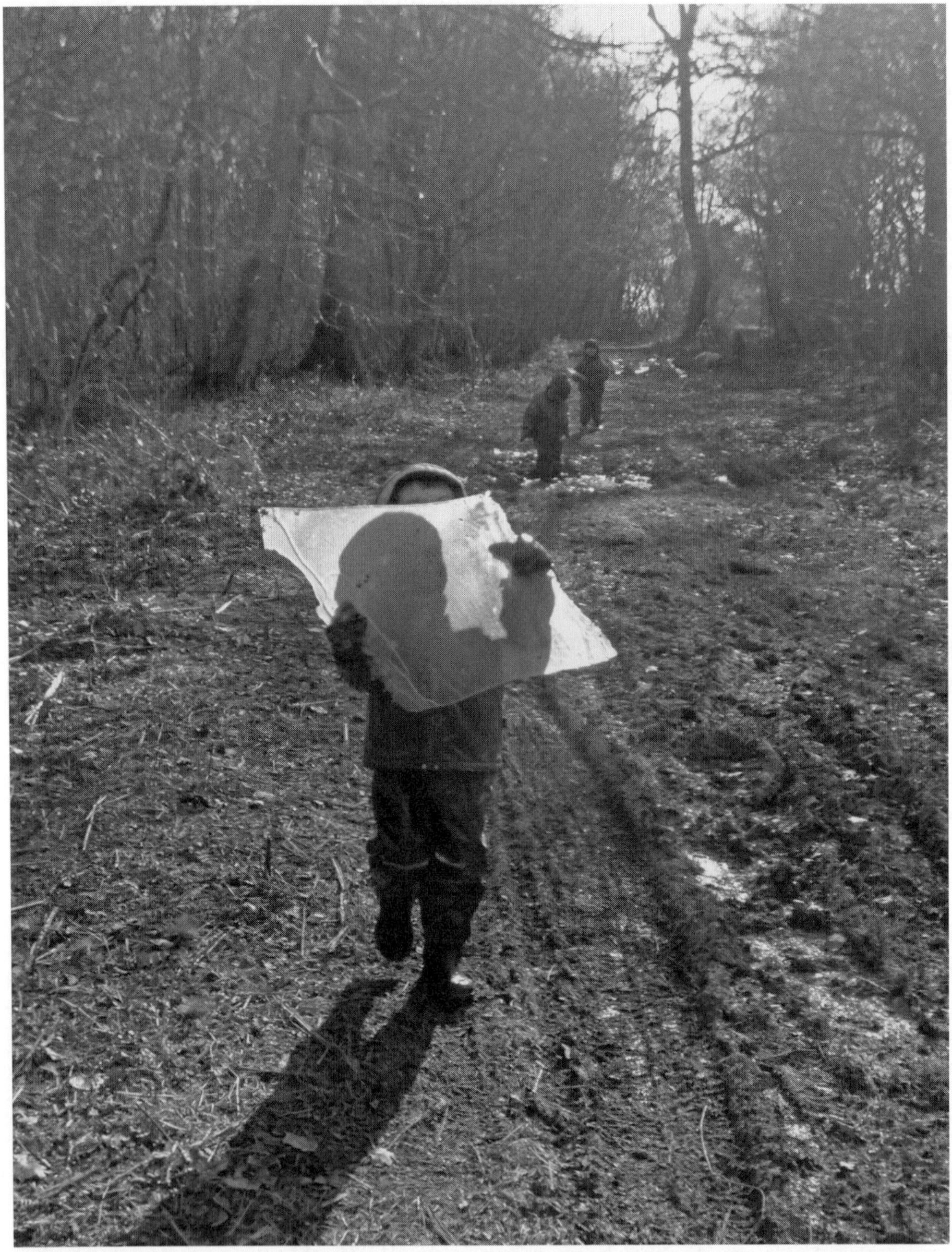

Figure 1.4 Ben discovers a sheet of ice

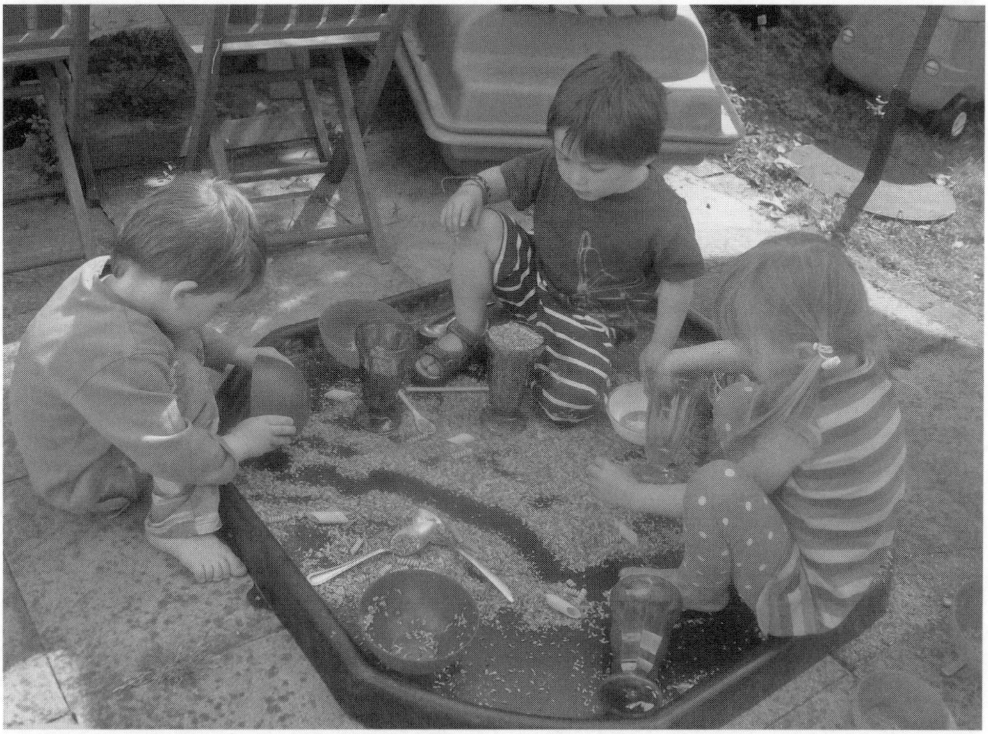

Figure 1.5 Layering and mixing coloured sand

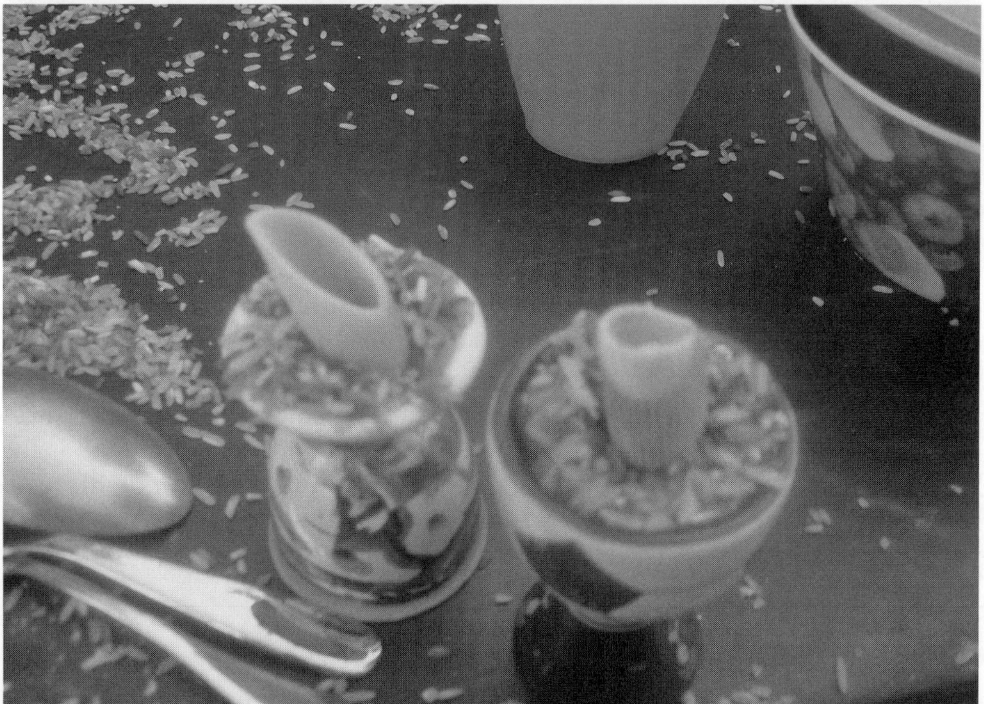

Figure 1.6 Creations in egg cups

Table 1.1 Imaging, imagining and being imaginative in aesthetic understanding and appreciation

	Ben	Daniel
Imaging	• Ice was spotted as a potential investigation. • The glinting ice caught visual and haptic attention and curiosity.	• Recognition of the colours and grainy consistency to touch. • An inference to previous play experiences.
Imagining	• The ice was examined and held in a variety of forms. • The light-related properties were understood and considered through touch, sight and even taste!	• A series of movement with hands running through, scattering and listening, mixing and pouring. • Volume of egg cups was considered.
Being imaginative	• Moving and dancing with the ice to capture the light and make sparkling lines which reflected onto others. • Smashing the shard to shimmering smithereens which formed a pattern on the frosted mud.	• Patterns conceived. • Layers made according to colour combinations. • A purposeful layered sculpture created.

If we now dissect these two experiences, we can see in Table 1.1 how the patterns of imaging, imagining and being imaginative emerge for these two boys and their developing repertoire of aesthetic understanding and appreciation.

Nourishing the artist's curiosity-driven exploration

Broadhead (2004) refers to children as 'astounding'. They are indeed this in their ability to capture the moment and make fast and furious connections. They are also astounded by the world itself and when we can recognise this, as practitioners, we too can participate and experience their engagement. We can never be children again, in the true sense of the word, but we can enjoy and recognise experiences of wonder through them. If we reaffirm this in our thoughts and actions, as the following reminders indicate, we remember why we wanted to work with them in the first place.

To get a sense of wonder in partnership and participation:

- Look at things with children.
- Value the moments when they stop and stare.
- Take time to watch and observe children's absorbed attention.

- Watch their gestures.
- Listen to their words.
- Give children time to look and ponder.

Although in our work we can plan and provide some excellent tools, resources and spaces, we can never be sure what the curious young mind will find out. Quite often when we observe a child's moment of absorbed exploration and are comfortably assessing what is being played out and surmising his/her route of learning, the enquiry will do something very different and go off on an alternative tangent that would have been impossible to predict. Our sparkly thinkers are at it again and their inquisitive search engines have found out something new and unique to them and characteristic of their way of learning.

If one takes time to picture that moment when the jaw is set, the eyes are focussed, the hands are manipulating, then we can carefully analyse what exactly is happening during the exercise of engagement. Laever's levels of child involvement (Robson, 2006), which are discussed in greater detail in Chapter 4, help us to track a child and observe their behaviours and gauge their engagement. This magnified observational technique affords a glimpse into a child's imaginative world, particularly in relation to their artistic endeavours. We can have a highly privileged view into their extraordinary interior landscape, which is full of contours, valleys and crevasses: each and every one unique to the child. We know that it is crucial for the child to be in charge of and in possession of their own endeavours in order to define and progress their own artistic prowess and character. We also know how important it is for us to understand this and embrace this ownership so that we value each new discovery and unravelling strand of curious engagement.

Curiosity and the young artist – 'the birth of identity'

Our initial thoughts in this text help us to consider the power of curiosity and the desire to find out when young. What we know is that as children enquire, engage and play with life, they start to define their characters and their ways of looking and perceiving. Simpson (2011) refers to this as the child's 'birth of identity' and such a title elevates the child's emerging character as something we must cherish and value. Their identity, as artists, continually threads through play and helps to define ideas, crucially aiding the development of confident children who are excited and driven to continue layering their knowledge and cognitive styles.

The inherent curiosity of young children, their propensity to ask questions and to be intrigued, their uninhibited fascination with all that is around them, their sense of being, must not be ignored or neglected. The freedom to roam through ideas and imagination from sparks of curiosity forms the symbolic markings of the artist in a child. Children freely, without hesitation, find what most interests them, what captures their thoughts, and these are intimately linked to their sense of aesthetic understanding and appreciation. They will use their own developing cognitive enriched sense of beauty – visually, haptically, aurally – and run with these in order to create and produce things that are absolutely intrinsic to their artistic natures and tendencies. As Cornelia Parker, stated in *The Daily Telegraph*, 'There's such a freedom about being an artist . . . You're not accountable – you're this renegade thing'.

Conclusion

We have, in this chapter, contemplated the powerful drive called curiosity. It is a very personal experience but one that can be enjoyed individually and collaboratively. If we reflect on our own practice, we need to recognise the importance of curiosity-driven creative experiences. Curiosity:

- feeds the mind and imagination;
- is a young child's search engine;
- ignites research;
- stimulates discovery trails;
- is endless;
- finds meanings and rationale.

We know that it is at the heart of how young children investigate and to so operate it occupies a space in their bodies, where senses conjoin and present to gathering rhythms, hypotheses and images. Our chapter here ends with the words of Loris Malaguzzi, in which he reminds us to look through the extraordinary eyes of young children:

> From the very beginning, curiosity and yearning refute that which is simple and isolated. Children yearn to discover the measures and relations of complex situations, even seeking out the pleasure of transgressing these measures and relations, changing their meanings, creating their own analogies, metaphors, and anthropomorphic and realistic-logical meanings.
>
> (Quoted in Filippini and Vecchi, 1996: 30)

In the next chapter, we will consider in more detail what happens with young children as they explore and emerge as artists. Their personalities, characteristics and idiosyncratic tendencies will be examined in relation to their image-making and developing creative cultures.

Reflection

Reflect on your own setting and environment and, in doing so, contemplate, with honesty and a determined, new-found energy, whether you observe the following curiosity-driven hooks into learning:

- When they do happen? Start to examine why and how they took place.
- What opportunities were available to the children?
- What spaces were they contained in?
- What time of day did they happen?
- Who were the primary players?

Further reading

Broadhead, P. (2004) *Early Years Play and Learning*, London: RoutledgeFalmer.

Craft, A. (2002) *Creativity and Early Years Education*, London: Continuum.

Dowling, M. (2005) *Young Children's Personal, Social and Emotional Development*, London: Paul Chapman Publishing.

Prentice, R. (1994) 'Experiential learning in play and art', in J. Moyles (ed.) *The Excellence of Play*, Bucks: Open University Press.

Prentice, R. (ed.) (1995) *Teaching Art and Design*, London: Cassell.

CHAPTER 2

The idiosyncratic child

Schemas and styles

> Personal style, be it that of Michelangelo, or that of Tintoretto . . . has always been that peculiar personal rapport which has developed between an artist and his medium
>
> (Shahn, 1967: 73)

Introduction

Schemas are not simply threads of cognitive learning and thinking, they are also inextricably intertwined in emotional development and personal exploration. In Chapter 1, we considered how play can assist with the growing confidence of a young child in their experiences and further employment in art-making; the kind of confidence that helps them to believe in themselves as artists from a very young age. In this chapter we contemplate the repeated schemas and behaviour patterns that are reflected in their art play and how these increase the sense of assuredness in their creative actions. Their repeated actions help them to feel secure in their artistic endeavours and to be resilient in their thoughts, style development and experimentation.

What is a schema?

From birth, my daughter Maia, not unusually for a young infant, was a prolific mark-maker; whether throwing stones into puddles to create ripples, drawing on paper, poking holes with sticks in mud or stirring patterns with her spoon in her food, she was fascinated by the power of A causing B. What was distinctive about her particular journey as an individual image-maker was that her marks had an identifiable and repetitive theme to them.

Her images were made of circles, arcs, dots, spirals and rotund figures. Her 2D image-making reflected this repeated behaviour and it was also a characteristic prevalent in her movement. She would toddle around circles on playgrounds repeatedly, make a bee-line for a tambourine if there were a selection of instruments on offer. One of her favourite toys, when very young, was a plastic concoction of spinning wheels and cogs.

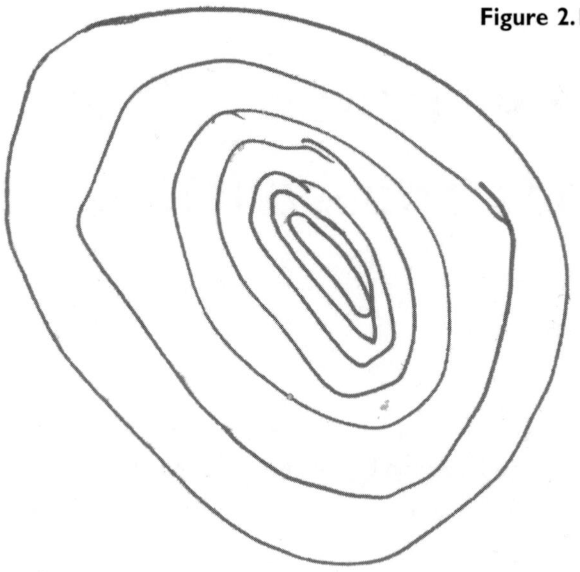

Figure 2.1 Maia's concentric circles

Figure 2.2 Maia's rainbow arcs

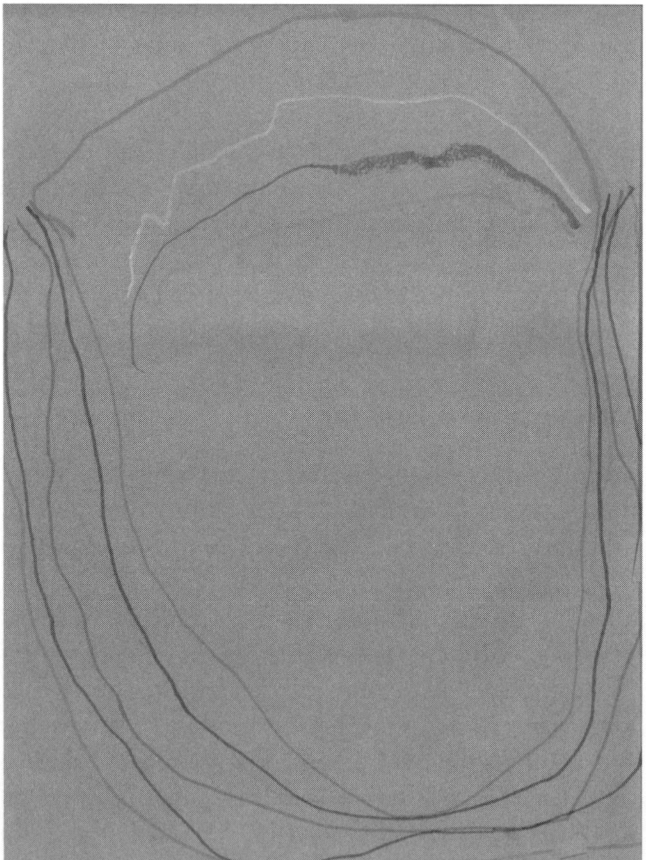

Figure 2.3 Maia's circular pattern

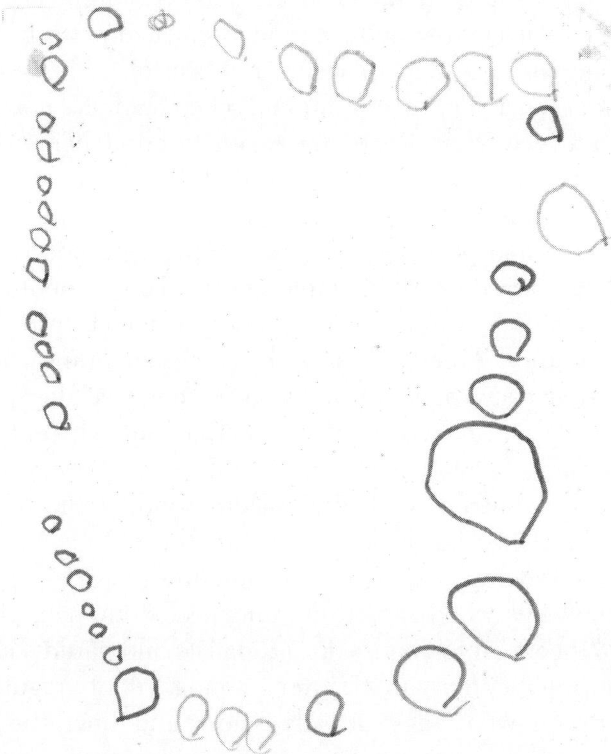

Figure 2.4 Maia's circular study

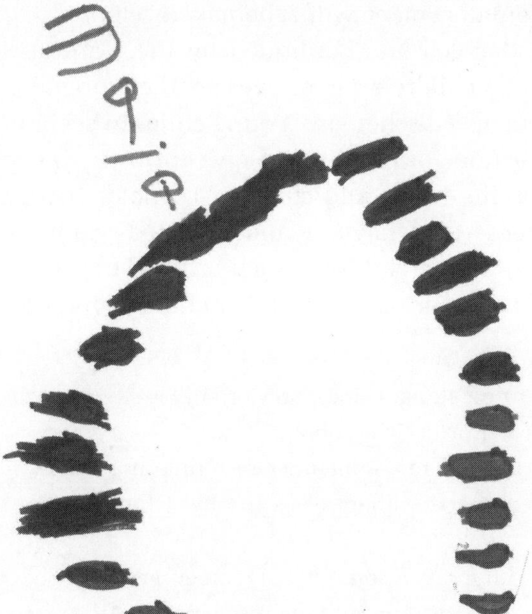

Her visual and tactile character had found a particular style, interest and focus. The circular and rotational repeated pattern that emerged in much of her young life's participatory encounters afforded her an understanding of the world through her very own rotational schema. Maia's particular schema was indicative of the way she viewed the world around her and how she understood and interacted with its vast playground. It is testament to her 'rotational' style that she continued to increase and understand line and form as she drew, whether abstract and playing with shape or with purposeful intention of outcome.

Our introductory example encapsulates a definition of schema: patterns of repeatable behaviours, the layering of which inform new ideas and new paths of enquiry. Athey's seminal research, spanning the recent decade, portrays a positive view of young children's cognitive development and their ability to actively seek new content to assimilate into current structures – schemas (Athey 2007).

This resonates with the Piagetian view that, as human beings, we build up working theories through repeating our actions. We 'assimilate' into our current ways of doing (schemas) and sometimes have to 'accommodate' our actions and knowledge when something unexpected happens (Piaget, 2001 [1950]). Piaget's is a theory which both educationalists and parents can recognise whilst working and interacting with children. Young infants regularly encounter the interface between what they already know and how the knowledge increases once interaction has occurred. Piaget's definition, however, has come under critical scrutiny in its conception of children with deficits of knowing – their schema is repeated and only with social enhancement will schemas develop.

More recent research such as that led and continued by the team at Penn Green Children's Centre credits the children themselves in their ongoing use and investment in their very personalised schemas: 'Young children seem to use schemas or repeated patterns of action for comfort, to give form to, to explore and begin to understand complex life events and changes' (Arnold, 2010: 11).

The following observable patterns of behaviour and repeated actions are a suggested list of schema we see in young children. Such a list is not definitive and some schema are more familiar in our observations of children than others.

Lines – making lines with objects and string.

Trajectory – moving in or representing straight lines, arcs or curves.

Oblique trajectory – moving in, using or drawing oblique lines.

Dab – making stabbing trajectory movements, sometimes resulting in a mark.

Connecting and disconnecting – connecting themselves to objects and objects to each other and disconnecting.

Proximity and separation – before children can connect, they sometimes place objects or marks in 'proximity' to each other or represent them separately (Athey, 2007: 73).

Enclosure – enclosing oneself, an object or space.

Enveloping – enveloping or covering oneself, an object or space.
Containing – putting materials or oneself inside an object capable of containing them or other objects.
Inside – being interested in the inside space of a container.
Subdivision of space – being interested in the subdivision of space, for example, upstairs and downstairs.
Transporting – carrying objects or being carried from one place to another.
Going through a boundary – causing oneself or some material to go through a boundary and emerge at the other side.
Classification – when objects, people or materials are grouped according to their similarities; the classifications become increasingly refined.
Seriation – ordering objects or people according to size or other comparative features.
Rotation – turning, twisting or rolling oneself or objects around.
Circularity – the shape through rotation.
Grid – vertical and horizontal parallel lines or bars, which intersect at right angles to each other.
Positioning – children position themselves and objects in different ways, thereby gaining different views of the world and of objects. Some objects can be placed in vertical, horizontal or oblique positions.
Core with radials – a coordination of a central core (enclosure) with radial appendages (trajectories).
Transformation – transformation occurs as a result of some action.

(Arnold, 2010: 21–2)

The significance of understanding schemas in art

In Chapter 1, we considered the idiosyncratic learner whose enigmatic and somatic approach to exploration was powered by irresistible curiosity. In our commitment to understand our young inquisitors, we need to be able to deconstruct what it is that determines their creative interests, tendencies and motivation. Each child is a unique learner and explorer and so will have a particular style that may be similar to another, but never identical. Whether we refer to their unique behaviours as 'ways of looking', 'behaviours of learning' or 'schemas', each child is layered with their own way of perceiving and conceiving ideas.

The significance of schema recognition to the art experience is that as these schemas layer and extend, further repertoires of understanding form. If we watch carefully, the investigation of knowing through repeated behaviours is a constant force in the progression of learning. Eisner (2002: 54) reinforces this point when he states:

> Each of these repertorial acquisitions becomes an integrated part of subsequent repertoires. Thus, children's development in art can be seen as an expanding collection of increasingly refined and diversified repertoires that widen their visual options.

From beautiful green to sludge brown

It is undoubtedly a familiar and, if we have to be truly honest with ourselves, rather aggravating moment when you watch a colour emerge which has been mixed and crafted by small explorative hands, and then transformed from a beautiful sea green to a sludgy brown. The desire to step in and freeze the beautiful colour is immense in us as observing adults – we want to let that child know that the colour is of great aesthetic value and how wonderful it would be to retain it, look at it and enjoy it. But we know we must not intervene in this very important sequence of events. By considering this act within the creative domain of the layering schema, we begin to appreciate that the child who mixes from beautiful green to muddy brown is someone who, although they may afford an appreciative eye over the colour produced, is also in charge of a process which is not just about creating beauty and aesthetically pleasing visual results. Their intent is a series of endeavours which spans the sound and visual experiences of mixing colours and also the power of layering – continuous covering to see what will happen – greens, blues, turquoises, sludge and brown are all a part of this sequence.

In contradiction, we must note here that there are moments during art exploration where we do permit ourselves, in the role of scaffolder, to alert young eyes and minds to aesthetic moments in creation. Our 'directed' teaching towards quality should exist, but it is the point of entry that is key so as not to disturb the flow of a particular journey. In this case, the child's intent is to investigate the layering process and our sensitivity to this moment is key. If layering is the quest, a nudge towards the quality of aesthetics is inappropriate. The question of intervention is examined further in Chapter 5.

A child's visually and haptically charged interior landscape has a vast appetite for this sequential act. It is possibly one of the most frequent schema sequences we see at play in early years settings and one that has immense intrinsic satisfaction for the child. Their continual layering refines their visual and tactile sensibilities; the rivulets of colours mixing, the sound of sticky paint congealing and concealing. We can consider the following sequential inferences in this layering process, as also referred to by Cox and Watts (2007):

- layering and covering;
- exploration of colour;
- in the present moment: alive and alert;
- internal drive to find out.

Adult eyes can misconstrue such semiotically driven events. Recognising a child's perceptive encounter will help us to 'feel' what it is they are doing and what they are finding out. Eisner (2002) reminds us to be moved by what children do, and in doing so we relive their experiences and so can appreciate the often quiet elation to be had when the covering starts and continues until the experience is fully saturated with satisfaction. It is a wonderful gift that young children have, to just keep covering and layering with no worries or anxiety about what they think they should actually be producing. The absence of worry celebrates the occurrence of those small eureka moments, via a practice that is repeated but not predictable in its findings. As Gentle (1993) suggests, within these acts of colourful and dense layering, young children can initiate whole new ways of looking.

Observing art-related schema

> We cannot decide in advance what they will learn but feeding their current schemas seems to go some way towards helping children to learn in a deep way.
>
> (Arnold, 2010: 25)

Each day of a child's life will bring different emotions and different desires. Their day may be shaped by incidents at home that morning, occurrences on the walk to their setting, excitement about some imminent event. Quite often, emotions in young children will be affected by things out of *our* line of vision, not physically but psychologically; things we have just overlooked now we are adults. New brightly coloured shoe laces, hair plaited in a different way, shiny sparkles on a jumper, puddles gathered on a playground and chairs round the wrong way all cause a spark of recognition and then interest in the young child. Recognition of these momentary sparks helps us to consider the design of our space, the layout of the furniture and utilisation of the environment so that opportunities provided are in direct response to children's emotional and motivational experiences.

It is difficult, sometimes, to consider how to get it just right in your environment: furniture, layout, resources, activities, spaces for expressive play and continuous play. There is certainly no golden rule that can be adhered to each day because we all work with different spaces, different adults, and, most importantly, different children. What we can be completely sure of, however, is the fact that we need to be guided by our young investigators and how they see and feel the spaces they work with. Examination of space is a continued focus in Chapter 6.

We can only achieve this organisational dialogue if we know who children are by listening to them and understanding them. Our developing relationships with the children we work with will take a meandering road with diverging and unexpected paths, but our tracking of their development allows us to draw up an empathetic and holistic picture of them. The picture will change, be adapted and extend to a variety of pictures but they all remain part of that child's individual portfolio. Glimpses into these experiences of children show how concrete and realistic exploits, which may be planned or serendipitous, can nourish the exploration of ideas – both fantastic and factual.

Their repertoires will often have signature characteristics, their schemas. As we all have different ways of seeing and doing, so do children. Their young characters are finding ways to define the world they experience and quite often, their search for this definition is guided by their exploratory behaviours.

An engagement in an art-based activity will see a child actively demonstrate particular styles and inclinations in desires. Many children have a whole variety of learning styles and it is not always possible to focus on one in particular, unless a particular style or *schema* is so prevalent in its repetition that it cannot be ignored. 'When children are involved in a schema they are engaged in a creative process, as they are making new connections and reaching new understandings' (Duffy, 1998: 84).

For a child to ascertain how something works, they tend to 'have a go' over and over again until the mechanics of the 'something' is realised and understood and can then be used to inform another layer of learning. She/he uses the familiar to understand the unfamiliar (Bruce, 2001). Children, from the moment they are born, are adept at trying again and then succeeding; a whole understanding of life based on active engagement and inference of experience. These repeated behaviours are born out in an important process of engagement and they are particularly prevalent during an artistic endeavour, where hand, mind and emotions are entwined to produce something uniquely individual to the maker.

The important thing about schema, when working with young children and their art, is to watch and recognise it. It can be a fleeting moment that is repeated daily, weekly, monthly or perhaps only twice in a term. By allocating time to observe, listen and note then we can respond in the most appropriate way through our planning, our talk and our growing and developing understanding of the child. The EYFS (2012) guidance reminds us of this. It advises: 'Support children's interests over time, reminding them of previous approaches and encouraging them to make connections between their experiences.'

This chapter opened with Maia, who had a very clear and recognisable schema in the way she constructed and played with materials in her early image-making. Rotational patterns were clearly distinguishable in her explorations. The following two case studies similarly present children who have clearly defined characters which emerge from their visual and tactile expressive play and exploration.

So what is the significance of the schematic habit in Lotta's (case study 2) emerging talents and skills as a young artist? Tracking a child's schematic journey is fascinating. In response to Lotta, we could ask the following questions:

- Did the rows and ordering appear in the marks she made on paper, walls, in clay and playdough?
- If they appeared, was there a reoccurring pattern involved and did she order the art materials according to this idiosyncratic repetition?

Case study 1: Noah's story

Noah would transport and layer in all aspects of play and engagement, making roads, layering wooden blocks, creating tracks and moving his body from one area to another on a very regular basis. The commonalities in his art-making were on a large, active scale, where objects and construction played an important part. On this particular occasion, there was an artist-in-residence working at the nursery for the week. The focus of colour-mixing on a large scale had dominated the week, which had been in direct response to inclinations in interest as indicated by the children early in the residency. Noah had worked for a little while in the studio space, mixing colours with a variety of materials on different surfaces. He had a particular interest in the misters which sprayed and dispersed the 'brusho' colours in myriads of patterns and splashes, and, importantly, at intriguing distances. One morning, with paper and brusho-filled mister in hand, he began to move around the nursery's inside space, trailing the paper around furniture and doorways and then spraying the colours. His journey took him outside and he continued to unravel the paper, gradually speeding up his process, until he had created an enormous spider web sculpture of a sprayed paper trail. His friends were fascinated and followed the path he created, moving along the journey of paper and around the objects and the people caught up in the web. They were inspired to join in with the colourful and growing creation. His 'transportation' instinct was at work and had inspired him to embark on an exciting, unravelling and creative adventure.

Case study 2: Lotta's story

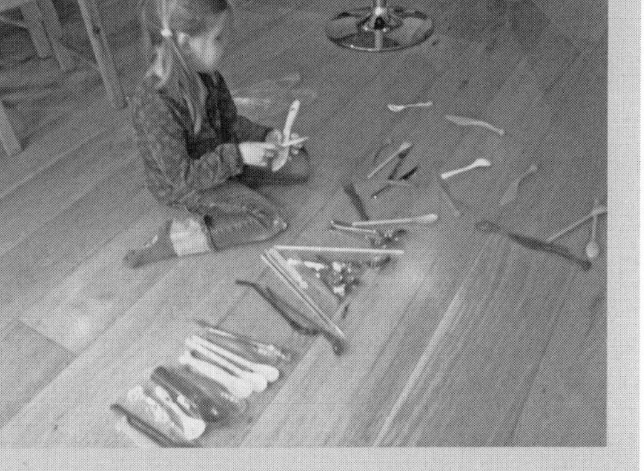

Figure 2.5 Lotta orders a collection of spoons

From around the age of 18 months, Lotta developed a very keen and regular habit of lining things up. These 'things' could be anything from people and chairs to cutlery. She could not start a meal without lining up all the spoons and knives – to the adult, there did not seem to be any order to the lining up. As this act began when Lotta was still pre-verbal, words were not a part of the process, nor did she seem to desire anyone to comment on it – but she was adamant that it had to happen. If she was in a room where there were chairs randomly positioned, she would pull them with all her strength to order them in a circle, in rows, in twos; no particular regular sequence could be afforded here, except that the ordering was very important to her. The linearesque sequence would always precede an event: before a meal, before singing in a group, before stories were told. She had also, on occasion, positioned a group of children on the carpet. Her parents also said she would position the family as they sat down to watch television or other such social family activities.

- Did her unspoken and very physically active row-making and line organisation have an impact on her choices of materials – was she particularly interested in a certain type of resource because of its potential qualities relating back to the desire to order?

Depending on the answers, we may be able to identify a progressional pattern and journey of development that can be supported through the correlation of experiences.

Our three children, Maia, Noah and Lotta, remind us that we must get to know our children. We need to be able to understand what makes them tick, what interests them, whether there are clues in their art-making and creative activities which express them and who they are. If we are able to understand this about them, we can then be far more intuitive about planning for them, responding to them and, very importantly, celebrating their achievements and developing creative mastery.

An important note here is to be mindful of the fact that this development and progression is not always explicit to them or to us, so we must not expect them to assess themselves in this way, nor indeed should we do this at every opportunity. If we over-analyse the schema and ways of thinking associated with one child, we could assume a child's identity and so dilute the very essence of 'her/him'. Claxton (2006b) reaffirms a wariness of assumptions as he debates the acquisition of personal identity. He reminds us not to assume a child's identity as this can narrow their own self-reference and so forsake the essence of 'me'.

As the adults who have got to know the child, we have the privilege of being witness to the moments that they actively define. Our observation will help us to reflect and connect their learning experiences to progression, aptitudes and skills development. This is looked at in more detail in Chapter 4.

Schema and physical development

As we are considering schemas of a symbolically suggestive nature, we recognise that these semiotic signatures of idiosyncratic artistry and emerging styles are housed in the bodies and minds of young children. A significant aspect here is the relationship between what the child has in mind 'to do' and consequently 'does'; their bodies physically responding to the mind's desires. The cognitive exploration of the young mind is translated and made public by subsequent movement. Internal actions are interpreted through motion to produce the repeated actions, the pattern of schemas. Goddard-Blythe (2004: 28) clarifies this relationship:

> Increased control of movement is indicative of strengthening connections between the brain and the body and within the brain itself. In this way, movement helps to map the brain, and the reflexes provide a child with his earliest vocabulary of movement.

The relationship between and reliance on cognitive development and motor control is at the very heart of the child's development and enquiry in art. As their reflexes and motor control develop, their ability to divulge more of their complex thoughts onto paper, in clay or with paint develops. Their physiological development is so very closely tied up in how they interact and pursue their schematic mark-making. Maia, our rotational image-maker, was a child who worked in a circular style not only in her drawing, painting and sculpture work but, as aforementioned, in her physical activity. Her rotational schema was made possible by her ability to use her motor skills in a particular way – she knew how to make her body work for her and performed in a way that suited her interests. The repeated actions were a direct result of her cognitive search engine and her physically developing limbs and motor skills working in unison. Goddard-Blythe (ibid.) associates this with the reflexive development of balance:

- spinning;
- turning movements (ring-a-roses, circle dancing);
- carousels;
- rotary boards;
- rolling (linear).

Maia's circular and rotational movements are performed as she develops as a physically able-bodied child, who can balance in particular ways in order to perform her artistic skills.

The relationship between the young mind's creative cognitive development and movement is of course closely linked to play in art, as introduced in Chapter 1. Whether it is repeated pouring of water, splashing dabs of paint, or dotting a strip of paper with similar charcoal marks, the playful element of this purposeful marking can only be executed by the partnership of physical involvement with the mind's ability to play creatively. Somatics and schemas are joined to produce images for the child as their body movements directly compute their thinking. Wright (2010: 170) refers to this as thinking with the body and says of these moments:

> Manipulating art materials integrates sensorimotor skills and other forms of reasoning, feeling and learning to emerge . . . a somatic knowing – exchanges between the psyche (mind) and the soma (body).

Schematic non-verbal communication through art

'Actions speak louder than words' is a phrase that resonates with the picture of young children engaged in creative and active play. Observing and analysing the body language, the visceral interpretations at play, tells us so much about the child in a way their spoken language cannot and is often not able to. As they actively define their ideas and imaginative endeavours, they, as with our three previous exemplifications, as young artists cling to characteristics which they are comfortable and familiar with, and therefore this repeatable confidence gives them the internal power to continue image-making. They are becoming 'descriptive symbolists' (Cox, 2005) in their art and use these repeated symbols to develop and progress. It is a personal journey indicative of symbolic and signature actions unique to the individual and one that continues to be communicated as they continue art-making.

Schematic art-making can be revealed through the language spoken or gestured. We follow two examples in Case studies 3 and 4 of children whose journeys were captured and observed by others. The very fact that a social interaction impinged on the journeys meant that at some point a message between the work being produced, the producer and the onlooker took place. This message was at times spoken, at times observed in a reciprocal action of gesture. The commonality in both examples is the visible schematic symbols used to inform both the maker and the audience.

Reyna (case study 3) had told a story about *her* drawing. She had worked on this illustration in her own way, in her own time, and had encapsulated a style that was hers. It was full of her own idiosyncratic style – the variety of bold marks, which increased and moved as she indented the page with her pen. Her teacher revealed in further discussions following this story dialogue that Reyna would ritually draw at the same time, with the same materials. Routine contact with the pen and paper had significantly impacted on her development and individual style of drawing, which she owned and used with purpose to tell a variety of stories through her images on a daily basis.

Our second example in this study is Jonah (case study 4). His schematic story tells a very different one to Reyna's. He had not been a child who prolifically produced marks and images. He had, prior to our featured episode, not employed the use of mark-making resources on a regular basis. In fact, little interest and little time had been spent in any type of image-making. At four years, three months, having very rarely scribbled, drawn or played with marks, Jonah produced the giraffe in Figure 2.8. This first image was fully formed and included facial features and careful colour selection. The same image was then repeated continuously with varying alterations and alternative features for several weeks following the initial episode. Perhaps he was responding to the pleasure of his adult and child audience who thoroughly appreciated this wonderful and humorous image. In the first drawing, not only was there a giraffe, long neck and extended snout included, but there was a happy spider alongside the giraffe.

Jonah, in contrast to Reyna's quiet and discreet image-making which often continued without the presence of any audience, responded to external recognition and rapture. It encouraged him and this appreciation was concurrent with his own developing self-esteem as a young artist, defining his own style.

Case study 3: Reyna's story

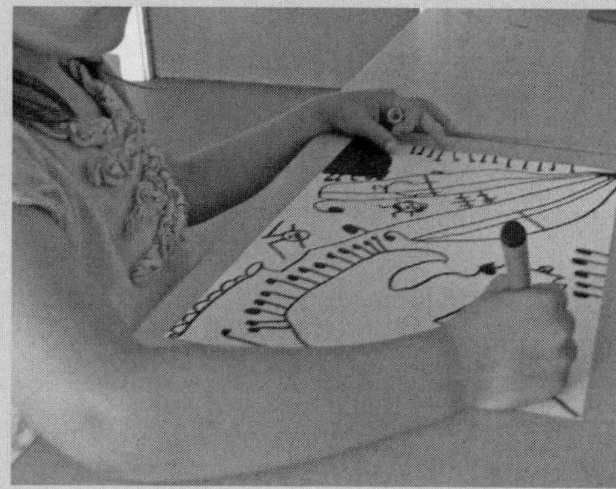

Figure 2.6 Reyna at work

Reyna (three years, five months) sat in deep solitary concentration for almost 45 minutes, graphically developing and following through the story that emerged in her image-making. She used a black pen and white paper to play out a drama through marks. The adult who sat with her was welcome to be there, acknowledged through eye contact and a small nod from Reyna. But here body language made it clear that she was not going to speak, she did not want to engage in a conversation. The adult could stay as an audience to the drama on the paper but nothing more initially. Big bold black marks with fluid shapes and patterns began the paper tale. As the shapes became more solid, little characters were also drawn. At this point, the drawing became too tempting, too fascinating for the audience to hold back, and a question was asked. In this instance, the question was genuinely provoked by interest and perhaps Reyna knew this; therefore she was open to a small dialogue.

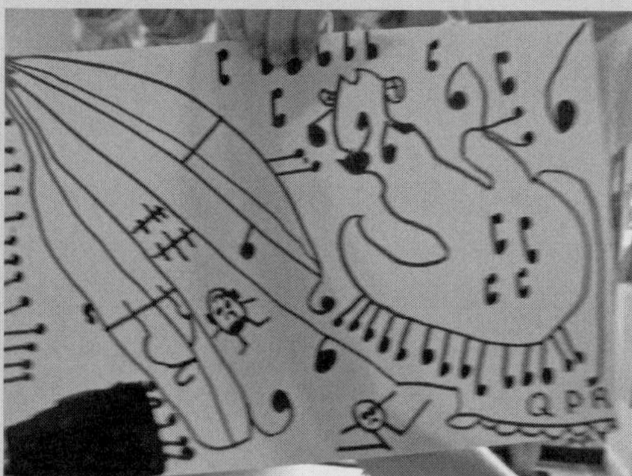

Figure 2.7 Reyna displays her drawing to the audience

A story was offered in a very serious tone: 'The little sad faces . . . they fell out of the lines and couldn't find their way home. These are lots of acorns – they are hanging.' The 'acorns' were significant and repeated marks – formed like musical notes.

Jonah's giraffe iconically continued to feature in his art play and image-making as he also experienced other forms of visual life ranging from the everyday of people's appearances and media-related images such as television programmes and book illustrations. Two particular influences were possibly at play if analysed in the dialogue below. Jonah had watched a wildlife programme where two giraffes had fought for their territory by thrashing their necks at each other – a violent image to be associated with this four-year-old's current vision of drawn giraffes. In addition, Jonah's father had just started a new job and he may have been conscious of adult nerves and anxiety – hence the giraffe 'on his way to work'.

Case study 4: Jonah's story

Jonah, always open to discussion, chatted with modesty and clarity about his giraffes, talking about seeing them at the zoo and his like of the book *Giraffes Can't Dance*. Interestingly, Jonah was a child who enjoyed climbing up, making paper aeroplanes and watching balloons float up into the sky. We could hypothesise that the giraffe and its long neck were a part of a 'trajectory' schema – a keen interest in the 'upness' of the world around him. Certainly, the 'giraffe' weeks that followed were a part of Jonah and his own, very specific, idiosyncratic mark-making. The fact that this development was watched and enjoyed by those around him was undoubtedly a part of his journey. His repetition was not so much visible in the actual specific marks, but was evident in the interest of subject he chose to draw about.

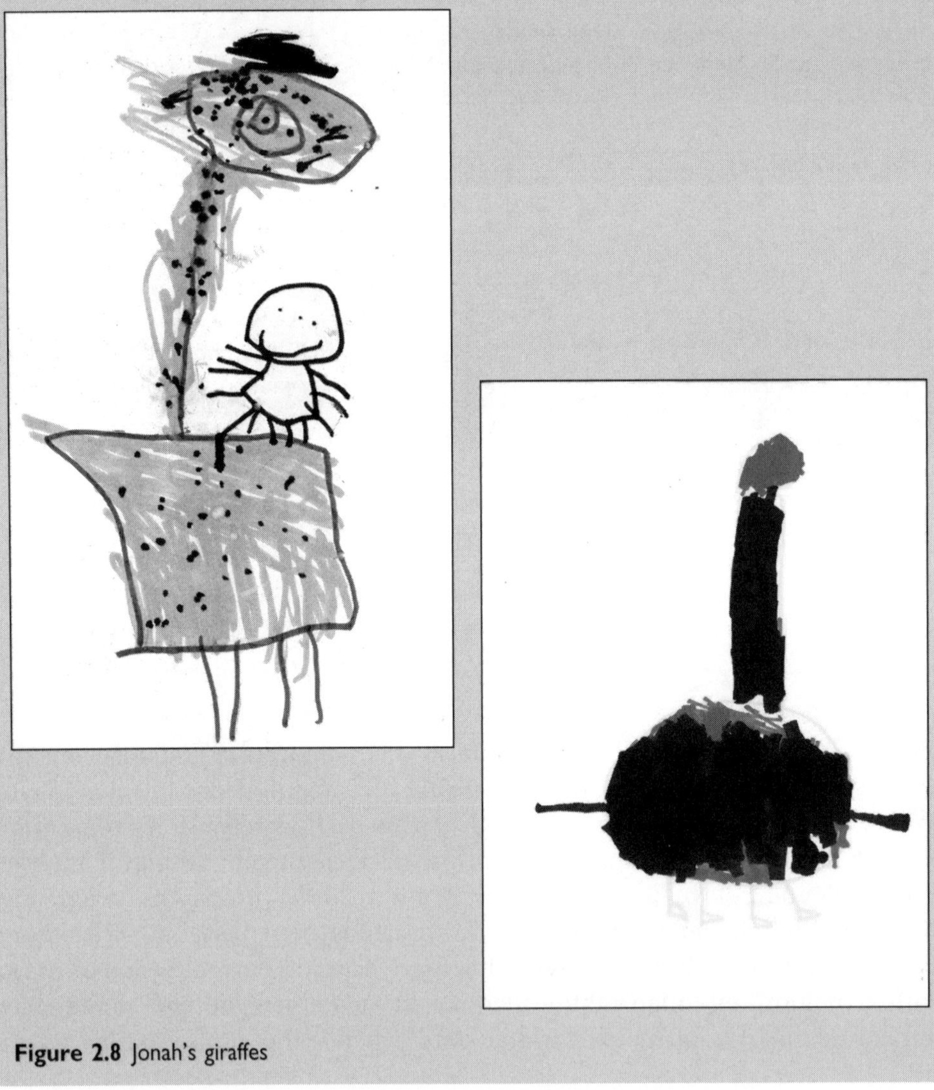

Figure 2.8 Jonah's giraffes

Box 2.1 A conversation had about a black and red giraffe

Jonah: A big lion came and killed him – blood on his face and then his neck and then his back and then his tummy.

Mummy: Is that where all this red comes from?

Jonah: Hmmm *(nods an affirmative)* and it goes all over the black because the giraffe is wearing a suit. He is on his way to work when the lion comes.

Mummy: On his way to work? How scary to be on your way to work and then the lion pounces.

Jonah: Yes on his way to work like Daddy . . . *(he moves his hands down the body of the giraffe and says after a silent time studying his picture)* He was a big big big lion and now the giraffe is dead.

Roots – stems of artistic confidence

In Chapter 1 we referred to the very important aspect of 'root' in the art adventure. We focus here on the core – the foundation of an artistic character. From the core, paths will meander, transform and merge but always doing so with the confident assuredness and anchorage of the 'root'. Take time to picture the child who transports A to B, a movement that is repeated several times a day on a very regular basis. This is not only a very familiar scene in an early years setting but one that is viewed, in abundance, in outside spaces. The physical space generates much transportation of objects, a very active schema that lends itself to the transportation of mark-making where lines are taken for a walk or sticky tape is pulled and stuck down onto a long surface. The outside space also offers many resourceful advantages in schematic transportation with its wealth of natural objects to be moved about. The ritual dance we often observed taking place is invested with patterns and idiosyncratic expression that can be related to our study of art schemas.

Each art encounter is expressed in multi-imaged forms translated by the child from what is being played out in their minds and imaginations. With each encounter children build on what they already know. Previous knowledge grows from a root knowledge base and relevant here is the value and recognition of the rooted path of children's artistic development. It is a bedrock seed that is deeply embedded in the child's cognitive and physical being and is integral to their artistic development. In the action of putting an idea onto paper, we see the fusion and entwinement of cognitive thought and purposeful action borne out of a characterful and personalised schema. This creative infrastructure is confident, self-assured and steadfast and, as such, sustains many paths and veins to diverge and meander from it as the child continues to investigate. Karmiloff-

Smith (2013) reminds of this in her studies of young infants' minds: 'You have to understand the roots because that's the only way to understand the outcome.'

Investigations remain in the domain of the root schema but can take many directions and possibilities. The root schema affords a depth of knowing in a repeated theme or medium as layers build up (Duffy, 1998). The commonalities and continuities of their 'styles' are captured at each event but are built on little by little and so the schemas merge with new nuances of style and understanding.

Incubation – a magnified moment

Repeated actions which stem from a root schema can be magnified to understand just what wondrous human actions are taking place in that one moment. By looking through a giant magnifying glass, the confident advocacy with which a root schema permeates within a child sparks reactions richly abundant in thought, creativity and reflection. Both Claxton (2006b) and Duffy (1998) refer to an incubation process indicative of a young child's creative spirit, which is mindful of time, space and process.

Duffy (1998: 79) refers to this incubation process as she describes a creative moment in slow motion:

> During this [creative] process we need to saturate ourselves with ideas, to become so familiar with the concepts involved in the particular problem that we are solving that we can recall them automatically.

Claxton (2007) discusses how ideas and creative thought 'bubble up' to the surface and need time to be digested and projected through a variety of stages, such as intuition, imitation and imagination. Claxton's reference to the mnemonic layers of knowing can build a picture of these moments in time and, when magnified, contain a whole complex strata of knowing and memories which form the emergence of the action, the thought, the idea. The end reaction or product can come to fruition, having stemmed from the idiosyncratic root.

This creative incubation process is present in children's actions in their artistic endeavours and can last a minute, an hour, a day – it can span a whole series of moments and weeks. There is no defined time attached to this processional conquest of understanding, but a generic route of experience and understanding takes place. As a child 'wallows' (Bruce 2001) in their moment of 'doing' we see different states of being emerge and each state triggers another. Figure 2.9 offers a flowing dynamic of 'thinking' and 'being' when wallowing in art experiences. Some moments may be more prominent than others and some only fleeting but their fusion is what makes a creative moment so very rich and interesting and why we repeatedly visit and indulge in these moments.

Inquisitiveness – a state of active curiosity

↓

Exploration – travelling in or through an unfamiliar area in order to learn about and analyse it

↓

Investigation – observing or enquiring in detail

↓

Immersion – deep mental and physical involvement

↓

Inspiration – mentally stimulated to do or feel something

↓

Imitation – using someone or something as a model

↓

Inference – reasoning from factual evidence or knowledge

↓

Imagination – forming new ideas, images and concepts

↓

Creating – bringing something into existence physically

↓

Reviewing – looking over, examining and considering change

↓

Refining – adding to and satisfying

Figure 2.9 Artistic wallowing – an incubation process

Looking back – a layered portfolio

It is interesting to ponder whether styles and particular recognisable and familiar patterns that we associate with celebrated artists, both classical and contemporary, can be tracked back to childhood schemas. As a child, did Bridget Riley respond to marks with a regular and ordered vertical and horizontal schema as her paintings and prints convey? Were the densely coloured canvasses of Mark Rothko inspired by his young 'layering' self? If you create your own art as an adult, take a moment to survey how you apply yourself to production and also the work you produce. Does a recognisable and particular pattern or style emerge that you can relate back to your own childhood days of exploring and investigating art-based ideas?

The artist Carl Andre reflects on a clear connection between impressions and experiences of childhood and his own giant, metallic sculptural art. The journalist Emma Brockes (2013) reflects in her interview with the artist:

> Those ideas were established early on, when he was growing up in Quincy, Massachusetts, around abandoned granite quarries and the shipyard where his father worked as a draughtsman. Andre remembers with awe 'these great blocks of rejected granite lying around'; at the shipyard, he says, 'all these steel sheets would be lying out in the weather, rusting.'

Our own memories, and those of celebrated artists, can serve as clues as to whether we can recall styles prevalent in childhood and relate them to our present-day actions in the art-making process. Memories, though, can be vague, skewed and not always reliable, but still fun for us to indulge in. Perhaps if we had all kept a portfolio of our image-making, photographs of our creative actions, we could then trace individual schemas back to childhood exploration – a huge and mighty wealth of analytical evidence swims before us!

However, retaining and reviewing the actions of children is very possible. Portfolios, for want of a better word, that house a child's images, actions and imaginative endeavours, are a hugely rich resource – not only for the adult who wants to understand and support the child, but also, and most importantly, for the child to observe themself, reflect on adventures had and see the artist they have become so far on their journey. Children enjoy, for good reason, the opportunity to look back at what they have done, to see the process of development emerging. They often find this very amusing and make fun of their young selves and how they interpreted life through their art-making.

Reviewing themselves as developing artists through hard-copy evidence provides a basis for self-recognition as image-makers, shape-creators and artistically imaginative beings.

Pedagogues working in the Reggio Emilia schools are dedicated to the historical and cultural heritage contained within the documentation of artwork. Through purposeful retainment of art, a sequence of images is kept as a rich resource of referral and celebration. Laura Rubizzi, a teacher at the Diana Preschool in Reggio Emilia, comments on this aspect when she reflects: 'The multiplicity of documentation materials enables the pulsing of shared moments between different educational contexts . . . and the identification of different paths' (Giuidici and Vecchi, 2004: 151). The role of documentation and the portfolio will be further considered in Chapters 4 and 8.

We have evidence of Maia, our first example in this chapter, because hard-copy evidence was kept and so reviewed and discussed with her. She is now eight and finds it very amusing that she drew, painted, sculpted and danced in circles. She is also, importantly, fascinated by this. When she looks at her past rotational creations, she sees the patterns that are pertinent to all that she did and also relishes the fact that she was prolific in her art production. The continuation of 'looking' and reviewing is something we need to retain as the artist ventures through the primary school system, and this is something we will consider in more detail in Chapter 7.

Conclusion

As schemas emerge in art-making, the outline of the individual artist simultaneously and consequently starts to become more focussed. As we have seen, one particular schema may be very distinctive in one child and a multitude of repeated behavioural actions and ideas may be prevalent in another. We can be sure, however, that what is common to both scenarios is that our 'young artists' continue to define their creative paths and mastery of skills by making full use of their internal behavioural resources. Children are very resourceful in their ability to tap into something they know, something they feel familiar with, and then, by using their confident and physically active mind, they schematically create and make. Charged moments of incredible art-making have so much invested in them – the magnification of which should continually influence the way we see the young committed visualisers with whom we work. Crucially, our observations and consequential understandings tell us about what children 'can do' as young artists and not what is in deficit.

Reflection

- Identify three children to track and observe – find out what they do. Are there repeated patterns that you can see in their artwork? Which ones are most relevant to the child?
- What could you use to extend their learning and involvement in art through your own recognition of this?
- How would you discuss this with a parent?

Further reading

Arnold, C. (2010) *Understanding Schemas and Emotion in Early Education*, London: Sage.

Athey, C. (2007) *Extending Thought in Young Children*, second ed., London: Paul Chapman.

Young children as artists

Duffy, B. (1998) *Supporting Creativity and Imagination in the Early Years,* Maidenhead: Open University Press.

Goddard-Blythe, S. (2004) *Well Balanced Child,* Stroud: Hawthorn Press.

Mairs, K. (2013) *Young Children Learning through Schema,* Oxon: Routledge.

CHAPTER 3

The world of senses
Transforming the consciousness

Mine is the squashest.

(Enrique, aged 3)

Introduction

In the previous chapters we have referred to the rich sensory world that our young children live in and how this gratifying habitat stimulates their cognitive development through experimentation and exploration. In this chapter, we focus on sensory awareness as the enlightenment of infant discovery and the process it takes.

Eisner (2002), amongst many, informs us that the senses provide the first avenue to consciousness. To understand this, we need to examine the relationship between very young children, toddlers and babies and their interpretation of brave new world which confronts them from the moment they come into the existence. Their contact is saturated in the various senses that are awake and alive each and every day. Some experiences are familiar, routine and everyday and so are ritually exercised, adding a layer of security to the multiple experiences of sensory awareness.

As they touch material, smell cooking food and hear loud sounds, their small bodies are energised with a multitude of complex known and unknown perceptible encounters. Familiar and unfamiliar enterprises and interactions continue alongside each other, each one informing the other, and so a personalised repertoire of understanding starts to emerge.

Senses and the developing brain

This repertoire is a direct consequence of the power of the senses and the connections that are being rapidly and busily made in the brain. Gopnik *et al.* (1999) liken this fast and furious cell connectivity to the intricate and complex paths of a telephone wire; wires that communicate with one another in order to speak, be heard, to listen and to make sense of the dialogue presented. Gopnik *et al.* (1999: 70) further maintain:

> In the first few months of life, babies already seem to have solved a number of deep philosophical conundrums. They know something about how those objects characteristically move. They know those objects are part of a three-dimensional space. And they know the relationship between information that comes from their different senses.

Babies are born with over 2,500 synapses – connections where nerve impulses are transmitted and received. These synapses actively multiply between 0–3 years of age, increasing to over 15,000. Such immense numbers alone can help us to appreciate the enormous and astonishing development that is happening within the young child's brain and mind. All these connections are being created during the interface of contact with new endeavours and are spurred on by the hungry, omnipresent senses.

> What was first a reflex response, a function of instinct, becomes a gradual search for stimulation, differentiation, exploration, and eventually for meaning. Our sensory system becomes a means through which we pursue our own development.
>
> (Eisner, 2002: 2)

Eisner (ibid.) also reminds us that sensory enterprises can be evanescent in their existence – fleeting and momentary but the essence of the discovery will remain within the domain of the moment, embedded in the mind's connections. Claxton (2006a: 3) further defines these momentary confrontations as:

> perceptions and sensations of which we are aware; images and memories and thoughts that flit across our minds while awake . . . and those more indistinct creatures that lurk on the margins of consciousness that we call hunches, inklings, glimmerings and intuitions.

Sensory mnemonic image-making

> Discovering the emotions that enquiry evokes, experiencing the feel of paint, the aroma of linseed oil, the touch of wet clay – these are a part of what is learnable from art and collectively contribute to meaning.
>
> (Eisner, 2002: 58)

Visceral and sensorial-driven interaction is a somatic act where the young child is involved, for a variety of time spans, in an embodied physical and mental experience of finding out. Paolo Cavazzoni of Reggio Children (2012) refers to this experiential and raw actuality as the integrity of the child. He goes on to discuss how the separation of body from mind for children is a non-sequitur; their bodies and minds are inextricably connected in a sensory juncture of discovery whether through touch and thought, sight and colour connections, or smell and memory.

The five senses commonly referred to are:

- visual – sight;
- auditory – hearing;
- olfactory – smell;
- gustatory – taste;
- haptic – touch.

Each of these is powerful in its ability to connect the young child to the world around them. We are each uniquely different in our make-up so our various senses will affect us in different ways. A food connoisseur is a master of taste and flavour, a sculptor owns a haptic ability which leads to an aesthetic knowledge of form, shape and space. It is the olfactory sense, however, that evokes immensely power images, and one that we often underestimate. The sense of smell has an ability to jog a memory or recall something from the past quite out of the blue.

Recalling a situation and feeling an emotion long past is quite a moving experience. We do it all the time, when our own sense of smell recognises something from the past and takes us back there, fleetingly but with a great overwhelming power; it is, at times, somewhat amazing to contemplate. The sense of smell can be extraordinarily evocative, bringing back pictures as sharp as photographs of scenes that had left the conscious mind. Such time-travelling phenomena often vanish as soon as they have appeared so they cannot crystallise as a perfect memory. But these fleeting olfactory recollections can evoke a feeling of warmth and comfort as they often draw on our fondly recalled exploits. Not all such evocations are positive of course, but they nonetheless have a very powerful reaction in our bodies and minds. They constitute our embodied knowing where we allow ourselves to focus on a process brought about by the simultaneous ignition of the body and our senses. Claxton (2006a) refers to these as mnemonic residues of experience. They are part of the vast tangle of momentary memory-based impressions that are based in passages of time and responses, forming part of our subliminal perception and unconscious registration.

If we now consider this scenario in the lives of the very young, we are able to have some kind of understanding of how much their powerfully driven sensory endeavours shape their early existence:

- Babies know how to find a mother's breast through their sense of smell.
- They recognise a father's voice which they also heard pre-birth.
- They can turn their eyes in awareness of a bright light or colour.
- They stroke and cuddle soft toys and blankets.
- Their mouth is often the first port of call for an unknown object in order to consult their gustatory glands and ability to touch with tongue and growing teeth.

Babies and young infants start to develop a conceptual clarity in the early stages of life by way of their sensory exploits. Their interactions steer perceived thought to a more concrete stage, and conception of ideas can be generated, as Figure 3.1 suggests:

A progressive flow of perceptive visual understanding and intent:

Sensorial exploration ⟶ Concrete understandings ⟶ Expressive intent

Figure 3.1 Perceptive visual understanding and intent

The development of tactile, visual, auditory, spatial and movement perception has an impact on their experiences, as considered in the stages above. Babies cannot synchronise their eyes, for instance, but by the sixth month they are able to reach for an object they see, and at about a year they can follow rapidly moving objects. Astoundingly, human life's ability to find a sensory base of habitat begins in the womb. Goddard-Blythe (2004: 193) states:

> In the embryo, awareness of and response to touch begin with the mouth from as early as 7 weeks after conception, spreading to the hands and the feet until eventually the whole body surface becomes responsive to touch.

A three-year-old's visual perception is similar to that of an adult. Their ability to see with understanding has a direct impact on their ability to represent and conceive thoughts and ideas (Duffy 1998).

Sensory modalities and aesthetic understanding

As children use their senses to learn and understand, they begin to develop an awareness of aesthetic appreciation. Senses are the channels through which we learn and they also awaken the world around us. A young child will begin to learn how to use their sensory powers in order to select, see, hear, observe, distinguish and feel in art. Aesthetic experiences bridge the sensory encounter with an ability to see, touch and hear further than the original moment of interaction. These states of being can facilitate discovery and examination and enable children to see and appreciate beauty. The beauty may come in all shapes and sizes, from a banana skin to a dried-up leaf.

We are reminded of the spiritual character of a young child, as examined in Chapter 1. Aesthetic experiences can be fleeting and we all recognise them: a breeze on your face, hot sand between your toes, a warm bath after a hard day's work, fresh sheets on the bed. For that one moment, all your senses are open and impress upon you overwhelming feelings and emotions. Eglinton (2003: 37) defines this journey as '[i]ntrinsically valuable sensory experiences that absorb us, awaken us, and elicit a response and an understanding of beauty found in both the natural and the constructed environment'. She goes on to consider the essential and powerful relationship between aesthetic experiences and understandings and those of children in their art development. A growing perception in aesthetic appreciation encourages children to expand their already natural sense of wonder and this often leads to art-making. The power of the experiences is often so all-consuming and overwhelming that they are naturally motivated and compelled to respond both verbally and, importantly in the case of art, visually.

If we consider the motivation and inspiration of living artists, it is often the essence of a sensory moment that has compelled them to put paint to paper or chisel to wood. The environmental artist Andy Goldsworthy encapsulates this motivational force:

> A snowball is simple, direct and familiar to most of us. I use this simplicity as a container for feelings and ideas that function on many levels. Occasionally I have come across a last patch of snow on top of a mountain in late May or June. There's something very powerful about finding snow in summer. It's as if the whole of winter has drained through that white hole – a concentration of winter.
>
> (Goldsworthy, 2001)

To maximise these moments and provide opportunities for children to indulge in them, we need to consider the how, what, where and when of sensory-based engagement.

> It is our job to put in their path objects of wonder, beauty, and awe, to point out the brilliance of the everyday, to notice the unnoticeable, to seek subtlety in the obvious, to be inspired by ordinary events, or sense the unfamiliar in the familiar.
>
> (Eglinton, 2003: 37)

We do not seek to direct or usurp a child's initial response. Our role here is to support this initial response and take it to the next realm of engagement, in order to expand aesthetic understandings and possibilities. The experiences still maintain a very personal quality and the origins remain true to the founder of the awe-inspiring moment. We do not pertain to seek ownership of their moments, but to engage with them and provide opportunities of space, time, resources and dialogue in order for children to unravel, examine and search for the jewels of the art-inspired stimuli. Adult collaboration and co-exploration is examined in Chapter 5, as is the consideration of space, time and resources in Chapter 6.

What we can consider in this chapter, in relation to sensory-awareness and its relationship with art development, is the emerging understanding of elements in art. Art-bound elements and their existence within experimental and experiential play are the result of linking aesthetic experiences with sensory engagement.

> Handled in such a playful way, objects cease to be context-bound, and we can change their colour, texture, scale and function. Objects can stand for anything we choose; they become visual metaphors invested with personal meanings which suit our present purpose.
>
> (Prentice, 1994: 128)

Combining experiences:
Sensory engagement + experiential art play = understandings of aesthetic appreciation

Figure 3.2 Understandings of aesthetic appreciation

The above combination of experiences produces processes and results pleasing to the eye, hand and ear. This successful partnership provides a concrete creative platform for young working artists who are beginning to train the eyes and hands to work with visual and tactile elements. They are energised and ready to explore as young artists and experiment with colour, shape, form, mass and space. This creative hothouse of active inspection finds in its path the elements of art: line, tone, colour, shape, space, texture, pattern and form.

Sensory-provoked language

A good old wallow in a sensory moment can provoke a strong sense of alertness, so much so that words or noises escape our mouths in appreciation or, at least, some felt recognition of that moment. The wonder of sensory indulgence in young children is the adventure through vocabulary as experienced when they touch, taste or smell something that is new and previously unknown. They are able to magically create new words to onomatopoeically describe the essence of the exploration such as the words spoken by a three-year-old – 'mine is squashest' – whilst he manipulated gloopy, paint-textured sponges. A child once invented the word 'stringly' to emphasise the stretchy length of clay being rolled between palms. We all know, recognise and sometimes smile fondly at such invented words. They dwell in the minds and thoughts, however, of our serious young artists. We, of course, can enjoy them, but we must also see how very crucial they are to the aesthetically experienced articulation which is abundant in art exploration. What better way to incite and inspire vocabulary, communication and language. Motivational forces of sensory experiences bring to life the brain's capacity to find descriptive words that are just as enjoyable to say as they are in their tactile existence. We continue to examine the articulation of visual and tactile vocabulary in Chapters 4 and 6.

The serious 'mess' of sensory-based art exploration

The application of sensory discovery is of the utmost importance in children's endeavours to play with all the elements which make up art play. In Chapter 1, we defined the act of art play as children physically and mentally exploring a material and thus becoming acquainted with its properties and possibilities. We have also considered the magical excitement and curiosity of young children as they venture forth in artistic activities. We know that discovery, reflection and practical experiences are at the very heart of young children's learning. But, somehow, when we are caught up in the everyday life of planning, preparing, observing and assessing we can become controlling and careful, often directly in response to the humdrum existence of these very words and what they symbolise. By this I mean we can lose the ability to let go, see what happens, be flexible and allow for chaotic experiments. Perhaps we do this because, in our adult minds, chaos can lead to huge mess and disorganisation that needs tidying up, compartmentalising, sorting out. Our adult embedded 'eyes' may view it this way, but what we really need to do is see it through the eyes of the children. The young minds and bodies caught up in gloopy paint play, mud pies and shaving foam glitter are involved quite seriously in investigative understanding – their engagement is not so much messy chaos, as adventurous meaning-seeking. In *The Scientist in the Crib,* Gopnik *et al.* (2001: 186) talk about brain activity and the rapid development that is taking place in the young child:

> Children's brains are much busier than ours. By three months the brain areas involved in seeing, hearing, and touch are burning up an increasing amount of glucose. The brain's energy consumption reaches full adult levels at around two years of age. By three the little child's brain is actually twice as active as an adult brain. This bristling activity remains at twice the level of an adult until the child reaches the age of nine or ten.

The young brain is fertile ground for experiments, exploration and discovery. Young children's minds are working it all out and they can only do this if they are able to get tangled up in the finding out. We refer back to 'the mess' and 'the chaos' as before: a stage that is vital in art-making in order to then filter through and find out the answer. As Gopnik *et al.* state, our adult brains have worked things out and have pruned the cells that are no longer necessary. Children are not there yet; they have not started the pruning process because they are still growing the cognitive and creative branches. Messy art play precedes and predicates the child's growing ability to prune and filter.

Young children as artists

In the context of the young artist, this tangle of spaghetti (Moss, 2004) is a hothouse of thinking for young children. They examine and analyse materials, experience visual and tactile sensations, find their own style, experiment with their own schema and start to find and make genuine marks and personal interpretations. There is often no clear focus, and the play can be uncontrolled and turbulent as they search, delve and fumble for their own glimpses of understanding. But there are also, conversely, purposeful moments where intent is real, as we know from our observations, further considered in Chapter 4. Duffy (1998) discusses the importance of this haphazard, pleasurable and lawless play as she says of the active involvement:

- children use all their senses in the process of exploration, especially the sense of touch;
- offer children plenty of opportunity to mould and manipulate materials;
- don't have a focus on making or producing something.

Creative connections and pathways of cognitive conceptions are fusing as children grapple with new tactile and visual experiences. They are making fundamentally important steps in their cognitive concepts of the world. Playing with a variety of materials can also be surprising to the touch, the smell, the eye and therefore can instil a moment of cognitive disequilibrium as children connect, often internally, the concrete relationship they are experiencing at the moment of interaction, adding their own thoughts, ideas and explanations to that moment. Messy play is the cognitive disequilibrium that allows for clarity of understanding. There is not a set answer, there are no set rules but there are ideas and discoveries to be surmised and found through the wonderful chaos of participative play.

An important aspect to note here, too, is that mess allows for mistakes and risks to be taken. With no fixed route or exact intention, playing with the infinite possibilities of the 'mess' is highlighted and gives rise to the implausible and odd. The brain is given permission to be sidetracked and the potential for creativity and originality is increased. 'Messy' art-based activities afford the freedom to explore the fantastic, the not-straightforward, and so excite the stirring imaginations of young risk-taking artists. We need to be able to play and create without preconceptions and then, as a consequence, those less likely patterns and connections will come to the surface.

Creating with the mind and body – sensory-rich explorations

> The power of discovering a concept, which is a mental category, orients the eye and the sensibility; it is at once knowledge of an object and of one's own potentials, and opens up the experimentation to different and deeper possibilities of investigation.
>
> (Giuidici and Vecchi, 2004: 56)

Consider the examples of children creatively participating in adventurous colour-seeking missions in Box 3.1. The examples respond to extending and enriching the sensory experience through tactile art experiences. In addition, and very importantly, they positively promote the potentiality of investigative-based results, which can only be reached through free and potentially 'messy' exploration.

'Messy art play' should conjure up an image of rich and colourful learning pathways, way beyond the confines and anxieties of mops, brooms and boundaries. 'Play helps children dare to learn, even when they are uncertain about what will happen. It creates an attitude of mind which is curious, investigative, risk taking and full of adventure' (Bruce, 2001: 47).

The words in Box 3.2 are just some of the justifications associated with these rich chaotic tangles and have been collected over time by both teachers, students and children. It is not a definitive list – it can be added to and continued if we ensure we value the 'open-endedness' (Broadhead, 2012) of these spaces and interactions. They are words that we associate with the visual and tactile play in art in Box 3.2.

Contained within art-based scenarios, where rich sensory development is at play, is the very important aspect of 'ownership'. The explorations of tactile adventure are manipulated by hands that belong to the artist – whether the child or the adult. The words in Box 3.2 are a part of that 'owned' moment and, though they may not be verbalised, they are contained in the application of doing and feeling for that individual at play. Art projects in Reggio Emilia are very adept at recognising and valuing these owned articulations and documentation relates energised experiences which form a part of children's individual tactile development as artists. The following excerpt describes an instalment in a sculptural project where children combined materials to discover tactile qualities:

> In contact with the children's hands, the material underwent yet another transformation. These were the first gestures, the first forms. We made a sort of catalogue of them. The children experimented with resistance, lightness, and delicacy; it was often the material itself, reluctant to be modified, that surprised them.
>
> (Giuidici and Vecchi, 2004: 29)

Again, we are reminded of the sense of trepidation, surprise and unpredictability that richly abounded in the sculptural adventure told. A concluding message as a result of the combining project tells of the relationship of child, tactile process and end product and, importantly, the ownership and identity of tactile-based artwork and child.

> The final compositions were the result of agreements reached, a sort of pact of alliance between the children and the material. Each composition bore the personal traces, thoughts, and imprints of the children and the quality, identity, and peculiarity of the materials.
>
> (ibid.)

Box 3.1 Adventurous and positive mess art play

Rainbow rivers

Trays of water and white sheets of plastic lie horizontally, vertically or diagonally. Water is continually poured down onto the sheets, as are droplets of coloured ink. The continual flow merges colour trickles and rivers and so colour-mixing explorations occur in amongst a very visual, tactile and aurally rich sequence of physical encounters.

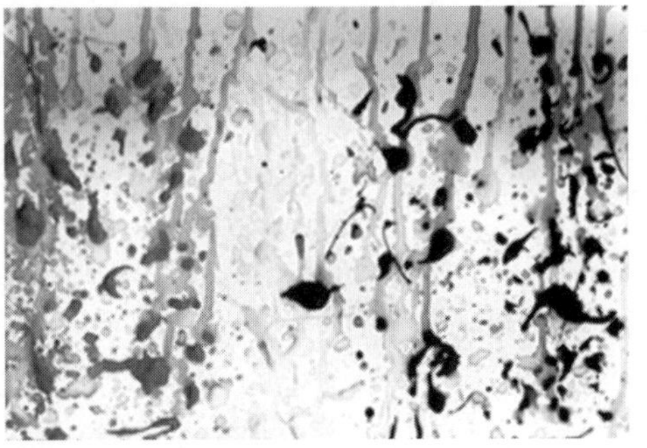

Figure 3.3 Rainbow rivers

Pots of colour

As opposed to the thick encrusted paint pots which allow a small hole for a particular-sized brush, children mix their own colours in glass jam jars – consistencies of paint dependent on measures of powder and water can be shaken and stirred and gazed at through windows where light filters through to illuminate the various colours created.

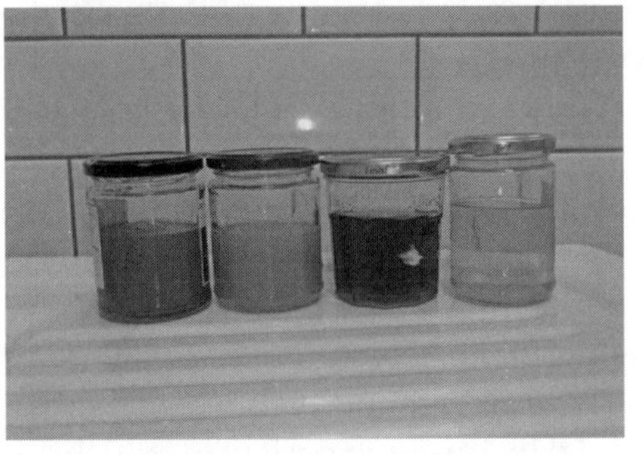

Figure 3.4 Pots of colour

Spread the colour

Enormous pieces of paper lie on the ground and these require big body and arm extension movements to make long defined marks with primary-coloured paint from the centre of the paper. As the paint is spread with large wallpaper brushes from the centre in a variety of marks, the lines mix and the colours merge. If the paper is appropriately large in area, feet and hands explore all the spaces with the paint and continue to merge colours on a grand and sweeping scale. Body parts will now also have the newly created colours imprinted on them, ensuring ownership and evidence of interaction.

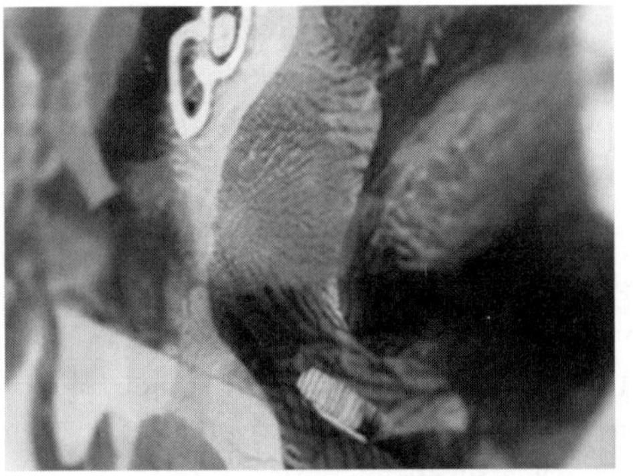

Figure 3.5 Spread the colour

Box 3.2 Associated words for visual and tactile play in art

banging	bending	breaking	brushing
carving	combining	continuing	cutting
dissolving	dragging	dripping	flopping
folding	holding	joining	layering
lifting	melting	mixing	modelling
moulding	parting	patting	pinching
poking	pounding	pouring	pressing
printing	prodding	pulling	pushing
reshaping	rolling	rubbing	scattering
separating	shaping	shining	slapping
smelling	smoothing	sparkling	spiralling
spreading	squashing	squeezing	squidging
sticking	stretching	stroking	tearing
tracing	thumping	wiggling	zig-zagging

Letting go

The majority of these tactile-rich experiences, as discussed, cause a disequilibrium in the residing adult. The message is that we need to go with the child and, in truth, let go a little. Wright (2010: 176) comments on this inter-relational balance: 'In the pursuit of understanding, the interlocutor [adult] must be willing to "go there" with the child.' For many adults 'letting go' pertains to 'losing control'. It is a difficult and disquieting teaching approach for some adults; but what we have to distinguish is what we are actually letting go of. Is it the adult-set rules, or is it the boundaries that prevent creativity flourishing? With careful management and classroom environment organisation, we can enjoy 'losing control' but within a secure domain. All too often in classrooms we live in fear of the cleaners and their comments. I remember very clearly that as a Year 2 teacher my classroom hosted 'messy play' as a rich and continuous feature of our art area and art experimentation. I was the least favourite teacher with the cleaners and no one wanted to sort out my classroom at the end of a busy day of experiential art learning. My constant defence was that this was a classroom, in a school – a space and place where children were 'learning' about the world and the mark they could make on it. It was not a space where carpets were to be kept pristine and table surfaces shiny and scratch-free. Hotels were for that purpose! As Hoyuelos (2004) stated, classrooms and settings should be seen as 'complex labs of constant experimentation and unexpected outcomes'. There is, of course, a place for systems in order to make the 'organised' chaos happen more harmoniously and for us to be able to feel secure in our role within this paradigm of activity. In Chapter 6, we focus on this aspect when we consider the environment, invitations and resources in more detail.

Energised states – unconscious and conscious

What we already know is that we are working with children who are committed participants in a world full of sensory adventures. Children's curiosity, as discussed in Chapter 1, spurs them on to find out and investigate. These investigations can be seen in many different forms and they nourish and feed the children's unconscious and conscious minds. If we consider our own explorations, we are not always aware, every minute of the day, of our mind's ability to retain experiences which remain latent but are fully submerged in our cognitive makeup.

> Consciousness is the product of attention, and attention is guided by past experience and moderated by current need or purpose. Consciousness is also a form of awareness, and awareness is fed initially by sensibility. Thus, sensibility is the mother of consciousness and provides the content for reflection, analysis, and the making of connections. Because consciousness depends initially on sensibility, the refinement of the sense is of prime importance.
>
> (Eisner, 2002: 108)

Small moments of energised existence can trickle through into our minds and unconscious thinking without clear definition or recognition, but they are there, nonetheless, and they continue to form within us alongside the conscious moments. Claxton (2002) refers to this as catching a gleam of an idea as it flashes across the corner of consciousness. We can link this back to our repeated interaction and layering of understanding through schema and continued play and practice with materials and experiences. As the children in Figures 3.6–3.9 luxuriate in the wet sand, they consciously:

- spread out their toes and imprint patterns in the sand;
- build small sculptures of sand on each toe;
- let the granules fall through their hands;
- add more water to make muddier, sludgier sculptures and ridges.

Unconsciously, they:

- continued to feel the sand under their feet whilst they discussed their next adventure, moving their feet and sweeping the sand up, then letting it cascade from their toes in unison with one another;
- rubbed sand between their hands and felt the different sized granules and crystals;
- had the tactile experience of sand sticking to skin and the water draining it off.

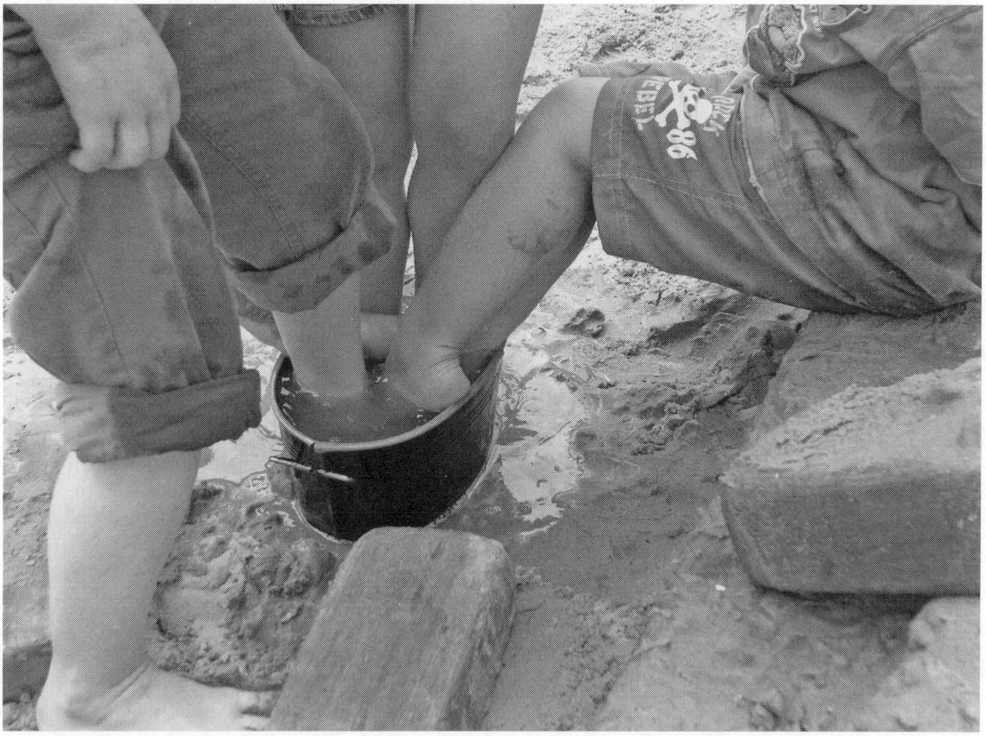

Figure 3.6 Washing feet in the bucket

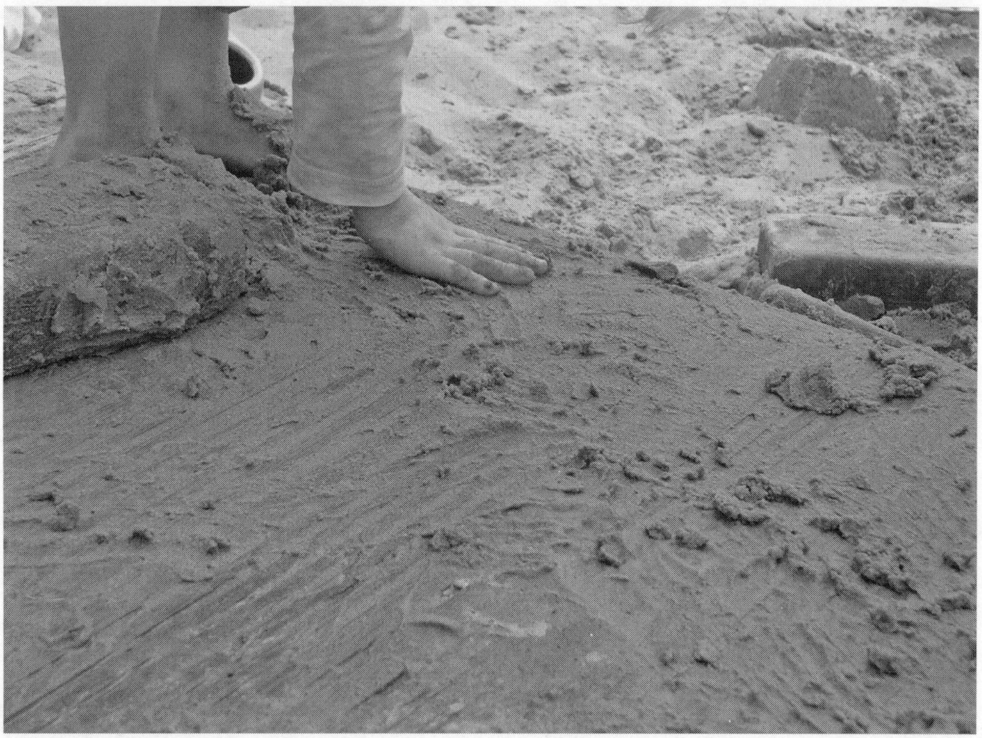

Figure 3.7 Sculpting the sand by hand

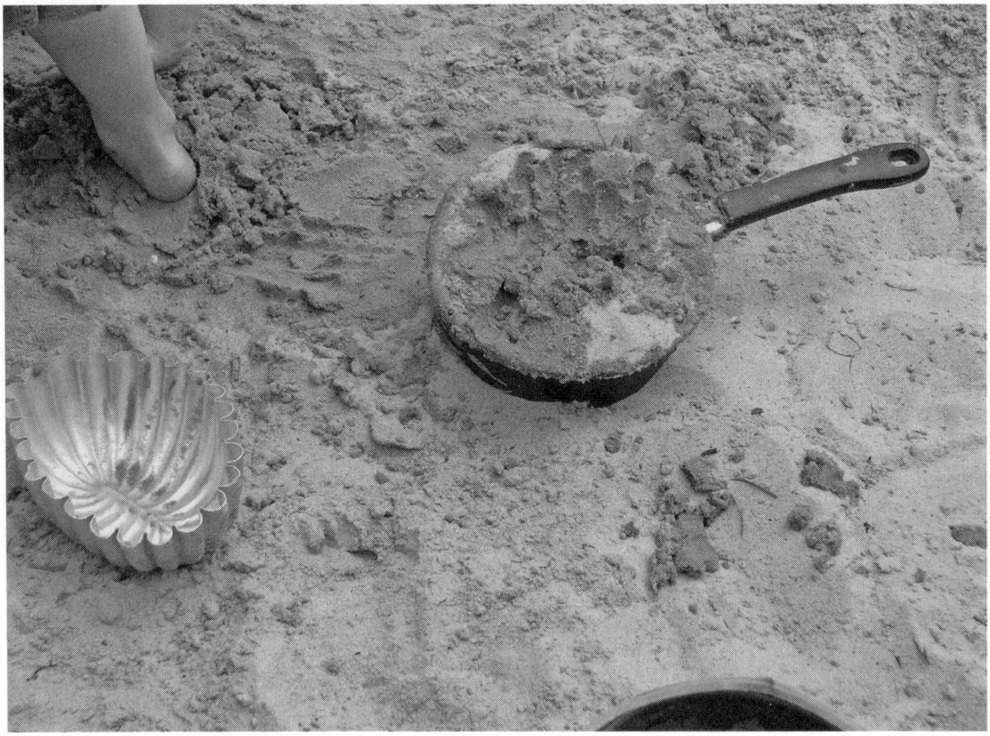

Figure 3.8 Using sand moulds

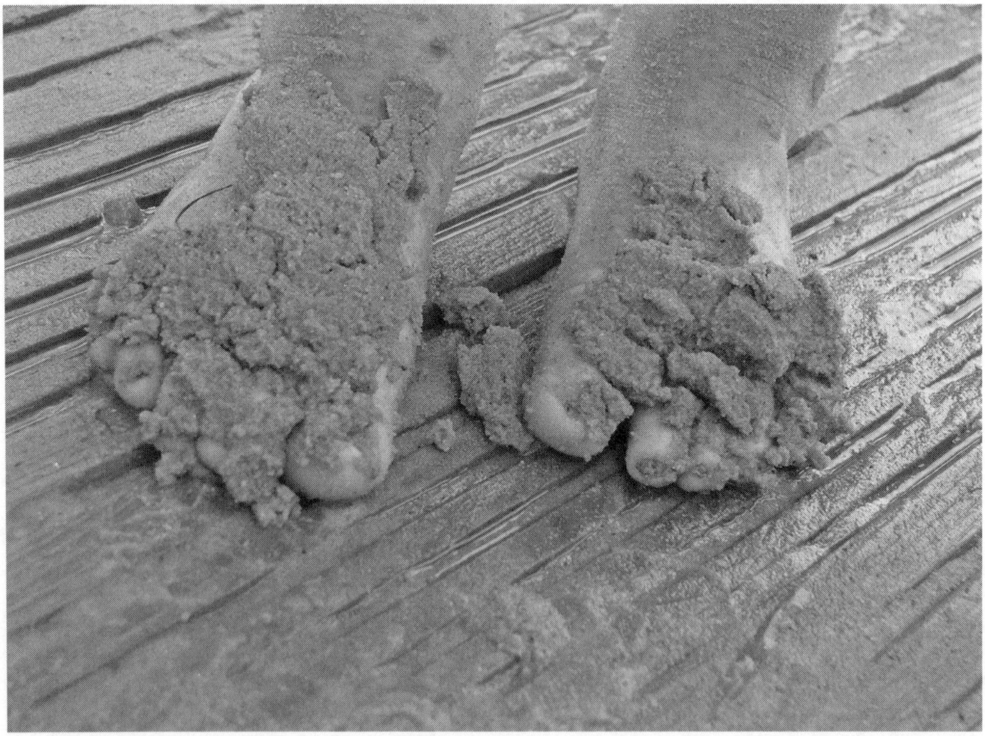

Figure 3.9 The tactile experience of wet sand on feet

All the children involved in this experiment were exuberantly committed to what they were doing and knew, from past interaction, that sand was an exciting and rewarding material to be working with. Sculptures were made and patterns created, all in the conscious mind. Their energised states of mind allowed their senses to penetrate the venture and hence their developing bank of knowledge deep within their unconscious and conscious states. Here we can appreciate the Montessorian view when Montessori, long ago (1995: 158), defined this adventure as simply 'passing little by little from the unconscious to the conscious'.

Other essential components were also at play in this scene: the collaboration of the children, the socially inspiring excitement and interest. The washing of feet in the bucket: how many feet can fit at once? Touching each other's toes and indulging in the grainy haptic experience: what does it feel like? Do I like it? What does it remind me of? All these questions could be heard and observed through voice and body language during the sensory-based dialogic exchange. Additionally they had the freedom and space to continue their explorations as a group of children, unhindered by boundaries. There was flow in this sensory investigation that followed a path of communicated and shared marvelling.

Not only was the entire activity alive with investigative intent, it importantly continued to build understanding and recognition of materials and possibilities. It is the latter which encouraged the children to create using their practised knowledge and further develop their skills as sculptors and transformers of shape and form. Eisner (2002: 12) refers to these undertakings as a way to:

> Invite children to pay attention to the environment's expressive features and to the products of their imagination and to craft a material so that it expresses or evokes an emotional or feelingful response to it.

Box 3.3 Shared marvelling moments in sensory sand and art play

- Socks off and feeling the sand: two children.
- Observed by others – two more join in.
- Children sit and lift the sand with their toes to sculpt little mounds on their toes: care and dedication awarded to the modelling of the mounds' peaks.
- Imprints made in the sand and ridges created by toes.
- Bucket of water added to the sandy ground to observe changes in the sandy ridges.
- More water added to create sandy puddles.
- Bucket becomes the focus of interest as all feet go into the bucket.
- Washing the sand off feet and rubbing the sand between hands.

Children place no restrictions on their adventures; they can experiment and explore without limits. Their ability to pick up ideas and refer back to previous sensory-driven escapades is without boundaries or caution. As Eglinton (2003: 29) states: 'A child's inner world is so spectacularly huge it could literally stimulate and motivate years and years of art experiences.'

The layering of sensory experiences in art

Creative adventures are filled with waves of engagement as the children probe, muse, evaluate – we are reminded of their ability to layer their understanding and draw upon their previous knowledge to inform the new. It is possible and often the case that we literally see 'layering' in the true sense of the word as children cover a piece of paper over and over with different coloured paint, or they continually wrap a box with more and more paper. The adventure in their quest to find out what will happen is valuable but, importantly, so is their need and desire to add more.

The dialogue in Box 3.4 follows a group of four- and five-year-olds as they relish a sensory-filled episode of colour, paint and water. Their encouragement of one another to first explore and then explore a little more is evident. Their investigations are dense with the 'feel' of the paint on the paper, the watery actions of the brush – sprinkles, splashes, flicks – and colour transformations. They investigate as a group in their awareness of one another's antics through dialogue and observation, but the individual quest is still very apparent. Each unearthing moment signifies an action that is engrossed in sensory awareness: feel, look, sound. This particular episode is one moment in time that will be repeated over and over, each instalment building on the former. The piquant understandings expand as the strata of experiences continue. Their journey is filled with revelations about consistencies, colour and, later, developing perceptions and purposeful actions in their art-making.

During explorations in art a child continues along stepping stones of discovery to see what happens next, showing full appreciation of the interactive material of the moment. Exploits have a perspicacity that we are to appreciate as senses ignite and explorations work in harmony. The feel and sound of the wrapping paper and the look, smell and applicatory quality of the paint drive an intense sense of adventure and ambition. Here we can see that sensory awareness is not only powerful in its ability to provoke understanding and memories, as previously discussed, but the *delight* encountered during the process drives the adventure and engenders further voyages of discovery. The sensory cognition is developing with determination and endeavour through committed investigation and revelation.

Box 3.4 Dialogue – colour, paint and water

Aimee: I'm putting oil on mine! *(Loads brush up with paint and does a flicking effect over painting.)*

Ella: How?

Aimee: Look *(shows her)*, you just sprinkle it!

(*Ella and Aimee both start sprinkling.*)

Aimee: These sprinkles are tadpoles! *(Adds another 'sprinkle'.)* There. (*Looks satisfied.*) Lots of tadpoles! (*Laughs and tries to pick up her painting.*) It's really soggy!

Ella: You put too much on!

Aimee: This is painty world where everybody loves to paint!

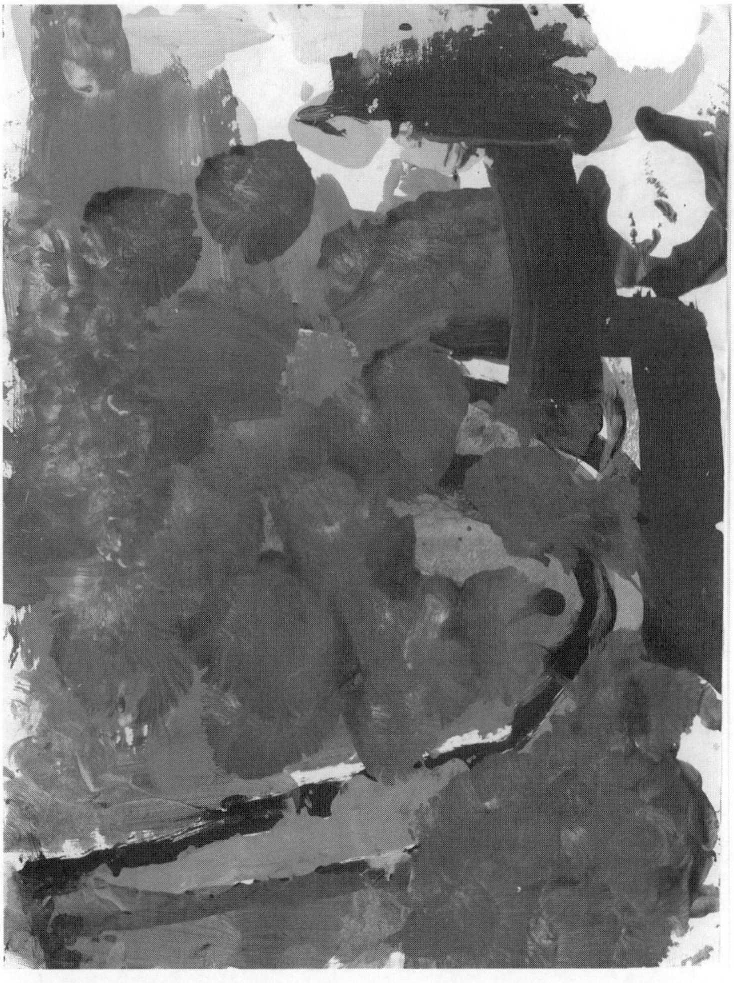

Figure 3.10 Colour dialogue 1

Ella: (*Screws up her painting and gets another piece of paper.*) I'm making a zoo instead. We are making a cave as there is going to be a thunderstorm and the animals need shelter. (*Looks at paper.*) I need a bigger bit of paper; it's going to be a big zoo! (*Gets another piece of paper and draws an outline.*) How do you like my zoo?

Charlotte: I'm drawing a spider – a big one in the corner of the cave!

Ben: I found a monster in my cave; I'm doing two black bits for eyes. (*Adds to black paint splodges.*)

Two girls clean their brushes: We've made black in the water!

Aimee: Now I need to wash it again!

Charlotte: (*Paints a line.*) Why is it blue?

Aimee: Because it already had some paint on there. t's all black, 'scuse me going to change it. (*Changes the water.*)

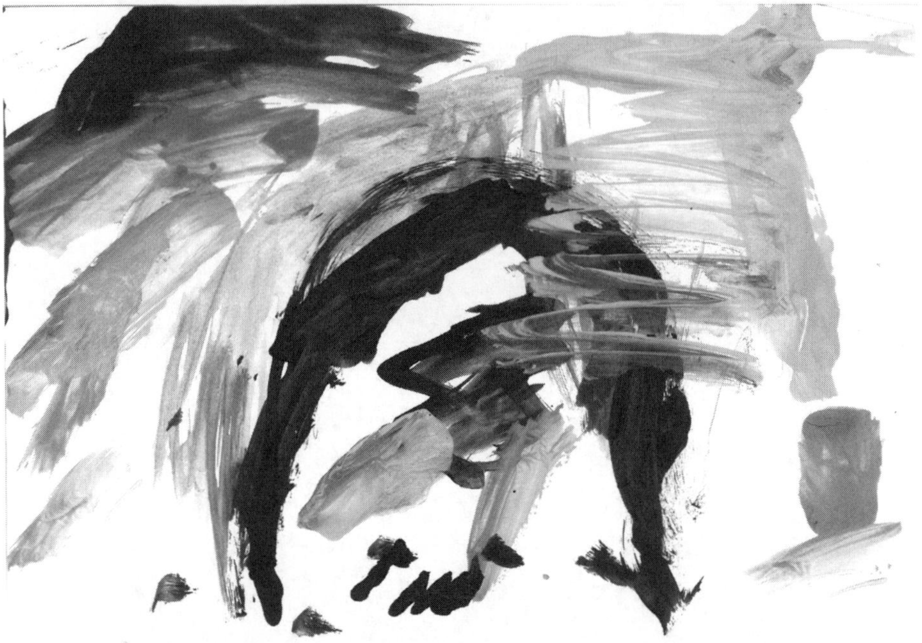

Figure 3.11 Colour dialogue 2

The wonderful 'surprise' of 'unchartered territories'

Surprise and revelation are intrinsically conjoined during infants' art-filled adventures. The physical and emotional sense of wonder that inspires motivation and discovery provokes surprise and unforeseen marvelling moments, as supported by Eisner (2002: 8):

> Surprise is one of the rewards of work in the arts. In addition, it is from surprise that we are most likely to learn something. What is then learned can become part of the individual's repertoire, and once it is part of that repertoire, new and more complex problems can be generated and successfully addressed.

A child struck by an unforeseen discovery is motivated to continue along that unpredictable path, as what can be more exciting than being surprised by something you have yourself provoked? The layering of paint not only changes the colour, previously unpredicted by its applicant, but it also transforms the stiffness of the paper into a gratifying surface of sogginess! A box gradually covered by multiple layers of paper alters the original shape seen, and creases, folds and crevices are created within the overlays, which offer a whole plethora of opportunities to poke and prod.

The actual exposure of the 'surprise' results from a making process that is owned by the child in their quest to experiment creatively. Surprise is a by-product of this process precisely because children are free to make up their own rules and take their own risks. Unexpected discoveries in art are what make the children feel confident and inspired to be in charge of their own journey as an artist. As they combine and multiply these moments of marvel, they gradually discover for themselves artistic possibilities and contemplate visual and tactile potentialities. They learn to see the previously unseen and feel the unfelt – richly rewarding experiences that are inextricably caught up in their own existence within the world.

Surprise is closely associated with *anticipation* in art. The unexpected lies in wait as a process is borne out and the result emerges. Some art media and practices afford this sense of anticipation more than others. A developing painting is visible to the eye, a mud pie gradually forms into a monster overseen by the sculptor, but the premise and process of printing expounds the delights of excited anticipation. The sequence takes the young artist through the important technical stages, rolling ink on the surface, making a pattern, placing the paper on top, and then . . . peeling it off to see what impression has been made. It is an activity where the end product is a relative unknown – the image or pattern has been drawn but the print will provide a different impression.

The revised EYFS (2012) responds to this in the guidance relating to 'Expressive arts and design' and positive relationships: 'This is about children's explorations into the world of pretense, building on their experiences of the real world and transforming them into something new' (earlyyearsmatters.co.uk, 2012). The guidance (British Association for Early Education, 2012) suggests to us that, quite rightly, a young child can construct and transform using materials:

> Children use what they have learnt about media and materials in original ways, thinking about uses and purposes. They represent their own ideas, thoughts and feelings through design and technology, art, music, dance, role play and stories.

We must ensure that opportunities to think in original ways and represent thoughts and feelings are numerous and progressively layered. Such consideration can be, oftentimes, noticeably absent from the wording laid out in curriculum guidance. In Chapter 6, we continue to consider our spaces and environment in response to this aim.

The abstract sense – awareness

We can recognise and value in children's creative experimenting a sixth sense – the abstract sense which is owned undisputedly by the young artist. The abstract sense is an intrinsic emotive domain that belongs to the individual. It is not always visible to an observer but it is a sense that refers to the individual's sense of awareness in a moment. This sense allows us to respond to a present episode in life and be alert to the experience of what might occur in moments of stillness, silence, gazing, touching and individual interaction. There is a sense of wonder at the interface between the moment and the individual – the transforming of consciousness as the two elements meet. Adam's wonderment was his initial reaction to the ice-tray colour experiment seen in Figure 3.12. He watched with intent curiosity as the colour he had chosen to drop onto the sheet of ice began to follow cracked rivulets, seep under the entire sheet and bleed into expanding shapes. His awareness during this episode was caught up in the coldness of the ice, the transformation from a clean sheet to a colour-ridden adventure, and the distinct relationship between him as the protagonist and the sheet of ice as his storyboard. His awareness-sensing was occupied by both an intensely visual and haptic quality and his own physically alert ability to direct his own body to pursue the moment.

We all possess a myriad of abstract senses that enable us to engage with and to interpret the world around us: some things which have no name but which we know we 'feel' and 'experience'. These abstract senses that children assimilate and digest offer infinite value to the art-making experience – inner resources are being utilised during deep moments of concentration and exploration. Children are not always aware of their ability to think in an abstract manner, making use of senses that do not have names but are acutely entwined in the very essence of who they are. This abstract or possibility thinking (Craft, 2002) is about the 'who' of the child in their actions and endeavours. It is intricately woven into their innermost beings, which are unique to them but come to the surface when

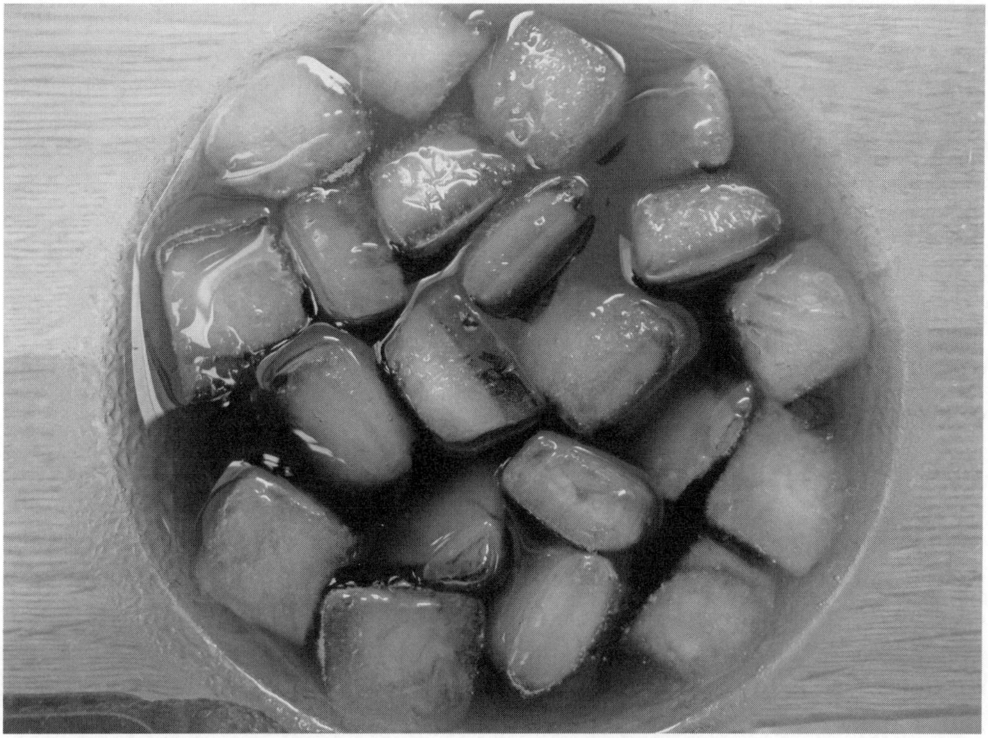

Figure 3.12 Ice-tray colour experiment

they engage and 'feel' the moment. This is a very personal and individual moment in which they understand themselves, sometimes as knowledge lying latent but present nonetheless. The strong subjectivity of their abstract senses defines moments with further understanding, silently flowing in and out of the dynamics of their intrapersonal experiences.

Sense of self – discovering an identity

We are reminded again of the spirituality of the child in moments of creative serendipity where children are freely and fortuitously following their own internal developmental agendas. This path emphasises their emerging sense of self and birth of identity (Simpson, 2011). Simpson (2011: 152) describes the relationship between the sense of self-worth and an emerging identity as being 'where mind, body, spirit are allowed to integrate, infused by the light of the soul'. A secure sense of self is what is at stake as children develop their identities as artists. The recognition of self allows them to follow a style, try out an experiment and take a risk, and thus self-confidence is positively pursued.

A young artist is working with their constantly defining sense of self – they can be affected, influenced and moved by others and the creative endeavours of people around them, but all this feeds into the promise of a developing artist. Craft (2005) refers to the intrinsic self of the young artist as consisting of seven aspects, all of which enhance the development of a confident, creative child:

- self-esteem;
- self-confidence;
- self-respect;
- self-will;
- self-actualisation;
- self-acceptance;
- self-discipline.

Intrinsically, rich layers of an emerging young artist, as Craft suggests, can be seen developing if we hone in on moments of experiences and instalments where a child recapitulates their artistic territory and defends their defining style. The clarity of their visual, tactile and spatial perceptions and conceptions are reiterated repeatedly and so confidence in their artistic selves grows.

A long time ago, I taught a young child, Jermaine. He was a very quiet and withdrawn child, who, at the age of five, had been greatly affected by his unsettling and somewhat stressful encounters at home. He lacked confidence socially and would look and observe others and their escapades rather than actively participating. There was, however, one area of the classroom where he would sparkle and transform in his sense of self, both internally and externally. In the art area, he experimented with line and space, form and shape, and his body language told us all of his enjoyment and satisfaction in this active engagement. He was still very quiet during these creative moments and fairly solitary but he was alive with ideas and, importantly, a self-confidence in himself and what he was capable of. He was particularly interested in charcoal and the marks he could make – big and small, thick and thin, bold and fine. Jermaine would use the charcoal to represent observed ideas and create enormous pictures of imaginary monsters, using the charcoal effectively to enhance and distinguish features. When the creativity was on a smaller and more delicate scale, so too were his artistic interactions and drawings, using charcoal lightly with a remarkable refinement of lines. The feel of the charcoal on the paper and the sensory pleasure and quality it owned had become a very strong focus and motivator in Jermaine's artwork. Whatever the artistic endeavour of the moment, his body was entirely confident in what he pursued – it was almost as if he grew ten inches in his self-esteem and self-assurance as he became the artist: 'We engage in a process through which the self is remade' (Eisner, 2002: 12).

Adventure in art helps children to formulate new concepts – concepts that they own. Their explorations are constructive in their developing nature and answers are found and imaginations stirred. The adventures are steeped in the child's entanglement with the sensory elements and as they play and explore they become aesthetically aware architects of their own artistic prowess. As Eisner (2002: 19) says: 'In a sense all these capacities for human experience are resources the artist can call upon in the crafting of the image. In the hands and mind of the artist they are avenues for communication.'

Conclusion

Children's opportunities to engage in aesthetically driven experiences are literally endless; true to the dynamic nature of artistic experience, aesthetic moments will prompt further learning and investigation. The more we allow these experiences to infiltrate children's (and our own) lives, the more we nurture the artistic education of young children and help lay the foundations for their lives to be rich in active discovery and response. Dowling (2005: 119) summarises just how special and deeply rewarding journeys filled with sensory perception and appreciation can be: 'It is about appreciating the journey through life in the deepest sense, particularly special moments, and recognising our own inner resources to help us cope with the journey.'

Reflection

- Track a child over a period of time and observe the various sensory explorations that take place. Consider, through body language, preferences and connections that are being made.
- Observe a group of children engaged in sensory-driven play and list the words and vocabulary used – share this with them to extend the language-rich dialogue.
- Review your setting – both resources and space – and consider whether you provide adequate opportunities for positive messy play experiences.

Further reading

Bruce, T. (2005) *Learning Through Play*, London: Hodder Arnold.

Claxton, G. (2006) 'Thinking at the edge: Developing soft creativity', *Cambridge Journal of Education*, 3: 351–62.

Eglinton, K. A. (2003) *Art in the Early Years*, Oxon: Routledge.

Eisner, E. W. (2002) *The Arts and the Creation of Mind*, Yale: Yale University Press.

Giuidici, C. and Vecchi, V. (2004) *Children, Art, Artists*, Reggio Emilia: Reggio Children Publishers.

CHAPTER 4

Observing the process

Analysing the experiences

> The creative process is a cocktail of instinct, skill, culture and a highly creative feverishness. It is not like a drug; it is a particular state when everything happens very quickly, a mixture of consciousness and unconsciousness, of fear and pleasure.
>
> (Francis Bacon)

Introduction

In this chapter, we consider the often simultaneous stories that accompany artwork and what this tells us about the child who owns the expressive fiction, both through process and end product. It will, as the previous chapters have done, equip us with an understanding of what is happening during the actions of art and, if our observations serve us correctly, how we can begin to layer our knowledge and understanding of the learning that is taking place. Observing the art learning process also enables us to consider how children perceive 'quality' and 'end product', with some suggestions on how to address this through longitudinal projects and shorter-term approaches.

One of the greatest and most rewarding pleasures as adults working with young children is observing energised moments of engagement, where imagination has been ignited and actions pursued. Children's bodies spring into thought and action as they are motivated to explore. This process can be fast but it also has the capacity to meander and ponder. We all have different approaches when we explore materials and art forms, and, in turn, as we contemplate the possibilities of what is being encountered. If we want to begin to understand and analyse something of a young child's art, we need to observe their actions. Whether these are witnessed through passive watching, attentive listening or active participation, the observer can ascertain a great insight into a child's temperament during the art-making process.

Process vs. end product

There is a lot of discussion and debate regarding process and end product in relation to young children and art experiences. Does there always have to be an end product? Is the process the essential element as it signifies the journey? As Eglinton (2003) confirms, there is often and inevitably going to be an end product – it is allowed, it is just that the process intrinsic to the artistic journey must be valued in order to reach the final product. What we do know about young children is that art is not a linear process with its peak visible at the end product.

Practising artists often talk about the relationship between process and outcome. It can be an emotional, tantalising and confusing relationship. Some say they start with an idea and pursue it, not able to conceive the final result; others have a goal they are working towards, with the end predicted and strived for. Artist Chris Ofili talked about his practice in a space that is considerate of process and thought:

> The studio is a place where I can experiment before I'm prepared for an idea to become a body of work, or a new way of working, or a way of working that can sustain me over a period of time.
>
> Sometimes, as I feel a door or an exit point in my work is closing, I'll try to create an opening so as not to stifle the creative process, which I see as a process that's never-ending.
>
> Often I think changes within my work have been seen as sudden changes or sharp changes, but for me they're not that sudden. They have been there in the studio, but not so much in public. The process of transition has to do with seeds that have been planted earlier on that can't always, and shouldn't always, come to fruition immediately. More often than not they are private gestation periods to see if there is mileage in something that goes beyond mere appearance.
>
> (Ofili, 2009)

Ofili clearly embraces the process as a relative unknown, where images unfold and then lead the adventure. The designer of the much celebrated 2012 Olympic Cauldron, Thomas Heatherwick, works in a very different way. His design process is almost the inverse of Ofili's; there is an end goal and this is how his creative process commences. It may meander in its genesis and evolution but the end product is at the heart of the designing and making:

> As to how he finds design solutions, he says the process is almost the opposite of having a 'Eureka' moment. 'It is more like solving a crime. The answer is there, and your job is to find it. So we go off and do bits of research that essentially eliminate suspects from the enquiry. And then you follow up leads and gradually narrow down the potential solutions. Ultimately what you're left with is the answer. Even if you'd thought of it at the beginning of the process, you could never know it was right until the end.'
>
> (Wroe, 2012)

Perhaps, for children, there is no definitive answer to this debate as it is entirely in the hands of the owner of the art experience. Children derive pleasure and individual discovery from an art experience and they exist in the active moment, doing and participating. Yet they can also feel proud, excited and interested in their final product. So, it could be said that the important aspect is that we, as the observing and engaging adults, understand and recognise those pivotal moments in both process and product. The journey has as many variables as it does individuals; the path may meander, diverge, end abruptly or tail off because the journey was the focus. The creative path may, in contrast to this, characterise a shorter, more defined route to production.

If we were to drawn a line to represent process, it is likely that the line would take a very different route for every individual, but the common theme to all experiences is the peaks and troughs, highs and lows, that are symptomatic of any creative process experienced. As Prentice (1994: 126) says: 'Starting a piece of work can be simultaneously exhilarating and unnerving: feelings are likely to oscillate between confidence and timidity.' Our emotions are inextricably entwined in the process of art-making and so it would be unusual for a direct route to dominate our lines of enquiry – in other words, true creativity is not a linear process. Claxton (2006b) likens a child's meandering and pondering during a creatively rich process to that of jazz musicians 'noodling' – an absent-minded improvisation which is key to their instrumental style and collective musicality. 'Noodling' is what children also engage in when they talk, doodle and play with art. Play, as previously discussed, is utterly caught up within the process of art. Only when children have playfully experimented with materials can they start to 'radiate' (Wright, 2010) ideas and feed their imaginations and thus commence production. Process will lead to production if the balance of time, space and engagement is appropriately maintained within a positive, encouraging and dynamic environment. Prentice (1995a), Eisner (2002) and Eglinton (2003) offer process cycles in art which form similar patterns, all of which are ignited by the exploration. Figure 4.1 suggests a process cycle as enjoyed in early-years-based art. The aspect of rich and playful exploration defines the beginning of this cycle and the other experiences follow on as a result. The rotation of learning activity will not, of course, follow in an exact fluid circular movement for all children – they move backwards and forwards in their endeavours – but the four aspects serve as a diagrammatical sequence. The oscillation of cause and effect leads to a progression where creative actions move from the playful art experience to the purposeful art experience.

'If you're not prepared to be wrong, you'll never come up with anything original' (Robinson, 2006). An unequivocal fact about process is that it will inevitably include some element of failure as commented on in Chapter 1. Colours mixed that are not pleasing to the eye, forms in sculpture that do not equate to the imaginative intention, lines that have taken a unintended route. Such ebbs and flows are all safely contained in the premise of the enquiry itself and are just as valuable as the successful moments. In the words of Albert Einstein himself: 'Anyone who has never made a mistake has never tried anything new.'

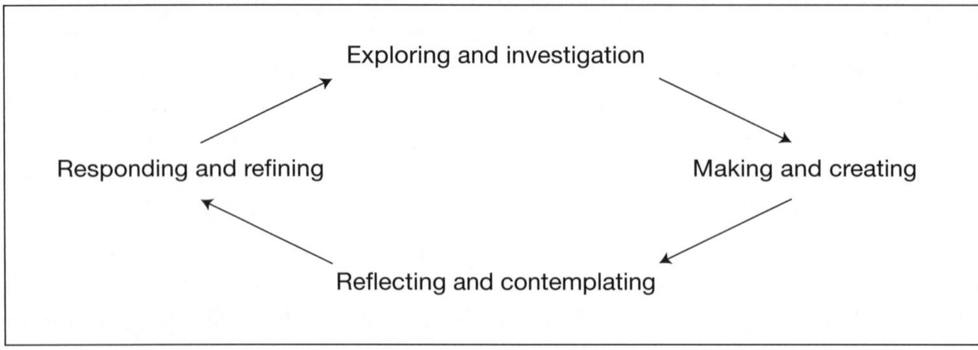

Figure 4.1 The quality of meandering and the positivity of problems

Children can become disheartened, irritated and inclined to refer to another when this happens. Their referral is a positive element in the journey as they can learn from the people around them, imitating how to work through errors and adding this to their knowledge base. We examine the role of the adult relating to the positivity of mistake-making in art in more detail in Chapter 5. Here we examine it as a quandary for the individual but, crucially, regard it as something natural and instinctive in the making of art. The conversational exchange a child has with himself or herself during the peaks and troughs of an art experience reciprocate their developing knowledge of aesthetic awareness and multimodal abilities. This exchange, whatever its time span, is an internally safe place, where a problem can manifest itself and a child can let a vague, messy sense of the problem form. Magnification of this personal quandary presents a seesaw of emotion where the child moves backwards and forwards through receptivity of ideas and solutions (Martindale, 1995). Their 'time out' moment feeds the quietness of the mind and this gem of solitariness is essential to the creative moment in the incubation process (as defined in Chapter 2). The moment a problem is digested a positive adaptation of its former self emerges. Prentice (1999: 155) echoes this cognitive rebirth:

> Uncertainties have to be lived with if situations are to remain open for sufficiently long periods of time to encourage explorations of alternative approaches, interpretations, ways of solving visual or technical problems that could not have been envisaged at the outset. Risks need to be taken.

Creative exploration can be slow in its progress as it welcomes doubt and uncertainty as well as wonder and marvel (Cavazzoni, 2012). The layers of reasoning and cognitive understanding develop our skills scape and lead us to new thoughts. Ideas come to the surface, change, become submerged and re-emerge over a period of time. This requires sustained involvement in the process and the confidence to take risks. Our classrooms should be vibrant hubs of processed risk-taking in the arts; hubs that invite open-ended paths and where challenges are seen as positive. We examine this aspect of our environment in greater detail in Chapter 6. Risks and challenges enable art-making to transform and transcend. Such are the features of experiential art play where children exist in a piece of work, combining cognitive, sensory and physical development learnt in the moment and remembered from the past.

The process timeline: the past, present and future observed

The definition of 'process' – a systematic series of actions directed to some end – suggests a timeline that is key to its sequential existence. The sequences or 'series of actions' tell of the importance of past, present and future that are involved in one activity. We know the inferences of daily experience, the layering of past understandings and the building up towards a new knowing exist very much as the body of a process in art. With this in mind, a piece of artwork contains a rich biographical story of the child creator. Of course, these art moments are often over as quickly as they started or they can stretch over a longer period of time with the involved child intent on seeing a process through over a series of encounters. In some ways the length is irrelevant here. Whether snapshot moments of creativity or longer periods of art action, the timeline of process is still in existence.

As we have previously considered from discussions in other chapters, children's explorations are rooted in what they already know – they build on the familiar to discover the unfamiliar. The roots are part of their past but are very current in the everyday of the present. Children are constantly finding theories about life in their discoveries and they will hang onto these theories for as long as possible. Their theories are very much bound in their ability to be carefree researchers; all that brain activity again at play as they find out, make connections and theorise about their encounters. Their theorising is key to the art process at stake. They will come across new encounters in art and use their existing theory to build on others.

Observing the narrative: stories from images

A piece of artwork tells the story of a process and the action that took place. Its production in the present is a result of the narration that often takes place during art-making where the marks made on a surface change and move as the story unfolds. These stories tell us an enormous amount about the focus of the child; not only of their artistic endeavour but also of their lives.

Young children deftly and skilfully tell stories. They are without inhibition to take a beginning and offer all sorts of whimsical features and unusual storylines. It is sometimes said that the art of storytelling is a dying culture in our schools and yet children respond with glee, pleasure and anticipation to a spoken story, watching the storyteller's face for clues, plots, hints. Perhaps it is the relationship of the aural and oral and also the language of gesture and the spoken word, but whatever the gold behind it, it is very powerful. Yet adults can often feel self-conscious, worried, awkward at the prospect of telling a story. A young child, however, feels none of the above. They are eager to tell and interpret, perhaps a story without a beginning, middle or end, but their storytelling has motivation. Props and resources may help with this and, as we have seen, their own artwork.

As we see in Box 4.1, a clear story was being told to the adult audience. The child relayed the story's adventures in conjunction with the action of drawing, both learning aspects happening in parallel with and as a consequence of each other. Not only did the narrated drawing have historical inferences relating to

Box 4.1 A white horse bited mummy – fantasy play through images

Ned: That's the horse there.

Mummy: Oh, and who is that next to the horse?

Ned: That's Mummy and me and it's the white horse, it bited Mummy.

Mummy: Ow, it looks like that hurt.

Ned: Yes, big sharp teeth, and it bited Mummy.

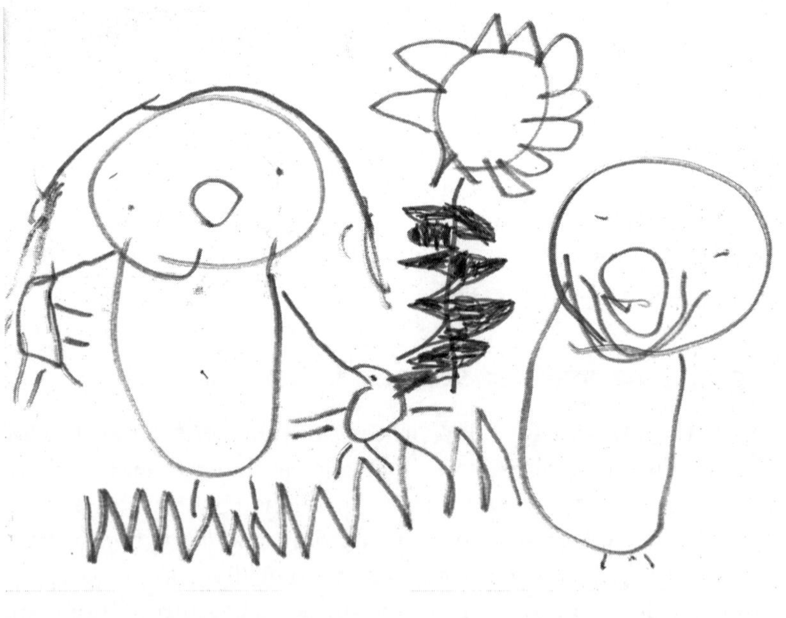

Figure 4.2 Ned's white horse

a visit to the circus, there was also a premise of danger, fear and excitement. This narrative had a beginning and a middle but there was not a defined ending, as there was not in the picture. What was also of significance here was that although the child was talking to his mother directly about the image, he spoke about one of the figures being 'mummy' in the third person, rather than 'you'. This was possibly because he was keeping the image in the storying of the picture, the fiction was being played out still from the page, not in 'real life' (or 'true life' as a child would refer to it). To have used the word 'you' would have merged the real mummy that he was sitting in front of and the mummy that lived on his paper. The image being told alongside the story became the more powerful element and the narrative sparked further conversations about the colours of the pens and the lines being drawn. The picture, during the whole sequence, was alive with talk, ideas, imagination.

If you listen, covertly or not, children weave stories and threads of imagination around images and marks being made. Matthews (2003: 120) refers to this as the dialectical relationship between their constantly changing understandings of the world and what is emerging as they make marks when he writes, 'It seems as if they realise that relationships emerging on the drawing surface are, in some respects, like relationships in the real world'. This 'synaesthesia' (Kress, 1977) emphasises imagination and cognition combining and converging during art activities. Children have an amazing capacity to transpose ideas from one mode to another.

Children's stories, images and words belong to the child and are often narrated in a babble that is not necessarily meant for an audience. The 'babble' narration is a form of verbal reasoning intended for the self. It represents the child's ability to transfer images and imagination into an art form. The stories or narratives may not be intended for an external audience as this is a very subjective and personal moment; they are playing out a fantasy, a story intrinsic to them and their experiences, likes, dislikes and moments of thought. Coates and Coates (2006) go as far as to say it is akin to active fantasy play but experienced in marks, images, shapes and forms.

For Vygotsky (1978) there is a syncretistic relationship between a child's play and art where the different and separate forms of art are not yet being consciously distinguished. Children's artful play is made up of many emotions, foci and genre. Children draw pictures and tell a story at the same time; they act a role and create their lines as they go along. Children do not always spend a long time completing each creation, but can often produce something in an instant, focussing all their emotions on what they are doing at that moment in time (Lindqvist, 2001).

There are times when children are able to engineer on paper what is absent or unreachable in their active fantasy play. In these instances, pictures can be complex, full of active detail of events and moments, as the fantasy play spills out onto the paper. Lewis and Freddy's shared drawing venture (Figure 4.3)

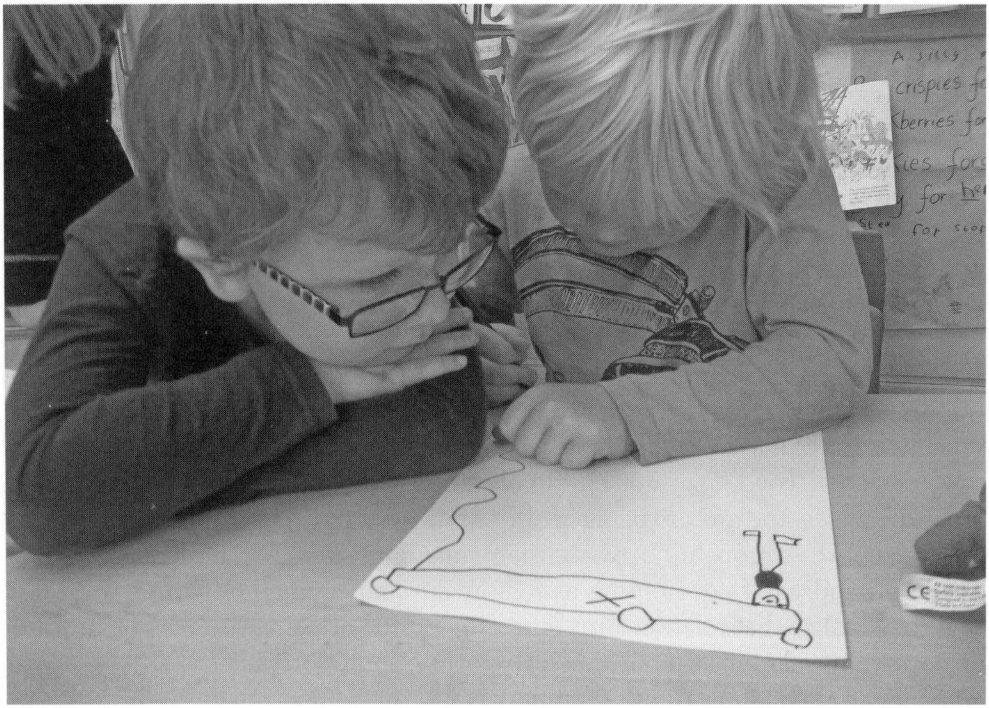

Figure 4.3 Lewis and Freddy's shared drawing venture

included a castle, with trap doors, knights escaping, fights taking place and a storm collecting with the noise of thunder in the background. This was all played out on paper with a rich dialogue of imaginative words and descriptive vocabulary. The two pictorial storytellers were layering their physical drawing experience with an imaginative storyline. Not only were they involved in a constructive process of visual and spoken thinking in action (Matthews 2003) but they were also experimenting with the language of the drawing materials and in doing so building new concepts for their story. Cox (2005) discusses the 'unfolding picture' as children interact with the entwinement of visual and linguistic commentaries. Images are layered, characters and situations transformed, as the ideas unfold through somatic involvement of art-making and image-making.

The child's visual and tactile interaction as an artist can be swamped with inferences from their own history, similar to fantasy and imaginative play. Quite often, children do not necessarily verbalise a narrative; instead their facial movements and body language may tell a story of the physical involvement in their art-making. But there are moments of narrative storytelling which form an intrinsic part of the art-making, which we, as engaged adults, are privileged to be part of.

As children create for themselves, they enrich their own images, their own fiction, putting their mark of ownership on the process. You can hear some really astounding figments of imagination and wonderfully illogical, abstract escapades as they chatter through what they do. Wright (2010: 172) comments on the imaginative play of art:

> Like film-makers: children can be the cast of one – taking on all the characters which live on their paper – multiple roles. Intertextuality – seeing life through an alternative prism. The use of quasi-human figures, hybrids of nature, offers the child opportunities to polarise between real and fantasy.

If we consider the fact that they are image-making, their dialogue of fiction relates totally to the moment their mind connects with the paper/board/clay and draws out the images and pictorial episodes. As children rapidly and enthusiastically make the connections between their physical and manipulative abilities and the marks they leave, they create images, pictures, shapes, signs and symbols. Although we know this interaction, whether original, repeated or progressive, is a vital aspect of their development as writers, to refer to it as mark-making compartmentalises it as a stage in writing and is coined as 'emergent writing'. As Hall (2009: 181) reminds us: 'Viewing drawing as a pre-writing skill undermines the complexity and richness of young children's drawings that often belies their apparent simplicity.' If we look at this interaction as image-making, we can then see the stages they are involved in as artists, writers, scribes and sportspeople to name but a few. Image-making encompasses a wider range of 'characters' and therefore makes the process less linear and rightly more illogical. Image-making is, after all, a very individual process, as we all have unique ways of seeing, doing, feeling and making. Image-making, in this context, is also importantly a reminder of the multi-modality of a child's involvement in art. They actively construct their current and expanding understanding of themselves and their worlds through involvement in many different forms of art. From the various forms ensues a preponderous fountain of images.

Crucially, young children can show a preference towards the manipulative ease and pliability of sculptural story-making where physical engagement in the tactile process of art affords them the somatically rich impetus to actively construct stories and tall tales. We can sometimes underestimate just how accessible this form of image-making is for the young child. Their enthusiasm may be partly due to their adventurous tendencies, which are motivated by physical enticement and also because they are inclusive of a wide variety of visual and tactile elements such as space, form, shape and volume. 'The tension and effort of children experimenting with a different material enables them to discover its true nature so that they can fashion their ideas from it' (Bloomfield and Childs, 2000: 89).

In Box 4.2 we witness an emerging story created by a group of children and an adult in a forest school setting. This particular creative experience was enhanced by the sculptural material supplied by the forest's natural resources. The group began to form a narrative as they felt, experimented with and sculpted the 3D, tactile-rich media. Tactile sense-making, and pretend and fantasy play were being performed on a small scale in amongst the theatre of large trees.

Box 4.2 The making of the wood family home

C1: I need leaves for the beds.

C2: Acorns for lunch.

C3: Can I help?

C2: Of course you can.

B: There are lots of dry leaves here. . .

C1: Well, we need dry leaves.

C2: There's a tiny baby.

C3: I want a tiny baby too, moss, we could use moss . . . for beds.

B: There's plenty around, so then we can wrap the babies up.

C3: I've found some.

C2: My baby has just been born *(finding a very small pine cone).*

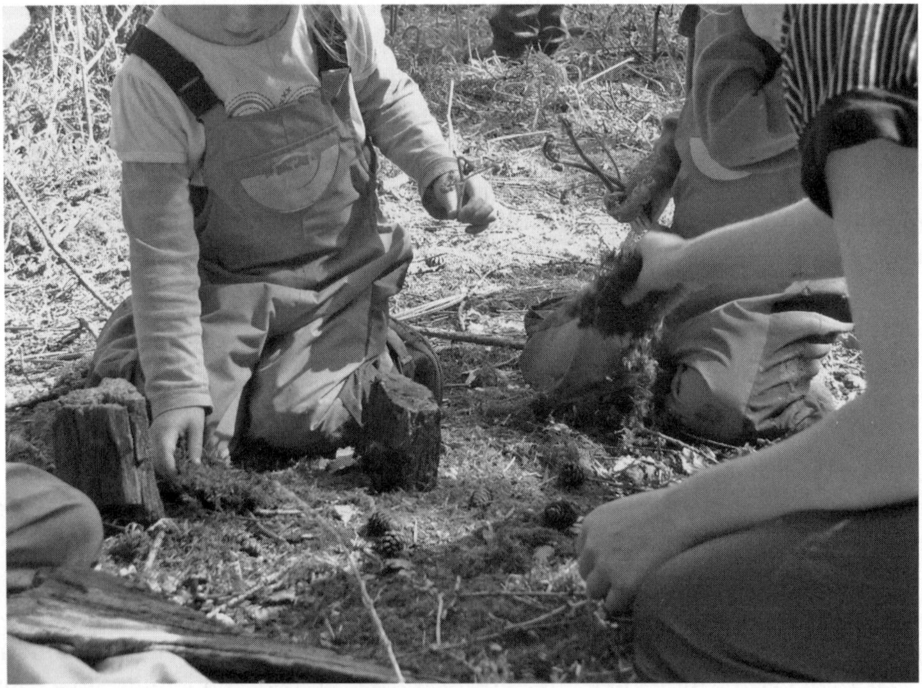

Figure 4.4 Tactile sense-making with moss and plants

The body tells the story

In our forest school group, one of the children, Paige, continued to construct the family home after it had been abandoned by the other original makers. She built the rooms and gardens and found some cylindrical bark peel, which she used in a game in the garden. She then proceeded to thread different sizes of found objects through the cylinder, all the while continuing to talk about the fantasy world of the babies who lived in the house, created by her and her friends.

Paige's actual physical activity is linked directly to what she is saying and necessitates the process of narration. Sometimes, however, what our hands do is not in accordance with what our heads are thinking about, the 'doing' and the 'talking' are actively engaged but work in parallel and not in unison. The actual physical motion of feeling an object may unconsciously stir active thought but the two actions are not complicit in their existence. Children are not always visibly or audibly thinking with a sophisticated purpose. Sometimes, their submerged state, when they have burrowed down into the activity or moment, means that they are simply refuelled and refreshed in a subconscious moment. As adults, it is not always possible to say what we feel or what we think and, for children, this is the same. If you imagine travelling on a long car journey, the road may meander through picturesque countryside where you spot a field

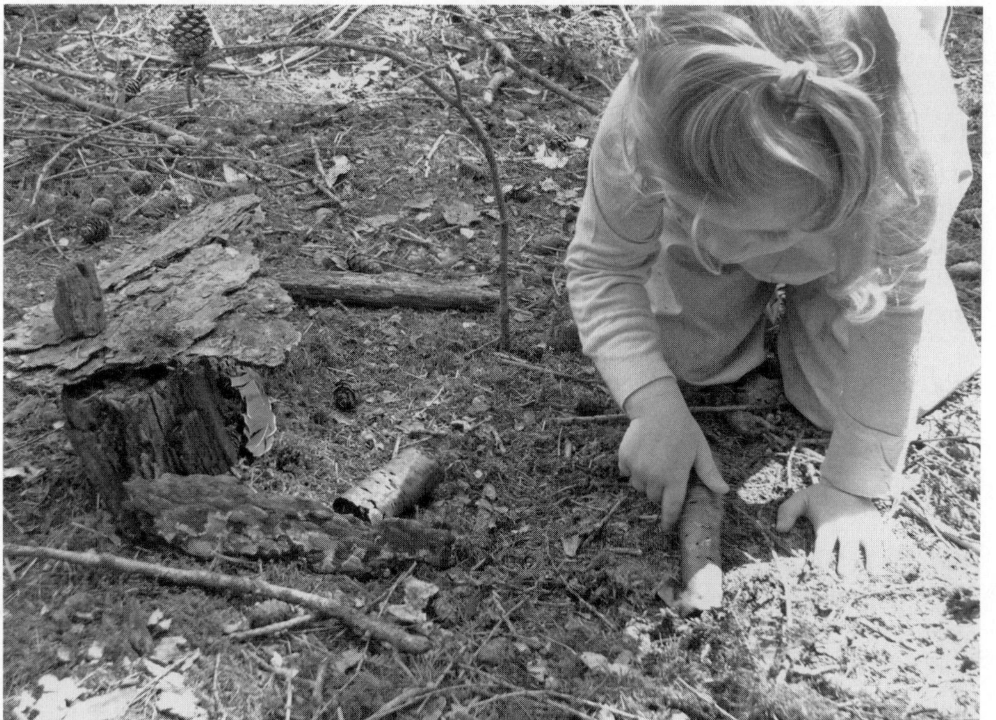

Figure 4.5 Paige explores the forest floor

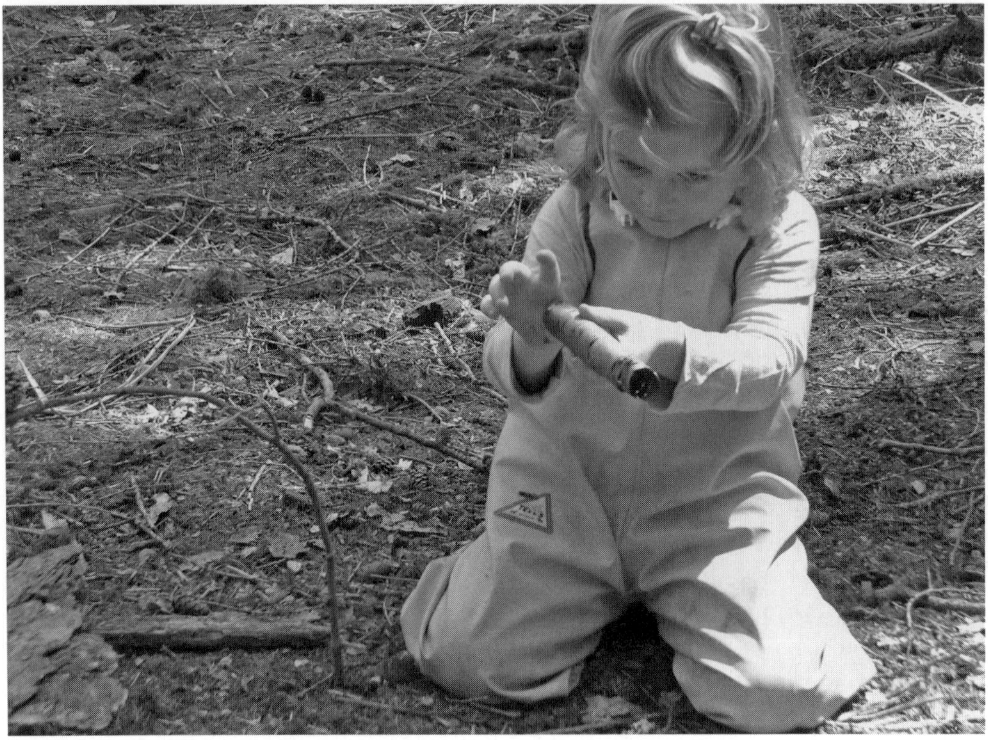

Figure 4.6 Paige experiments with found wood

of cows, a church spire, a village green – what you see and how it makes you feel is something that is fleeting and personal to you. You may not be fully conscious of that feeling or moment and you certainly do not always need to, or indeed wish to, verbalise it. If we empathise with that emotional and dream-like state of mind, we can have some understanding of our children's worlds. Their constant endeavours and observations are so numerous and complex that to verbalise and consciously narrate them would be a thoroughly exhausting process. But what does exist is a higher order of thinking for the immersed child, and extraordinary thought is very hard to define.

Child involvement in the art process

The act of art convenes a platform on which children's processes are played out – they can visualise as well as articulate and depict as well as describe. They often work as free-spirited artists, allowing the event to unfold before their very eyes. They may experience disappointment and irritation if there are intentional moments at the outset and the final result does not reflect this. This is less frequent with young children as their ludic play in art allows them to experiment, be themselves and image-make in harmony with their own thoughts and ideas.

Box 4.3 Child involvement – five levels

Level 1 – No activity
Level 2 – A frequently interrupted activity
Level 3 – Mainly continuous activity
Level 4 – Continuous activity with intense moments
Level 5 – Sustained intense activity

(Robson, 2012)

As we work with younger children, there is a whole range of timescales attached to their ability and inclination to sink into an art experience and 'wallow' in the exploration, or to touch upon, sometimes very intensely, but within a short immersed moment so that there is a defined end. Ferre Laevers introduced child involvement scales, which when adopted in an observed capacity can inform us about the involvement level of a child in their learning (see Box 4.3).

The levels of involvement are gauged by consideration of the signals displayed by the child (Box 4.4): the energised body, the jaw set in concentration or the ability to focus without distraction. We know that if we use this scale to observe children and track their involvement in activities, they are likely to oscillate from one end of the scale to the other. Their concentration spans and desire to become engrossed in a learning moment will vary depending on time of day, emotions, location and social awareness. This continuum of engagement is reflected in encounters in art as much as in any area of learning. But when involved moments

Box 4.4 Signals or indicators to ascertain involvement level

- Concentration
- Energy
- Complexity and creativity
- Facial expression and posture
- Persistence
- Precision
- Reaction time
- Language
- Satisfaction

(Robson, 2012)

do occur, fascinating insights for us as the observing adults come into focus: the timeline, the schemas, the developing sensory awareness. During that energised and engaged moment in time, a very intense and constructive synthesis is taking place.

Silent and energised concentration

It is important to remember that not all image-making moments will have a clearly defined spoken narrative. As Kudryavtsev (2011) discusses, creative ideas are not always tangible – conception and perception are not necessarily realised and then made public to an onlooker. Kudryatsev goes on to say that ideas are only understood consciously when crystallised. It could be argued that this crystallisation may not always be abundantly obvious to the adult observing, and that this moment is very much owned by the child. If we think about our own continuing development and understanding, we are not always aware of the moment when we 'twig' something, or when creative thought is crystallised, and, of course, this is exactly the same with children. Our job is not always to recognise and know these moments – it would be an impossible feat – but it is important we ensure that we establish and sustain an 'atmosphere' for these moments to materialise for children, unconsciously or consciously. There is a tendency for adults to ask children questions about a picture: What have you drawn? What is in your picture? Such interrogative questions can negate the impact on the storytelling as they probe and intrude on the process, often once the story is complete. The numerous images weaving through the story are quick moving and to retain the images internally, let alone in a verbal construct after the event, can prove difficult. The real quality of narrative and dialogue relating to story will happen during, not after. By listening to the running commentary the adult can pick up the intentions, the fantasy play, the imagination, but if they enquire for a description at the end, the story is over and the pivotal instalments lost.

Consider the child with pencil in hand, creating a picture that may start with a big rotational mark. The relational narrative may begin as the child animates this shape with more features and so brings it to life. The shape becomes 'something' and takes on a character or a function within the story taking place. Strokes may be added to the circular form, and the shape morphs into a spider character. This spider then 'moves' as the child draws more and adds actions to the story. The actual picture may not have changed drastically but a lot has taken place in the developing imagination and storytelling skills of that young child. It is a silent sequence, but rich with visual expression.

Active image-making, spoken or silent, can also be associated with the enveloping schema of the young artist, as they experiment with colour, shape and form. The actual movement of 'enveloping' depicts layers of the story being told. Again, this story may not be verbal, but each layer is being added as the image-making tells a story in the mind of the child, as examined in Chapter 2.

The dream-like state of the young artist

'The rights of the child should include the right to be a dreamer' (Oldfield, 2011: 186). Young children have an immense and wonderful ability to enter into dream-like ponderings and images as part of their internal story-making. They need no encouragement to switch off from the here and now and disappear into their fantasy worlds. It is an ability that we are quick to lose and so we can sometimes forget how rich and imaginative these worlds are. Children's ability and aptitude to dream is directly related to their thought and image-making and so is a central force in relation to their growing artistic temperaments.

Adams *et al.* (2008) refer to this spiritual dimension of childhood as the ability to connect the 'dream-like' state with the 'awakeness' of the senses. It is not a connection that can easily be defined, observed or known by the child-experiencer but it is described by Adams *et al.* (2008: 44) as '[a] myriad of abstract senses which enable us to engage with and to interpret the world around us: emotions, some things which have no name but we know we "feel", "experience"'. This is one of the true delights of working with young children whose fledging imaginative existence in the world has not yet been negated or deflated by self-perpetuating inhibitions or externally placed limitations – they still use their time wisely to dream, explore, consider, invent, as discussed back in Chapter 1. It could be said that perhaps adults who are still able to retain this dream-like perspective, who treasure and create time for colourful, individual and inventive interpretations, have kept hold of their creative identity.

An observing role

So what is our role as adults in relation to children's visual and tactile fiction-making? The role is brought into question in detail in the following chapter but we refer briefly to it here in terms of observing the *process*. We obviously listen and, importantly, enjoy but what other aspects of engagement are involved in our relationship with the process of the young artist? Are we allowed to suggest, guide, advise? Again, this has to be up to the child and the artist emerging. They will often make it quite clear if they want our attention and they are very skilled at guiding us and our interactions with them. Read the child and the situation and be astute to their body language, facial gestures and responses. Do they invite you in with:

- words;
- discussion;
- hand gestures;
- facial acknowledgement;
- silent agreement?

If one, two or all of these occur, then you are welcomed into a narrative dialogue. Illumination of a drawing may occur with a spoken story as you are recognised as a genuinely interested listener. You may be invited to join the story and add some ideas or it may be that your presence is irrelevant to the drawer in the moment of art-making. The latter is common and at times devalued or misinterpreted. We must remember that children like to be private in their development, discoveries and experiences, just as adults often are. So we have to be wise to the signals and observe quietly, instinctively and without being obtrusive. Fisher (2010) is candid in her reminder to the practitioner about choosing the moment you interact so that your action will 'illuminate' the learning process as opposed to 'interfering' with it.

Knowing children and their emerging artistic styles allows us to ensure that opportunities in the form of space, resources, activities and events are planned and available. Chapter 6 examines the environment further and highlights considerations for planning and resource organisation. Events and artists are also explored further as opportunities to extend the art experience in Chapter 7 (whole-school art – transitional aspects, learning from the foundations) and Chapter 9 (encounters with artists).

Valuing quality – editing and reviewing

How do we now make those observations significant in our work with the children?

In the final section of this chapter we consider how our observations can have an impact on children's art experiences and how we seek to extend and help plan for the next instalments in their journeys. Here we can introduce and contemplate the issue of 'quality'. This is a contentious aspect and we must be clear that we mean 'quality' of artwork as perceived *by the children*, not what adults may see as 'quality'. In its living definition, the word quality can often represent 'neat' and 'tidy' proprietorial aspects where a polished finish dominates. In this discussion, we are clearly defining 'quality' as part of a procedure where a child develops the skills to review, reflect and sometimes adapt, add and continue with a piece of artwork. In this act of artistic reflection, he or she is developing a capacity for aesthetic awareness and critical thinking. The quality does not, importantly, relate to the end product – it is the quality of the experiential process which can be enhanced; 'If you do this, you could also try this.'

Pursuit of an artistic encounter will lead a child to further discoveries, and in this protracted investigation a greater and more defined understanding will occur. As a child begins to understand the 'more' about a situation, he or she is able to filter and refine their understanding. This ongoing process is a part of what makes art so challenging, rewarding and in some ways infinite in its possibilities. Art experiences – and artworks need not always have finite endings

– can continue changing depending on the creator. As previously mentioned, this is of great importance in classrooms of young children when work is very often made and one of the following may happen to it: left on a drying rack to join the many forgotten layers of artwork built up over time, taken home that same day with little value afforded it between the making and the home taking, or put up on a display out of reach. In order to encourage a young child's understanding of review and quality, we can consider a range of positive and productive initiatives that help to promote self-reflection. Rather than artwork being stowed away in a home bag, and sometimes not to see the light of day again, consider the alternatives:

- Place it on a 'work in progress' wall – to be reflected on and thought about and returned to.
- Include it in a display which the child has helped collate.
- Add it to a portfolio – a sketchbook of work to be referred to in moments of past recollections and sharing evidence of progress.

Such scenarios allow and encourage a young child to return to a piece of artwork, and in doing this simple act, they review, reflect and consider their art, adding a dimension of signature quality to the process. 'It is in the process of editing that transitions are made graceful, colours harmonized, intensities modulated, and, indeed, seasoning to suit the palette adjusted' (Eisner, 2002: 6).

Sometimes, we need to purposefully create times for reflection and evaluation of artwork. It is something we do as adults when we look with a sophisticated eye and it is also something children will do if time allows them this pleasure. In a busy educational environment, we often rush onwards with whatever is waiting round the corner, whether it is playtime, lunchtime, assembly, target setting! We have to continually remind ourselves of the art of today, which should preoccupy some of our reflection time so that the child can respond and critique the artwork produced before they rush onto the next expectation. Time in reflection allows an understanding of editing and, as aforementioned, the ability to develop an aesthetic awareness. The three suggestions above illustrate purposeful events or approaches that respond to time and the value of reflection. We will now look at the suggestions in more detail, always keeping in mind your own setting in order to adapt and transfer these approaches to an environment that reflects your own ethos and community. One glove does not fit all, that we know, and adaptation is perfectly valid if the principles remain.

The work in progress board is a transient space where the artwork on view is for the purpose of browsing and contemplating its qualities and processes; for the child, other children and adults. It suggests both individual and collaborative reflections. The board affords quality reflection time and so constitutes an active task of reviewing artwork to be adapted, changed, transformed or left in its present state. Eisner (2002: 82) comments:

> Another quality that characterizes work of high artistic quality is that a percipient can return to the work over and over again and still find qualities and relationships that continue to nurture; *the work is not exhausted in one single glance.*

Shelves of work that display unfinished sculptures and models are also a welcome inclusion here as a further component in our attempt to galvanise a positive reflective dynamic spanning the panorama of art-skills development.

Awareness and caution are to be adhered to in relation to some of the art displays on offer in early years settings. They can, at times, with the greatest of creative intentions, constitute the creative work of the adult teacher rather than the child. This is often the outcome when an art activity takes place in order to create a display. Artwork solely created for display purposes more often than not prescribes an art activity with an intended and expected outcome. Anning and Ring (2004: 11) admonish the creators of such displays:

> At worst feeding the display imperative resulted in children spending hours aimlessly sticking squares of fabric or screwed up tissue paper onto adult drawn outlines of bunnies (in spring), the seaside (in summer), harvest fayre (in autumn) and snowmen (in winter).

As we have already considered, displays can be works in progress but if we use them as spaces to elevate pieces of artwork to the public domain we need to ensure the artists are included in this process. Allow them to choose and select, help arrange the display, participate in making labels and annotation as part of the design. This will enhance their ownership of the entire process of thinking, imagining, making, reflecting and exhibiting.

As children become active in creating displays alongside an adult, they are also taking part in a very important transition; the individual artwork made in private enters the public domain of a shared viewing space. Their personal imprint becomes a part of the cultural art community. The community may be the immediate space and those that dwell in it, but it can also extend to the whole setting or school. This is key when we consider the transitional issues of art and young children as they go from stage to stage within the primary school system. Such issues will be addressed in more detail in Chapter 7.

A crucial consideration in our discussion regarding process, self-assessment and self-reflection is the keeping of *portfolios*. Portfolios, or learning journeys as they are often referred to, are a familiar feature in most early years classrooms and settings, containing a wide variety of evidence that captures the essence of the child and who they are. Information stored illustrates the child's processes, makes learning tangible or can serve to enhance or connect future experiences. These portfolios may include a range of drawings, photographs of models, pattern-making moments and tactile-based adventures, all of which form a very rich repertoire of art skills and glorious moments belonging to the child. Eglinton (2003) refers to this autobiographical collation as a 'process-folio'. She goes on to consider the contents and lists what they could contain in their acknowledgement of the process of art endeavour and progression. Process-folios can contain:

- paintings, drawings, and other visual works that demonstrate cognitive, perceptual, and aesthetic growth or change;
- significant dialogue pertaining to all forms of artistic experience;
- video and audiotapes of dialogue and experiences;
- photographs of finished works, works in progress, temporary work and photos of the child participating in all types of art experiences (including encounters with art and aesthetic experiences).

Alongside the portfolio exists the *sketchbook*, a collation of workings and imaginings that depict construed enquiry and pictorial research. Prentice (1999: 153) affirms the importance of sketchbooks as a firm component in the investigation process:

> Sketchbooks are central to the development of enquiry in art. When they are used intelligently evidence of knowledge and understanding is revealed through personal responses to experience, traces of thought processes, insights into decision-making, and experiments carried out over a period of time.

Sketchbooks should abound in all schools from EYFS through to Year 6 in order to contain the visual 'workings out' that follow the child through their primary school experience. Where there is a dearth of sketchbooks, there is often an absence of a culture that respects and encourages 'working out' as part of its art process. Children who are introduced to the idea of sketchbooks when they are eight years old, for example, are of the delicate age, spoken about previously, where their inhibitions in art become evident. Their workings out tend to be the pencil line that is continually rubbed out. One Year 3 child (eight years old) said of her sketchbook at the beginning of an art project, 'I am going to tear this page out because I don't like my drawing – it's horrible, it's going to spoil the book'. So the issue here is about what a sketchbook is. Does it contain finished and perfected end products? Essentially this decision belongs to the sketchbook's owner, but what we can do, as the engaged adults, is create a culture in the foundations of education where children are more interested in using ideas and thoughts, which come from a selection of sketches, images and photographs.

These sketchbooks may be collaborative and tell the story of particular projects or they may follow a child through a year in their educational life. They may be individual and the sketchbooks themselves become the works of art in their entirety. The wonderful thing about sketchbooks is they define a space that belongs to the decision-making and hypothesizing of the young artist. Abbs (1994) eloquently inflated the importance of sketchbooks by calling them 'the larder of reflexive intelligence'.

Young children as artists

It is also interesting here to consider how famous and celebrated artists use sketchbooks and spaces to 'work out ideas'. Chris Ofili's words at the beginning of this chapter reflect the progressive value of his studio as his sketchbook. Rachel Whiteread, a Turner Prize winner in 1993, is fascinated by the relationship between herself as an artist and her sketchbooks as a collection of ideas. She says (Curiger, 2010):

> My drawings are very much part of my thinking process. They are not necessarily studies. I use them as a way of worrying through a particular aspect of something that I'm working on. Quite commonly, there will be a dozen or so drawings of more or less the same thing. I find it quite a therapeutic process, and it's something I've done for the past twenty years.

Conclusion

We end this section as we began it, by considering the words of Prentice (1995) as he reflects on the journey of practising artists:

> When describing their working methodologies, it is common for artists and designers to stress the importance of the periods of time they spend looking at and thinking about work in progress: making far exceeds the skills of mere production.
>
> (Prentice, 1995: 12)

Artists are multifaceted by way of the various personas they masterfully adopt during the very act of art-making: imaginer, constructor and producer. In amongst the many facets of their employment, there is the person and all he or she embodies. Deeply rooted in all our art-employment are emotions that come in many shape and forms. Their influential strength will naturally and undeniably impinge on what we create. Thoughts and feelings, the results of our emotional make-up, are oft-times expressed in very raw ways through art-making. Children's emotions are part of their everyday existence and are full of intense desires, deep anger, furious frustration and elated excitement. This myriad of emotions will emerge during the art process and the child will be aided on their journey within a cathartic and secure experience. We must not prevent such outbursts of emotion as they are vital to the art process as well as contextually essential to the moment during which visual expression takes place. We can sometimes be afraid of the entanglement of emotions but instead we must celebrate and enjoy their motivational force and how amazing some of the results can be. As Claxton (2006a) reminds us, emotions are not symptoms of malfunction; they are essential aspects of our all-round intelligence. Expressing thoughts and emotions in art happens during exploration, creation and review. We are reminded, once again, of the process cycle (as examined earlier in the chapter), which we must continue to refer to during our successful teaching moments in order to full engage with the who and why of infant art.

If we provide appropriate space and time for children to realise and tell their stories, young reflective artists will emerge who can begin to define a picture, a sculpture or a print in correspondence with sequential content and development of content, as is the case with story-making. A final thought is to remind ourselves of how enjoyable storying moments are for the teaching adult. Stories and tall tales which stem from a young child's imagination can delight and amuse as well as amaze and astound, and these particular moments are what makes teaching so extraordinary.

Reflection

Spend some time observing one child and consider the following:

- How does she or he use specific art media?
- How does she or he turn expression into form?
- What does she or he play with in art-driven moments?
- What particularly inspires her or him in their art-making?

Consider daily communication in art-making experiences in your setting and the dialogues:

- between children;
- between child and adult;
- from child to self;
- within a group;
- during artistic experience;
- during reflection.

Further reading

Anning, A. and Ring, K. (2004) *Making Sense of Children's Drawings*, Maidenhead: Open University Press, pp. 11–26, 116–24.
Coates, E. (2002) '"I forgot the sky!" Children's stories contained within their drawings', *International Journal of Early Years Education*, 10(1): 21–35.
Cox, S. (2005) 'Intention and meaning in young children's drawing,' *International Journal of Art & Design Education*, 24(2): 115–25.
Matthews, J. (2003) *Drawing and Painting: Children and Visual Representation*, London: Paul Chapman.
Prentice, R. (ed.) (1995) *Teaching Art and Design*, London: Cassell.
Wright, S. (2010) *Understanding Creativity in Early Childhood*, London: Sage.

CHAPTER 5

Adult interaction and engagement

I wanted to climb the ladder and it kept on growing.

(Moore, 2013)

Introduction

In this chapter, we examine the various aspects that help promote and maintain positive and proactive child–adult interaction, a joint venture in which, as Eglinton (2003: 26) aptly describes it, 'the child and teacher are thought of as colleagues searching, exploring, flowing with, and at the same time, guiding the experience.' It is important to establish who we are referring to when we use the word 'adult' in this chapter. Our considerations are in reference to the adult who engages with the child and their art outside of the home. The adult here could be a childminder, a pre-school practitioner, a nursery nurse, a teaching assistant or a reception teacher. The 'adult' can be associated with the person who shares an art-driven moment with a child. The skills and aptitudes considered in the chapter can, of course, be linked to family-related adults, as they are universal skills and generic to any shared adult–child art experience. The latter relationship, is, however, considered in detail in Chapter 8. Our focus in this chapter is on the adult in a setting. The variety of settings, of course, will have an influential bearing on shared explorations as the space and layout of a childminder's home will offer different experiences to that of a reception class in a busy primary school, for example. Throughout the chapter, as indeed the entire book, we have to read and cogitate discussions in relation to and adaptation of our own working experience and situation. The principles will remain the same, but manifested in a setting they may be different and varied.

The interested adult

Helping children to be creative is as much about encouraging attitudes of curiosity and questioning as about skills or techniques. Children are accomplished observers and often find interesting the everyday things that adults take for granted. Building on children's interests can lead to them creating amazing inventions or making marks on paper that represent for them seen and felt experiences. Encouraging children to choose and use materials and resources in an open-ended way helps them to make choices and to have confidence in their own ideas. Educators energise the child's artistic experience through dialogue, motivation, observation and documentation. Childhood confidence in their ideas and skills can easily be lost if others, often senior in years, 'take over' and try to suggest what the child is making, thinking or doing.

Children need to see an interested adult – someone involved who looks and makes comments that are individualised and thoughtful. They are far more aware of our reactions to life's explorations, sometimes far more than we imagine. They watch our reactions and emotions as played out on our faces, so they know a look of detachment, an expression of expectation – we must credit them with this sophisticated interpersonal knowledge. *Development Matters* (British Association for Early Education, 2012: 7) recognises this perspective in the guidance statement relating to aspects of 'Positive Relationships': 'Model being a thinker, showing that you don't always know, are curious and sometimes puzzled, and can think and find out.' An exchange of ideas that is honest and involved is far healthier and motivational than one that is tokenistic and detached from the actual event.

Trusting – letting go of control

> If we intervene with a view that the purpose of art is to produce an image that is as realistic as possible and therefore think of children as failed realists we may do great harm by imposing inappropriate expectations which do not match children's developmental stage.
>
> (Duffy, 1998: 91)

Free adventures in art-making is a liberating experience for young children, as indeed it is for children of all ages, where imagination and personal enlightenment are unencumbered by rules and regulations. This liberation, however, can also be a little unnerving to some adults as it requires us to 'let go'. It ultimately means that we have to divest some of our learnt 'control' of a situation, which is not so easy as this is what we have become accustomed to doing. As adults we have learnt to confidently take control of our lives, where possible. We know what we know and we have developed the tools and a capacity to understand situations and respond accordingly. A child who 'freely' makes art expects a very different set of skills from the presiding adult. The older human being needs to understand and recognise the balance to be had that seesaws between acknowledgement of a child's line of enquiry in response to their sense of wonder and excitement, and a sense that recognises the need to encourage absence of pressure or direction. The latter often cannot help itself; it wants to take charge and direct a situation that may, in our eyes, be 'out of control' – we often think we know what should be occurring because we see an end result or a way of doing something.

It is much like when you play a game of word association or character consequences. You think you can surmise what the next word will be, or what part of the body will be drawn, but actually how can you really know as your prediction crucially lurks in the mind of the person who owns that moment and it cannot therefore be predicted by you. You are often surprised and, importantly, humoured by the outcome and this surprise and unpredictability is the very essence of the game. We cannot control what happens next, each stage is in the hands of the stage's owner and belongs to them but is a part of a collaborative game, which belongs to everyone.

Of course, such an analogy does not purport to convey the deep and meaningful exchanges in teaching and learning, but it does highlight the fact that adults play a very important role, as both the presiding adult and the co-player. It is a role in which careful consideration and sensitivity overrides control, prediction or direct expectation; instead, recognition of the infant who co-owns the moment is our focus. Training ourselves to let go, and thereby disarming a sense that controls, could positively change our mindset in this area of teaching. In fact, by turning this sense on its head we can enjoy, nourish and maximise the moments and instalments in children's art in which we participate with far greater appreciation than if we were in control of their movements and endeavours.

> When adults' perceptions of children's creative efforts are clouded by their own aesthetic preferences or a narrow view of art, it is difficult for them to extend children's creative responses. By heightening their own perceptions of children's creative responses in art as in play, it is likely that practitioners will develop a more caring attitude towards the objects of attention. When things are cared for, it usually follows that their qualities are even more sharply perceived.
>
> (Prentice, 1994: 129)

We know that as engaged adults employed in a young child's learning journey, we are obligated to observe, scaffold, extend and enjoy. But the reality, when confronted with art and young children, is that we often find ourselves in the habit of interfering and intervening in order to bring a control element back into the event under the guise of adult-driven expectation. It is, as we have examined back in Chapter 3, inevitably caught up with the issue of 'mess' production in art-making. It is also, as remarked upon in previous chapters, entrenched in our aesthetic awareness and understanding. As adults we see a beautiful green colour produced and want to step in and prevent it from turning to sludge – this example is a repeated one because it is so familiar to us all.

At the heart of the situation is the understanding and value of trust. Trust within the adult that they advocate the observation and appreciation of the meandering paths taken, trust that the outcome is to be owned by the child, if there is an outcome at all. Trust also comes in the form of trusting ourselves not to interfere in order to allow the moment to take shape and find its way. If this trust can surface, then we can look forward to and fully enjoy the pleasure of the 'messy' journey. We will no longer look on it as mess as we can now see it as the workings-out, the rough sketching, the layering of art knowledge pursued by the child.

The child 'dances with the light'

How we perform this psychological mindset of trust and the surrender of control is more tangible to some than it is to others. It may be something we have to repeatedly train ourselves to do, as a constant reminder to ourselves that it is OK to 'let go'. We can do this by remembering what children are and how they live in the moment. We are reminded again of their sense of spiritual adventure, as examined in Chapters 1 and 3. Paolo Cavazzoni (2012) refers to the child dancing with the light, to remind us of the visceral movement of a child's interaction with sensory-rich moments. His words refer to a shadow projection project where the combined beauty of light and space motivated a pleasurable and dynamic movement of the infant's body, self-choreographed in response to the elements experienced.

> The children's bodies in movement formed a relationship with the material itself and transformed it into a whirlwind of gestures and actions . . . Body and material pursued each other, encountered and confronted each other, concealed and revealed each other, contracted and exploded, in a dance in which the children, it seemed to us, perceived an expansion of the dimensions of their own bodies, a projection that went beyond the physical nature of the gestures.
>
> (Giuidici and Vecchi, 2004: 62)

There exists a vivid quality to such a somatic moment, symptomatic of mind and body actively playing and creating. It is a beautifully composed metaphor that tells us of what we can 'see' and 'feel' when we engage and trust in children's embodied creative minds.

We respect and relish children's ability to luxuriate in a sensory-driven moment, as they excel in the delights of that experience and all it offers. Our debate in this chapter is to consider ourselves in all of this furious sensory art-making and spiritual adventure and how we relate to it as adults. How do we relive the moments, not just through the children's adventures, but through our own lives, so that we can engage and explore alongside children and reinvigorate our own aesthetically charged awareness?

It may seem frivolous, but by allowing ourselves to breathe in and digest some of the experiences suggested below, we reinvigorate the reunion of sensory pleasures and aesthetic awareness. Sometimes, in our busy worlds, we forget to value these moments and extend them on a regular basis rather than always

Box 5.1 Experiences for sensory pleasure and aesthetic awareness

Jump and run: get lost in the moment, feel every muscle, try to hear your own heartbeat.

Experience silence: close your eyes, and listen to the sound of nothing. Become absorbed in it.

Get dressed up: choose fabrics of personally pleasing colours and textures.

Water a plant: notice colour changes, watch the water as it splashes off leaves and is sucked into the soil.

Wash your hands: experience this very ordinary, daily task and awaken to the sense of the cool water, the foam of the soap. Build up lather, smell the aroma, make many bubbles, rub your hands together, rinse and watch the foam run off your fingertips.

Study your favourite object: what is so special about this object? Does it have a special smell, how does it feel, what colour is it, what does it sound like?

Build a tower: take a moment to build a tower. Work slowly and be aware of each piece being added on and keeping the balance. Knock it down and watch the building crumble and the sound it makes. Take in the moment when it has all crashed and the movement has stopped.

Watch a bird fly: look at the movement and the bird's smallness in relation to the sky. Consider the movement and shape of their flight and wings and wonder where they are going.

Take a train ride: look for moving patterns in the landscape and feel the vibrations of speed and the rhythm of the engine.

Taste the rain: let the droplets land on your face and tongue for a few minutes.

speeding along, ignoring what is at our fingertips. To indulge in such momentary pleasures, even if it is for a fraction of a minute, reminds us what it feels like to live in the free sensory world of the young child.

Vicarious expectations – liberation from the literal

As adults working with infants, it is essential to for us to recapture these aesthetic moments for ourselves if we want to develop our abilities and teaching strategies, which include 'letting go'. Of course, you are not actually literally and entirely letting go, but you are releasing yourself and consequently your children from the shackles of prescribed direction; the withdrawal endorses the more important growth of artistic temperament. Affirmation that creativity is about the liberality of the mind and has a potentially infinite range of contexts is at play here. By letting go you allow the artist to emerge and his or her own skills and imagination to control the process. We are reiterating one of the most serious messages here for those committed to valuing child art and all its worth. We are reminding ourselves about the infinite routes and outcomes an art journey can have. It is in the eye of the perceiver and the conceiver, not the observer. Imposed targets require children to stretch into the next stage of development rather than creating and supporting an environment which fosters self-choice and direction where a child works at their own pace and decides the rights and wrongs of the fruits of their labour. As Prentice (1995a: 127) maintains, '[p]rescribed procedures and preconceived ideas squash the spirit of spontaneous exploration fuelled by curiosity: thus imaginative possibilities dwindle'.

Re-focus on young children's art

It is not always easy to 'look at' young children's art for what it is, particularly if your background or experience has not penetrated this exploratory world. It may be that you have worked in the past with older children, possibly secondary level, and therefore your ceiling of expectation relates to a very different age group. Your past observations of more sophisticated markings and intentional, purposeful form and shape are required to be redefined when casting your eye over a young child's piece of work. Notwithstanding the importance of retaining a critical eye for the visual and tactile elements, you have to refocus and alter your understanding – the process of art is still very much alive, as with all ages of children, but it is one that belongs to the investigative energies of a young child who does not create a figure as the adult eye would, or indeed a 13-year-old would. I remind you of this as I remind myself, that the journey of a teacher to understand a young child's art is a liberating one, but one that sometimes has to be learned.

When asked to consider possible stories found in four-year-old Joel's drawn depiction of an elephant (Figure 5.1), a PGCE student, who had previously worked as a teaching assistant in a secondary school, honestly admitted to the fact that she was taking a while to appreciate what was in front of her. The emphasis of the image was the very large body and head belonging to the elephant – this to Joel was the most distinguishing feature. He knew an elephant was the biggest land animal and he wanted to convey this in the size of the body. The fact that an elephant also has a trunk and tusks were added as extra detail, but for the young impressionist this was not of primary importance, but the scale of size was.

Our adult eyes tell us, arguably, that when we think of elephants, we think of trunks as an immediately recognisable feature of this animal. We know they are large creatures, but then so are horses, cows and hippopotami. It is the trunk that we remember. Not so to this particular child. If you work with children of this age and listen to their commentaries and the way their minds interpret data

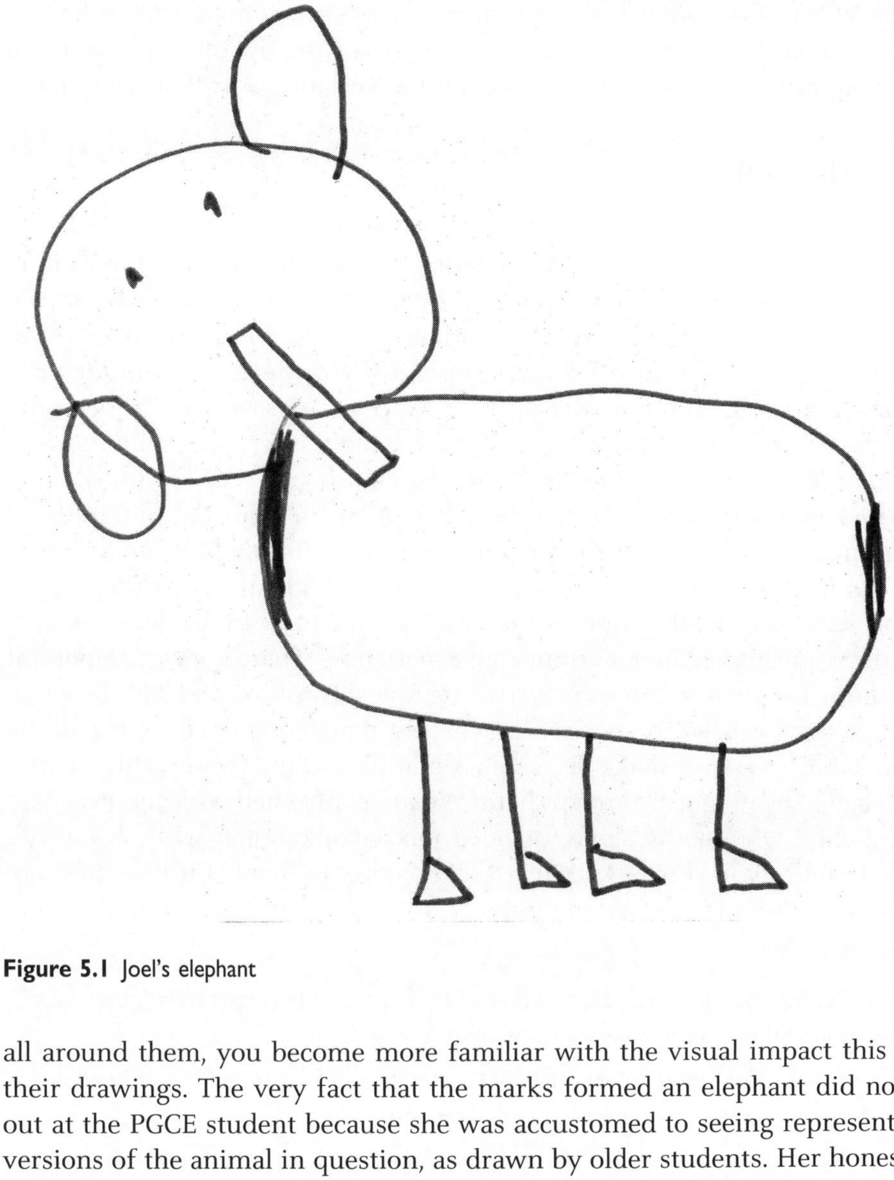

Figure 5.1 Joel's elephant

all around them, you become more familiar with the visual impact this has on their drawings. The very fact that the marks formed an elephant did not jump out at the PGCE student because she was accustomed to seeing representational versions of the animal in question, as drawn by older students. Her honesty was also a request for advice and help as to how to relate to this art, how to change her own way of looking and, in doing so, appreciate the artwork in front of her as a five-year-old's masterpiece. The owner of the elephant drawing had certainly shown great pride in his drawing. It again responds to the 'misunderstood gap' issue – the fuzzy misunderstanding that remains between what children do and how we adults perceive it. The implication here is to consider our overall approaches and strategies in our interactions with children and their art. If we talk to them, listen to them, engage with them as they make and create, we are then able to transcend to a practice which understands their motives, their representations and, most importantly, reminds us at what age they are operating.

We need to find the balance that encourages experimentation and which co-explores and shares the imaginatively charged art-making by following the route of the young artist and valuing and trusting the various paths that may take.

Finding the balance

A part of this careful relationship of trust is achieved through nurturing shared dialogue, actions and interactions. We are also charged with the role of modelling skills and techniques in our conversational exchange with the young artist. We are able to make suggestions and offer guidance – *when it is asked for.* We can place this energised, art-based exchange within the context of a vibrant early years environment. It is a reminder of the balance of approaches to all learning in an early years setting where the continuum moves between child-initiated learning and that which is more adult-led (see Figure 5.2).

Art-based exploration will rightly be situated in the arm of child-initiated learning on this continuum. In moments when the adult deduces and decides when a conversation, agreement or suggestion may illuminate a learning experience, the scale tips to the more structured right. This careful and sensitive relationship is magnified in our art-making experiences. There is a very important balance here between sharing and trusting the adventure and aiding when required. What we need to consider is whether that requirement is owned by the child alone, or do we make decisions sometimes to intervene? The theories of both Piaget and Vygotsky are apt here. We are confronted with the Piagetian view of a child who learns alone, unaided (2001 [1950]), and with Vygotsky's scaffolded child, who learns within a social context (1978). Duffy (1998: 90) refers to this conundrum as the role of the interventionist and the non-interventionist:

Non-interventionists: those who think that adults should not become directly involved in young children's creative and imaginative work.

Interventionists: those who believe that the interaction between children and adults are keys to children's learning and development.

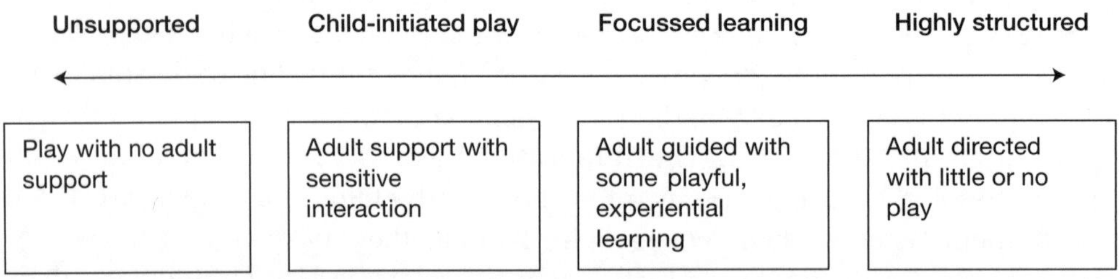

Figure 5.2 The continuum of children's experiences

We, no doubt, flow between the two roles when we support infant art-making. We learn to 'read' the situation and the episode being played out in front of us. Going with the child, responding to their investigations and providing an environment that fully endorses a child-initiated approach may all convey a non-interventionist persuasion. Conversely, to get this balance right, the interventionist approach is to be adopted with care and sensitivity as, whether we observe or physically interact, we are there as practitioners who can pave the way for great moments of insight and discovery.

Intervention is perhaps a harsh and intrusive description of the role we create for ourselves. Wright (2010) refers to the role as the 'interlocutor', which conjures up images of forensic investigations and secretive ponderings – quite an exciting image for both parties involved! Whichever term we wish to use, the essence of the adult's relationship with the young artist remains the same: the nourishment of the journey through appropriate interaction.

'Riding the waves together' – cooperative interactions

Positive engagement with a child and their art is inextricably bound within a mutual relationship of trust and cooperation – a shared understanding of what is being played out. The very Vygotskian model of socially enhanced learning is utterly implicit in these highly creative and participative relationships. During socially bound and critical art-making moments, we are able to 'ride the wave of discovery' with the child, as one teacher once described it. This teacher was someone who, though very quietly spoken and calm in her outward manner, was able to enter into a child's experience with total commitment and focus. She understood the need to balance a sense of listening, imitation and co-creation. Her co-existence with a child's art-making experience was welcomed by the children because the moments were chosen and identified carefully and sensitively. These moments could last a minute, the length of an activity or sustain the longitudinal pace of an art research project over a period of time. The quality of her cooperation was founded in her ability to 'see' the child in the art. To be more explicit, she recognised and valued the emerging styles, the various eccentricities that were being exposed through creative 'doing'. She watched these emerging patterns and followed them with interest. So when she entered into a shared moment, she was able to relate to the specific child and their personalised art play and creations. Her responses were guided by knowledge of the child, their creative character and the participative quality of the involvement of their body in their art-making.

The detail which is of importance in our 'balance' discussion here is that we need to be sure of the why, when and what of adult support. Again, this refers us back to the continuum from Figure 5.2. We have to learn to appropriately identify invitations, verbal or non-verbal, from children and when to conjoin

Box 5.2 Adult engagement

1. Sensitivity

This is the sensitivity of the adult to the feelings and emotional well-being of the child, including elements of empathy, sincerity and authenticity:

- A child's need for respect: giving the child a feeling of being valued and put on a equal basis.
- A child's need for attentiveness: listening to the child, acknowledging the need for attention.
- A child's need for security: recognising and responding to the child's insecurities and uncertainties.
- A child's need for affection: responding to the child with warmth and care.
- A child's need for praise and encouragement: giving the child praise and support.

2. Stimulation

This is the way the adult stimulates the child:

- introducing or offering an activity;
- giving information;
- intervening in an ongoing activity to stimulate action, thinking or communication.

3. Autonomy

This is the degree of freedom the adult provides for the child to experiment, make judgements, choose activities and express ideas. It is also how the adult handles conflict, rules and behavioural issues:

- the degree of child choice of activity;
- the opportunities for children to experiment;
- the freedom of the child to choose and shape the direction of the activity;
- the respect given to the child's work, ideas and judgement of the finished product;
- the opportunity for the children to negotiate and solve problems and conflicts;
- the participation of the child in rule making and enforcement.

(Pascal and Bertram, 2003: 82)

Case study 1: Samina and the dinosaurs

The children in Clara's EYFS classroom had recently become fascinated by dinosaurs. One girl, Samina, in particular, following a visit to a museum full of dinosaur skeletons, had excited and motivated her peers by bringing in photographs of what she had seen. This then snowballed and other contributions relating to the theme were brought into school, and books were found in the school library and class book corner. Huge paintings were created – one collaborative painting extended the length of the classroom as the children wanted to 'make it as long as a brontosaurus'. One of the final art-based activities that came about within this theme was a giant masking-tape-framed sculpture of a dinosaur. The sculpture was made from tables, construction blocks, masking tape and plastic covering. Samina, the original motivator and initiator of the dinosaur investigations, was also a leading light in the sculpture-making and in this case study we saw how very closely her teacher, Clara, worked with her, sharing her moments, offering encouragement when needed, and exploring the tactile and visual pleasures of the aesthetic adventure.

If we magnify a particular moment during the sculpture-making in this case study, key features of positive adult engagement are at play. During the making of the body, Samina was keen to breathe life into the dinosaur. She wanted to give him more of a character and somehow illustrate how dangerous and fierce he was.

These distinct features gave value to what was already an exciting and fulfilling art experience, but they added something extra – they gave the art-making a sense of importance and relevance. Clara's willing and participatory recognition of what was happening during the making elevated the experience to a new level of discovery.

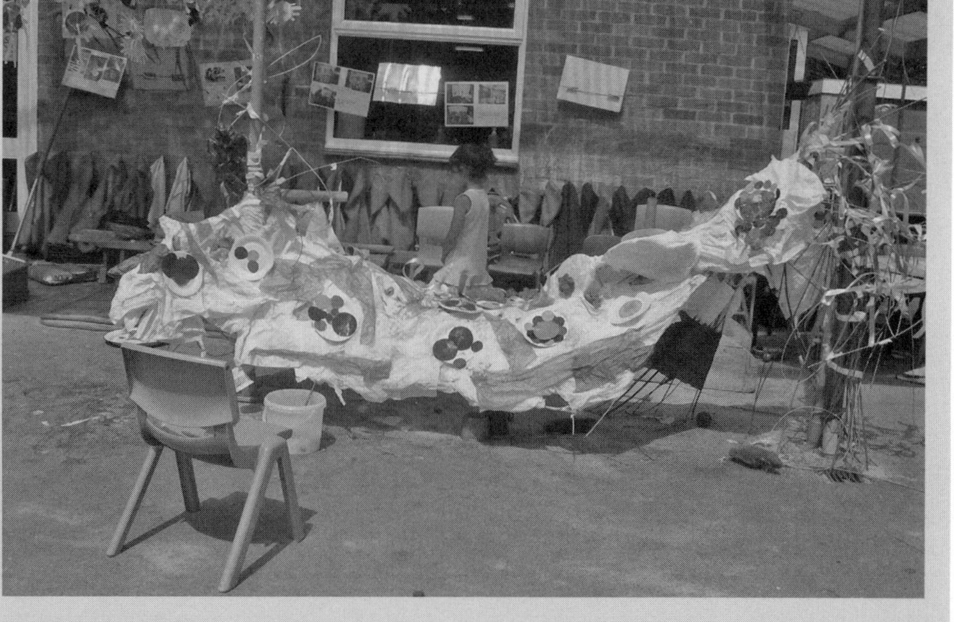

Figure 5.3 Giant dinosaur sculpture

Case study 2: The house with ears

Rayaz and his key worker, Jo, had set up a printing activity with rollers. The pre-context for such a task, from the point of view of the adult, was her recognition of Rayaz's fascination with sequence and stages of progress – he had a propensity to work through a process, layering each moment with enormous concentration and commitment. This was a repeated behaviour prevalent predominantly in his use of large and small construction kits as well as games with rules. His schematic behaviour had been reflected in this creative work with regards to art-making, but he would often become overwhelmed by the presence of others, making his work anxiety-ridden. At such points he would rush through a sequence silently, without his usual precision and dedicated endeavour.

The printing equipment had been very much on the agenda for the whole class and had been a focus for some of their art-making through observing patterns in the environment. Rayaz had shown an interest in the rollers and had handled them on previous occasions but without commitment to further investigation. Jo, identifying his interest and in response to the absence of others at this particular moment in the printing space, encouraged Rayaz to enter into an exploratory episode with her.

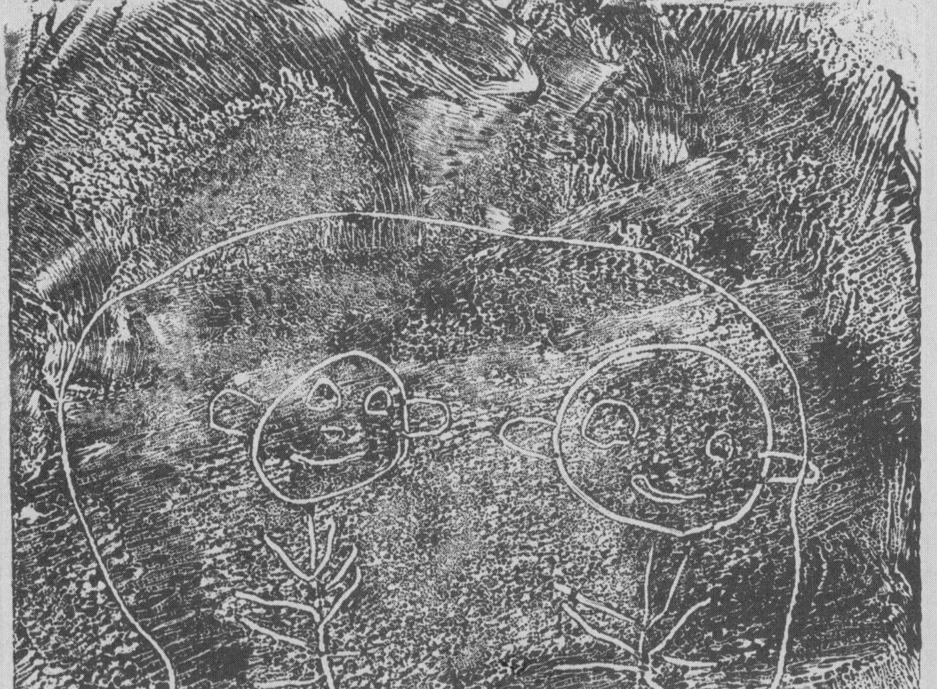

Figure 5.4 Rayaz's house with ears

In response to his interest in sequence, and to her as the adult with previously gained knowledge, she modelled the path of monoprinting, moving from one stage to the other until the final moment of revealing her print was conceived. Both parties took a deep anticipatory breath and Rayaz excitedly peeled off her paper to reveal the impression she had created. He was utterly motivated to then try out the procedure himself and went onto repeat the sequence with confidence and self-assurance, so much so that he would alter certain aspects in order to change the outcome.

Sequence, anticipation and the supportive presence of the engaged adult combined to ensure this was a richly rewarding enterprise. Rayaz responded with characteristic behaviour to the modelling, the techniques, the sequence and the physical manipulation of tools. Reciprocal creativity was very much at play as the roles reversed; the adult modelled the techniques and the child inspired the images imprinted. The adult stalled at the point of pressing marks into the inked surface, unsure as to what image to create. The child was alert with ideas and images took shape which were borne out of his vivid imagination.

Rayaz: Look, I've drawn a house with ears . . . and there are two people *(after he scratches out two figures)*. The house can hear them . . .
Jo: And the ears are big so it can probably hear everything that they are saying.
Rayaz: *(giggles)* Yes. And now. . . *(he lifts a piece of paper and places it on the printed surface, presses it down and peels it off)* Look there's lots of lines now *(looks a little confused)*.
Jo: Well, I think that's because the ink makes the lines when you lift it up.

(They look together and contemplate the product in front of them.)

Rayaz: It looks like rain – it's been raining.
Jo: Yes, it does look like rain, it's making the house with ears very wet!
Rayaz: And the two people.

An important aspect of this dyadic dynamic was the fact that there were moments of noise and spoken word and also very secure, energised moments of silence as the stages were carefully and securely played out for both co-explorers. This was a shared endeavour where participation and response were of equal importance.

with their adventure. If we know our children well, and have learnt about them through mutual responsiveness and understanding (Reddy, 2010), then we can identify intervention appropriately.

By sharing the adventures, we become part of them and this ensures we retain the adventures as part of the children's developing art abilities rather than imposing our own adult-based understandings. This does not mean to say we are not to value and be interested in our own view of art. Our own aesthetic appreciation, with years of invested interest, is of great importance. If we remain interested and alert to what is out there, this then helps us to retain awareness, a critical mind and a continual research facility. We will return to this later in the chapter.

'Riding the wave' with the children encourages both the child and the adult to engage in a respected union of interest – their responses to the art-making can be discussed, considered and employed, but all within a constructively mutual and trusting arena. This arena is one that we know is of immense importance in all of our workings with young children. The importance of creating relationships and shared moments that engage trust, autonomy and stimulation are vital elements of positive adult engagement.

If we refer to Bertram and Pascal's table of adult engagement in Box 5.2, we can start to relate this to the shared art experience. The previous case studies highlight the key features of positive adult engagement in action.

Responding and valuing

There has been much discussion throughout this book about our role as adults within the context of how we share experiences through the eyes of children. It is, however, essential for us to value our own personal responses. If we retain an interest in art-making and invest our own critical and culturally aware skills in art appreciation, it ensures we continue to develop our own minds in this sensory-rich aspect of life. Teaching, as we know, can be exhausting and strenuous. Its daily demands relating to a whole range of circumstances and expectations can leave us drained. So, it is therefore all the more important that we are mindful to bask in the enjoyable experiences that belong to us. Joining our own individual and adult-based searches in preferences of artworks, visiting art galleries and tinkering with art materials will keep us alert and energised in a subject which, as we have examined, is very personal and intimately related to the individual and all their values. I am not, by any means, suggesting that we should all paint, sculpt and print in our spare time, or indeed, insist that galleries are frequented and works of art viewed on a regular basis. I am merely stating that we have based, and rightly so, most of our discussion and thoughts around how we interact with children in relation to sharing their worlds and 'seeing' their viewpoints. This accepted, our own viewpoints and aesthetic understandings still matter. The shared art experience is all the more powerful and dynamic if we also have our interests and can recognise the feeling of what art can do for the soul and spirit.

So, as an aside, at this juncture in the book, do remember to value your own creative character. As we continue to define ourselves, our developing empathy with the creative quests of our children becomes more apparent and contemporary. Self-esteem comes from valuing our responses and if we feel confident about approaching art because we have enjoyed it in our adult world, then this positive regard will transfer to our engagement with children and their art.

Our own continual engagement with art appreciation, aesthetic awareness and refinement of creative criticality will also assist us greatly in how we discuss and critically reflect on children's artwork with the children themselves. Discussion and dialogue are at the heart of observing and engaging with children and their art. We have examined the narration of stories through drawing and image-making in Chapter 4, and now we consider this again but with the emphasis on the 'adult-speak', what this might sound like and how it might present itself. It is as much to do with our body language as it is with the words we select in consideration of a motivational and stimulating pedagogical dialogue.

The signs we can offer in encouragement are commonly recognised in relation to positive body language. An inclined head to indicate critical analysis, eyes alert with genuine interest, awareness of height at child level or the level of where an activity is taking place all play a part in the exchange of appreciation and discussion. Positive body language can also be displayed in our actions of 'doing', our *joining in* physically with the adventure. Here the active mirroring of our own creative and explorative movements reflects that of the child who is painting with a large brush, sculpting clay with both hands, peeling and unwrapping masking tape. Our cooperative and energised hands can tell a child how interested we are in the artistic journey that they are taking. Reflecting, copying (a positive term of acknowledgement in this instance) and simultaneously discovering a piece of artwork contain a very powerful teaching moment as they say to the child, 'I like what you are doing and want to do the same so that I can feel the shape, form, texture. I can see the lines you are creating – are they a bit like this?' Again, we are reminded that the choosing of this moment correctly, understanding when it is appropriate to physically join in and co-explore, is essential. It is a carefully monitored moment that will be welcomed if the time is right.

The shared physical exploration produces shared moments of tactile and visual discoveries. A joint journey between child and adult gives rise to a growing sense of self-esteem in the child as their adventure is being valued by someone else, and someone who, with careful and considered language, can extend the journey to a higher level of thinking. Young children are more than capable of higher levels of thinking. In fact, their spiritual mode of awe and wonder can oft-times afford them greater and more frequent episodes of higher thinking than adults. When the child is working alongside the reflective adult, the artistic mode of the moment is given the opportunity to expand and to reveal further layers of understanding.

Body language tells many stories of joint non-verbal participation, appreciation and investigation. It is a point of discussion that needs to be had regularly in settings where pre-verbal children make art and investigate aesthetic awareness: 'Children experience a softer and slower kind of grappling and groping for a way of articulating something that is currently and tantalisingly beyond their linguistic grasp' (Claxton, 2006b: 352).

Paired co-existence and co-exploration in a rich moment of art engrossment extends both the quality and the richness of the process. It is an immensely powerful companionship and one that affects both parties as they reaffirm their interest in one another (Simpson, 2011). As verbally active adults, we often feel the need to speak, to use words in order to form a dialogue with a young pre-verbal child.

Communication and language is enhanced through direct speaking, but what we devalue and ignore is the power of silent cooperation. Once again, we are reminded of the significance of 'awareness sensing' as discussed in Chapter 3. In this instance, the cooperating partnership offers a silent awareness of one another. But the silence is responding to the present time and the two are alert in those still and silent moments to the experience of what might occur.

The focussed one-to-oneness of a childminder and a 30-month-old child as they interacted with two pieces of wood, as I was privileged to witness, perfectly describes such an exchange of cooperation and shared interest. In this scenario, the childminder followed, with imperceptible awareness of intention, each move and inclination of body gesture that the child issued. The adult here operated with clear knowledge of the child and an understanding of what was at play: the wood's surface was a tactile space which had appealed to the little hands and eyes and the child had begun to peel away at the bark. The childminder peeled too, their movements coinciding and colliding, both showing pleasure and enjoyment through smiles, gesture and exultation at the extracted shavings.

At one point, the childminder gathered the shavings and sieved them to the ground with a rub of her hands. The child imitated the movement and once they were on the ground, moved them around this new surface to form a pattern. Pattern formed, she returned to the wood and peeled some more. Further shavings extended the picture on the ground and so this sequence continued, led by the child until the original piece of wood was too small to peel from – this decision made by the child.

The quietness of space, company and extension of time within the childminder's home environment had led to this very rich, very intimate exchange of ideas where concentration of mind, hands and emotions were all involved. The body language from the adult translated as actively interested and genuinely participative, and so there existed an energised air of intent for both parties. Their cooperative interchanges (Sharan and Sharan, 1992) presented joint creative and exploratory moments – their bodies mimicking each other as the marks moved and transformed.

Possibility thinking – an intergenerational exchange

Carefully considered interactions with children can help to develop their creativity and imagination and give rise to a whole world of possibilities and potentialities. At the interface of the social interaction, a different and new outlook is found and so another layer is built onto the experience. An interaction, if positively, willingly and cooperatively applied, should enhance the learning experience, not limit it. We have to know ourselves as professional educators who foster relationships with our children, where our actions and interactions implicate and value possibility thinking (Craft, 2002). In order to achieve this mutual thinking platform, we have to remind ourselves of the following, as outlined by Craft:

- openness: receptivity to germinate and assimilate ideas;
- releasing the unconscious: nourishing the unconscious self;
- self-esteem: valuing responses and endeavours;
- relationships: relishing dynamic interaction.

As we nourish our own thinking platform, we set a precedent in our own settings where 'possibility thinking' in art learning is at the forefront. It permeates the atmosphere and says to all that being imaginative is about what might be feasible.

This 'thinking culture' abounds in the entirety of art exploration whether spoken or silent. Silent here refers to action without words, certainly not silent

Table 5.1 Possible vocabulary for journeys of art discovery

Line	*Tone*
Angular Broad Broken Circular	Black Contrast Dark
Contour Curved Dark Diagonal	Grey High key Highlight
Flowing Grid Hard Horizontal	Light Low key Monotone
Light Linear Long Outline	Shade Shadow
Rhythmic Short Smooth Soft	
Spiralling Straight Sweeping Thick	
Thin Vertical Wiggly Zigzag	
Texture	*Pattern*
Coarse Dry Feathery Furry	Arabesque Border Decorative
Glossy Hard Matt Rough	Geometric Grid Half-drop
Scratchy Shiny Silky Slimy	Irregular Regular Natural
Smooth Soft Waxy Wet	Repeat Rhythm Rotation
	Symmetrical Tessellation
Colour	*Shape*
Bright Clashing Cold Contrast Dark	Large Made Natural Simple
Deep Dull Earth Hue Intense Light	Solid Small Tessellating Long Short
Pale Pastel Pallet Pigment Primary	Hard Soft Curved Straight
Rainbow Secondary Shades Warm	
Form	*Space*
Carving Cone Cylinder Cube Mass	Airy Atmospheric Broad Busy
Modelling Natural Organic Rigid Sculpture	Enclosed High Large Narrow
Sphere Structure Volume Weight	Open Quiet Small Wide

in what is being communicated – energised actions speak volumes about thinking processes. But applied to both forms of communication is the mutual and dialogue-rich interaction of the adult and child. The adult–child partnership can lead to thinking beyond the realms of the immediate. Our unified bodies and minds work together to find out new things. This is also creative and possibility thinking of which we are not always aware and conscious – the thinking flows and meanders around and through the living art process. A piece of clay can be manipulated by child and adult hands, the fine and exploratory sensorimotor movement can progress in skill steps by mirroring, reflecting and bouncing physically imaginative ideas off each other. This 'silent' but very physical cogitation has taken both parties into another realm of tactile investigation and, in doing so, has added another layer of knowing to the art in progress.

Our non-verbal and verbal dialogues empower young children to become acquainted with the language of art from a very young age. By using a rich vocabulary through movement and word, we are increasing a knowledge and understanding about what is possible and also, importantly, about quality and aesthetic contentment. Table 5.1 should serve as a guide, not complete or exhaustive, but a list of possibilities when on journeys of art discovery and possibility thinking with a child. Its foundations are based in the basic elements of visual and tactile art and this is a subject that we return to in Chapter 6. Some of the words are familiar and some more complex – the choice of use will depend on the appropriate moment of exploration. Some words will never come into play and others will be considered more regularly. Importantly, young children will create their own words to be included in our modern diction in response to exploration.

Mistakes are positive

Nurturing the development of language and articulation of visual and tactile vocabulary in response to art enables processes to become more 'meaty' (Wright, 2010). The episodes converge into enquiry-based experiences. As the inter-generational discussion continues through movement and talk, so it will ebb and flow through successes and failures. The dips and troughs are also key to developing a language in art that belongs to the artist: the ability to review, re-address and redefine a piece of artwork is achieved through self-analysis and constructive self-criticism. Claxton (2007: 2) says:

> To train young people that everything can be neatly answered within an hour is to weaken what Keats called their 'negative capability': the ability to 'be in doubts, mysteries and uncertainties without any irritable reaching after fact and reason.'

Possibility thinking in art is to encourage and participate in, as the adult, an environment and atmosphere that includes mistakes, errors, frustration, irritation and doubts. It is the doubts that have probably stalled many of us, back in our own childhoods, as to whether we saw ourselves as artists. One mistake that does not look right in a painting can linger for years as the reason for not taking up painting again. If the practitioner, however, identifies this moment of uncertainty and enters the learning moment, they can help to administer the negative sentiment, and use it to invigorate a positive response. Children need to know that the adults around them understand the importance of pursuing seemingly irrational ideas. When children are making errors they are operating at the limits of their abilities, whether cognitive or physical, and are stretching themselves (Duffy, 2006).

> Encountering problems during process; from skill limitations to expressional concerns; using discussion as a tool, adults can help children recognise artistic challenges and aid in finding subsequent solutions. Educators should seize upon these occasions and, using active dialogue, expand the given experience into further explorations and future artistic endeavours.
>
> (Eglinton, 2003: 33)

Our actions must replicate our words, so that children see us 'doing' what we advise them to 'do'. Claxton (2007) refers to this as 'walking the talk' or, in true creative fashion, 'dancing the talk'! Clarification in positive mistake-making is further enhanced by modelling similar 'error-enhanced' behaviour. Sometimes, we may have to be rather explicit in order to convey this as a learning strategy, but most children pick up on mistakes being made. They actually quite like it if adults make mistakes, particularly glaring ones. This can be of great amusement to them – how can we, the older people who know everything, make mistakes? But, on a serious note, it liberates their confidence to find out, to fail and to succeed.

The EYFS Characteristics for Effective Learning (2012) clearly advises us with regards to risk-taking, challenges and the positivity of mistakes:

> Encourage children to try new activities and to judge risks for themselves. Be sure to support children's confidence with words and body language.
>
> Talk about how you and the children get better at things through effort and practice, and what we all can learn when things go wrong.
>
> (British Association for Early Education, 2012: 6)

Joint possibility thinking could also be referred to as sustained shared thinking – a process much explored and celebrated in early years. Siraj-Blatchford *et al.* (2002: 3) define it as:

> an episode in which two or more individuals 'work together' in an intellectual way to solve a problem, clarify a concept, evaluate activities, extend a narrative etc. Both parties must contribute to the thinking and it must develop and extend.

Such an approach is one that allows for mutual debate, investigation and deliberation, thus reaching further into layers of understanding.

Praise: making it real and useful

Both sustained shared thinking and possibility thinking present us with another contentious point of discussion, which we sometimes have to train ourselves to respond to correctly, and that is the question of praise. Praise in art can be difficult and confusing – it is, in its very definition, a word that summons up an assumption held by an observer, a subjective comment placed on something they do not own or necessarily understand. The assumptive nature of praise, as well as the blandness of praise often associated with art-making, needs to be considered and examined in order to make it purposeful and non-judgemental. It does have a place, but not as a statement from teacher to child, more as a conversational exchange in shared moments during or at the end of the process. It is an opportunity to engage with the young artist and their work through words, critical appreciation and empathetic perceptivity. When praise is continuous or repetitive, it can sound monotonous and banal – the words lose their power and the experience loses its meaningfulness.

> Observation reveals that children are perceptive and can usually tell if adults are being thoughtful and sincere in their comments. The EYFS (2012) recognises and advises on the issue of praise in consideration of positive relationships and characteristics of effective learning: 'Be specific when you praise, especially noting effort such as how the child concentrates, tries different approaches, persists, solves problems, and has new ideas.'
>
> (British Association for Early Education, 2012: 6).

Our dialogic relationship with a child and their art provides exciting and tangible opportunities to make sincere comments count and to cherish these shared moments as meaningful. This can be achieved if we choose and consider the appropriate language so that we are offering relevant and constructive messages.

Whatever the encounter, our message of encouragement remains the same. Dialogue should maintain the open-endedness necessary for an exciting interchange between the educator and child – a balanced diet of analysis, description, solution and discovery. The offerings of banal praise such as 'that's a nice picture' or closed questions have no place in this sort of dialogue. Open-ended praise is something that is not finite and what we say should initiate further conversations so that we are training children to use their critical eye and their developing understanding of visual and tactile elements in art-making. As Schirrmacher (1986: 93) confirmed:

> Rather than resorting to platitudes . . . of children and their art, adults can respond to children's creative endeavours by commenting on the artistic elements in their work. When used sparingly, this approach will help facilitate children's artistic and aesthetic development.

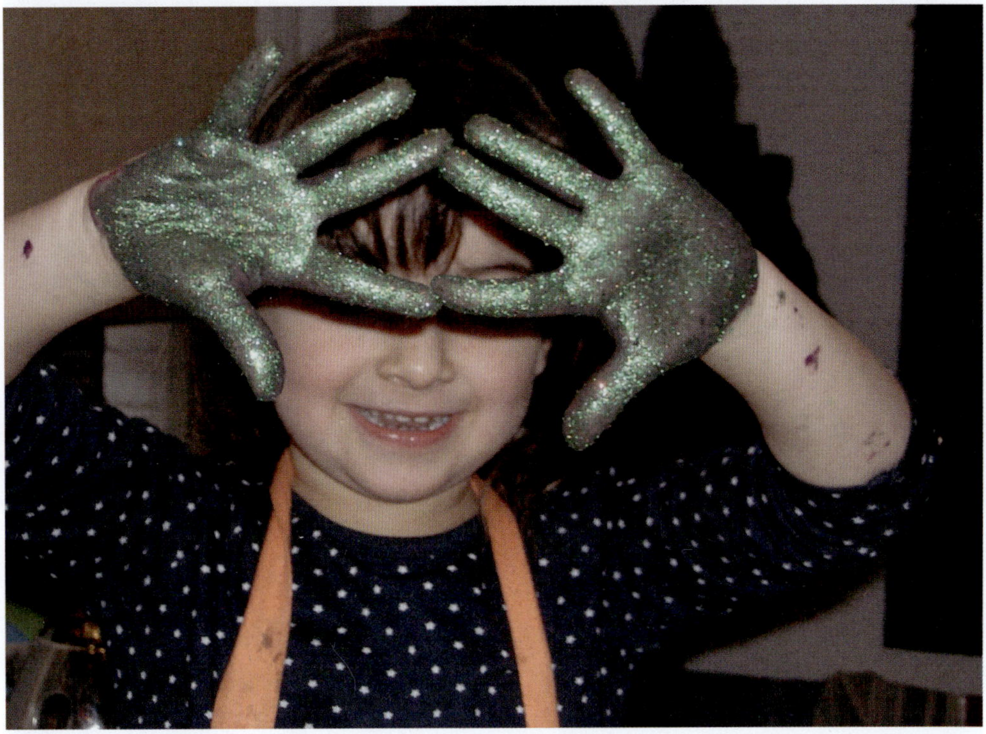

1 Sparkly investigations

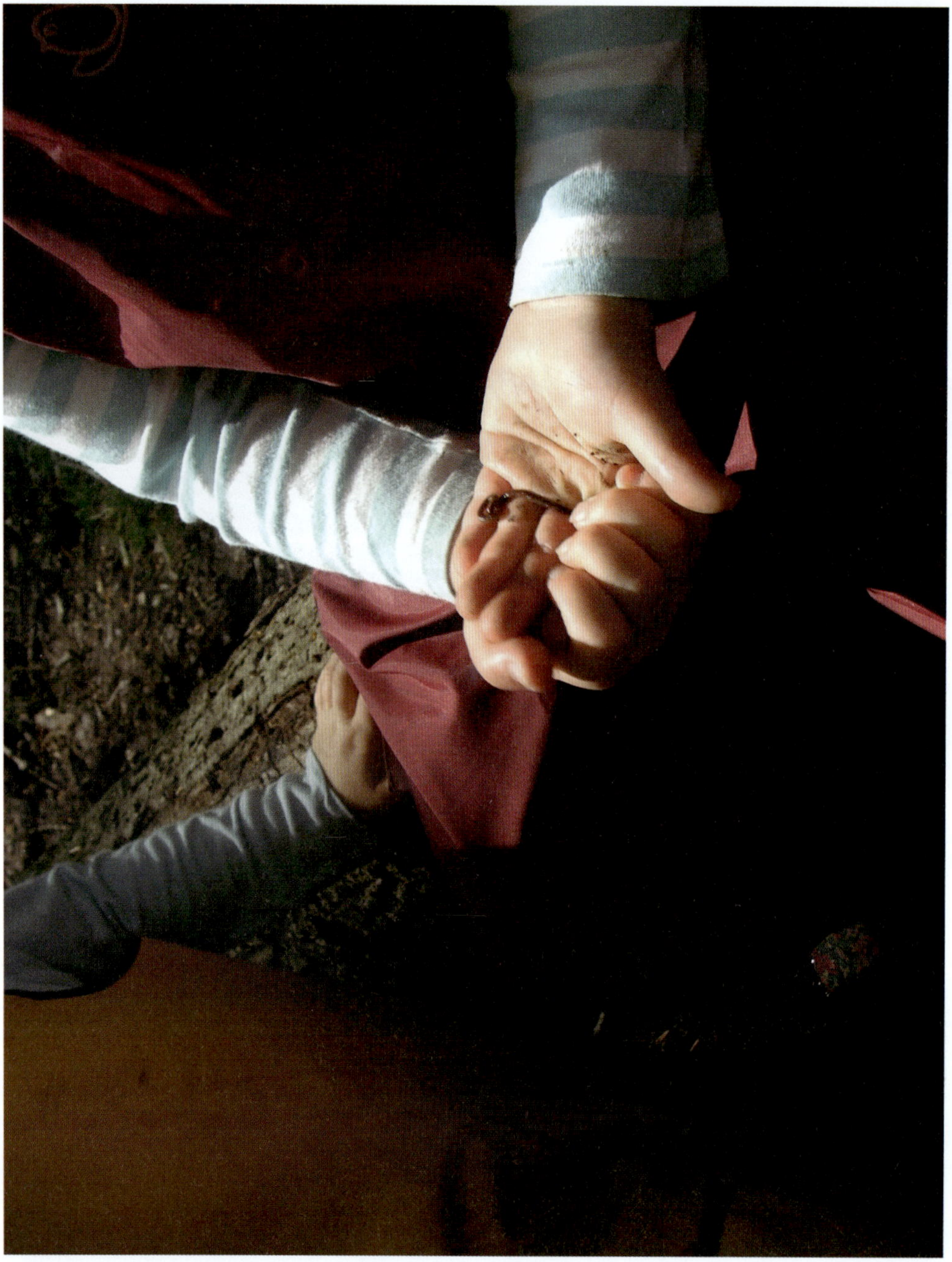

2 India discovers a woodworm

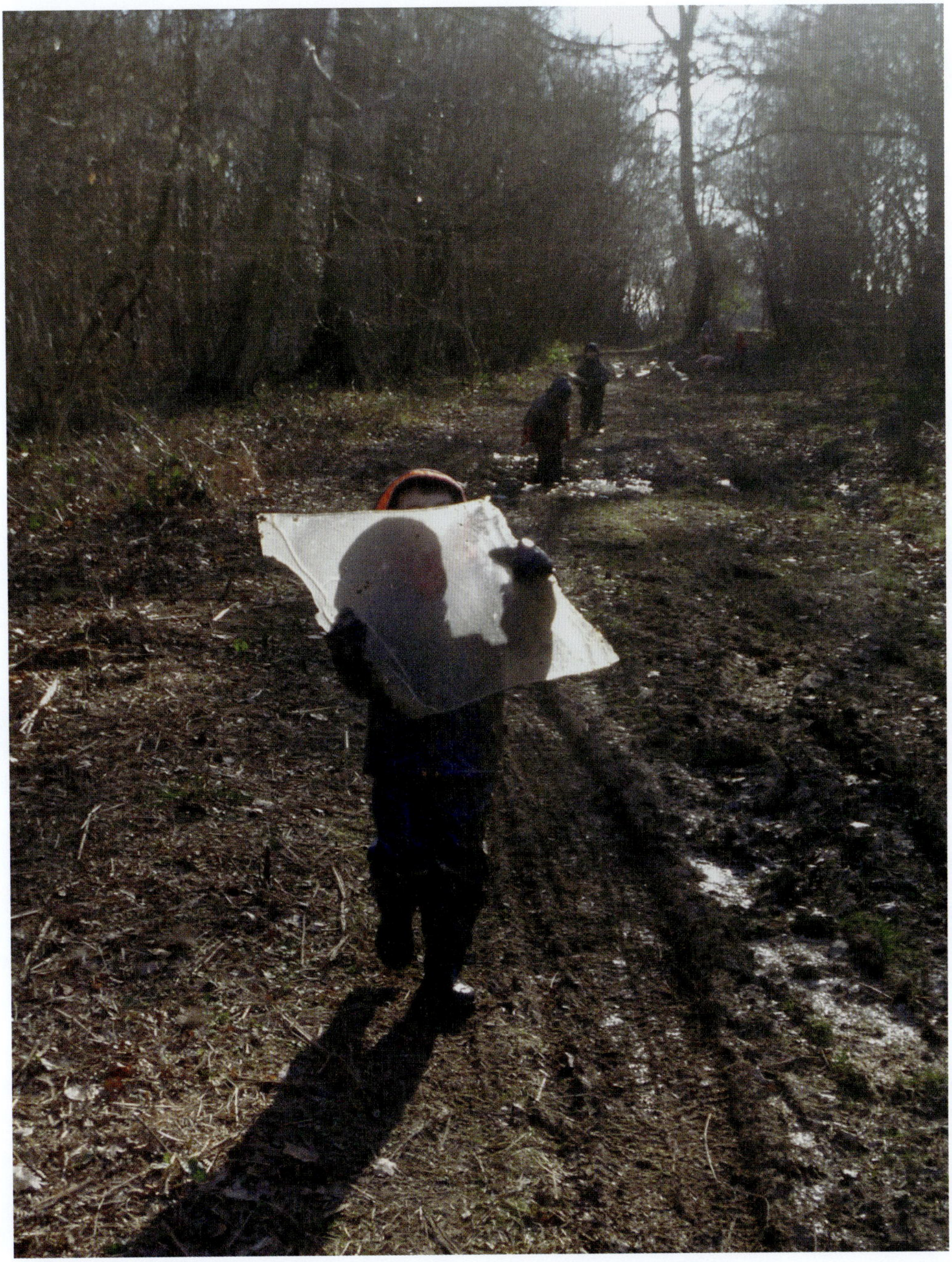

3 Ben discovers a sheet of ice

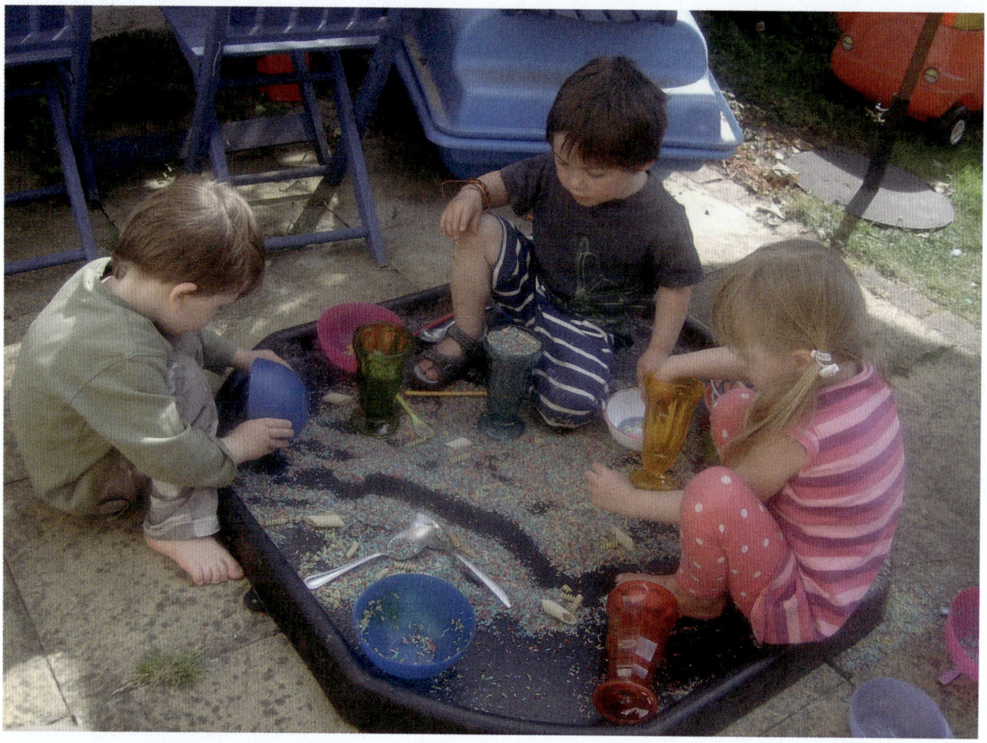

4 Layering and mixing coloured sand

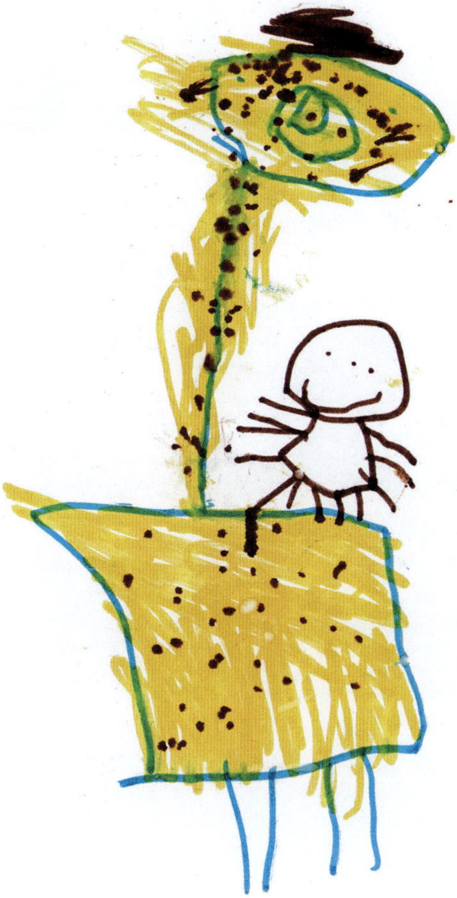

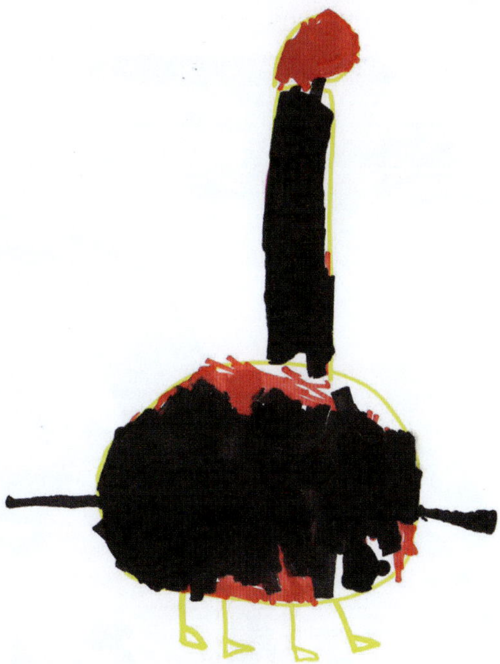

5 Jonah's giraffes

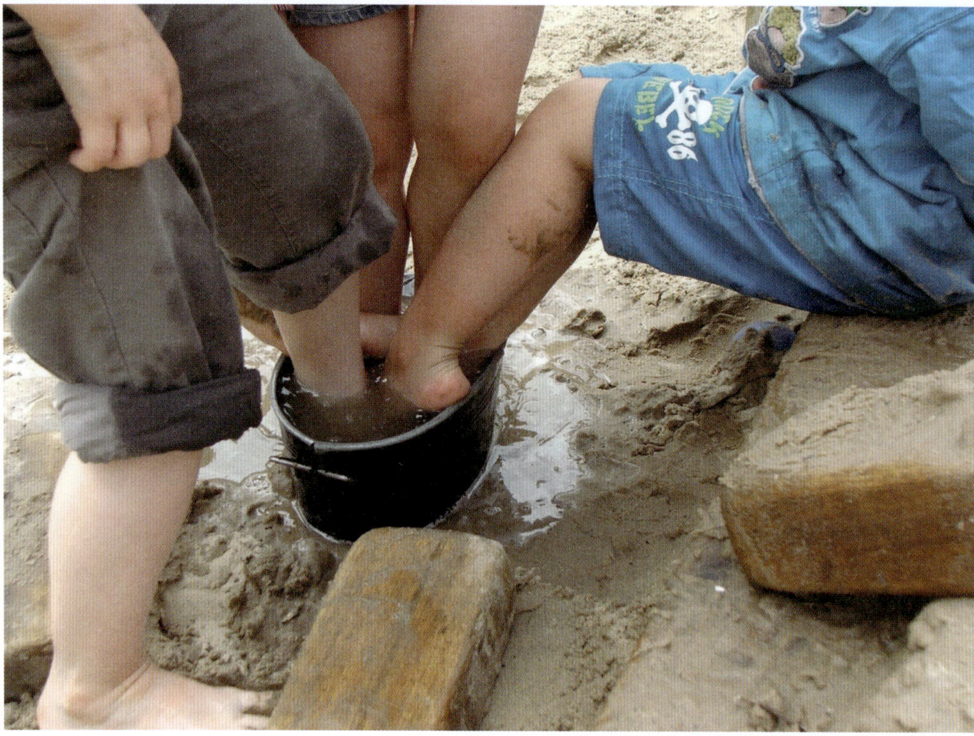

6 Washing feet in a bucket

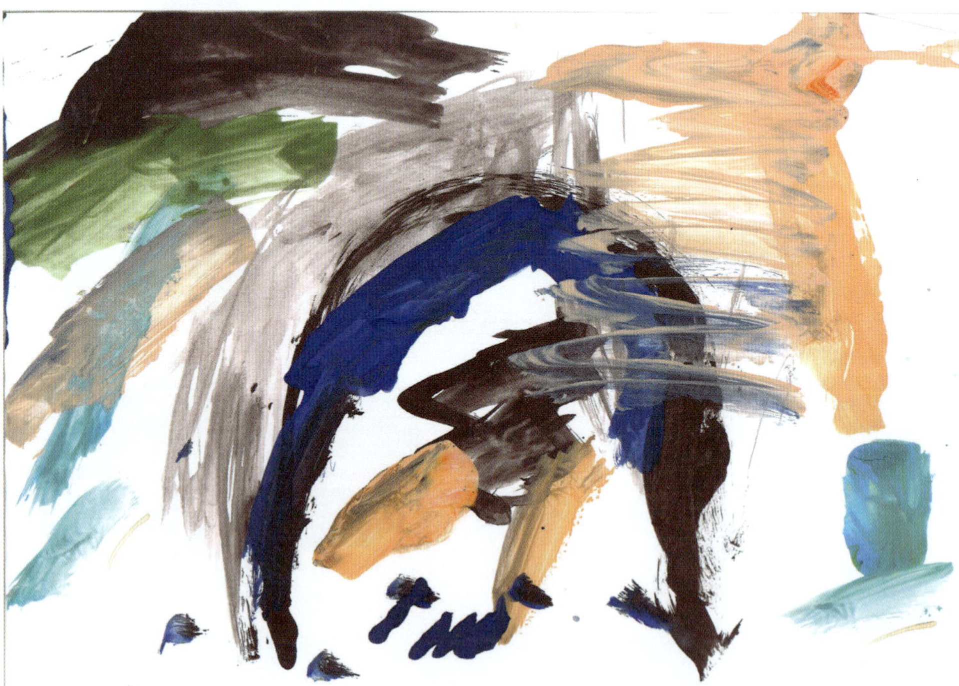

7 Colour dialogue

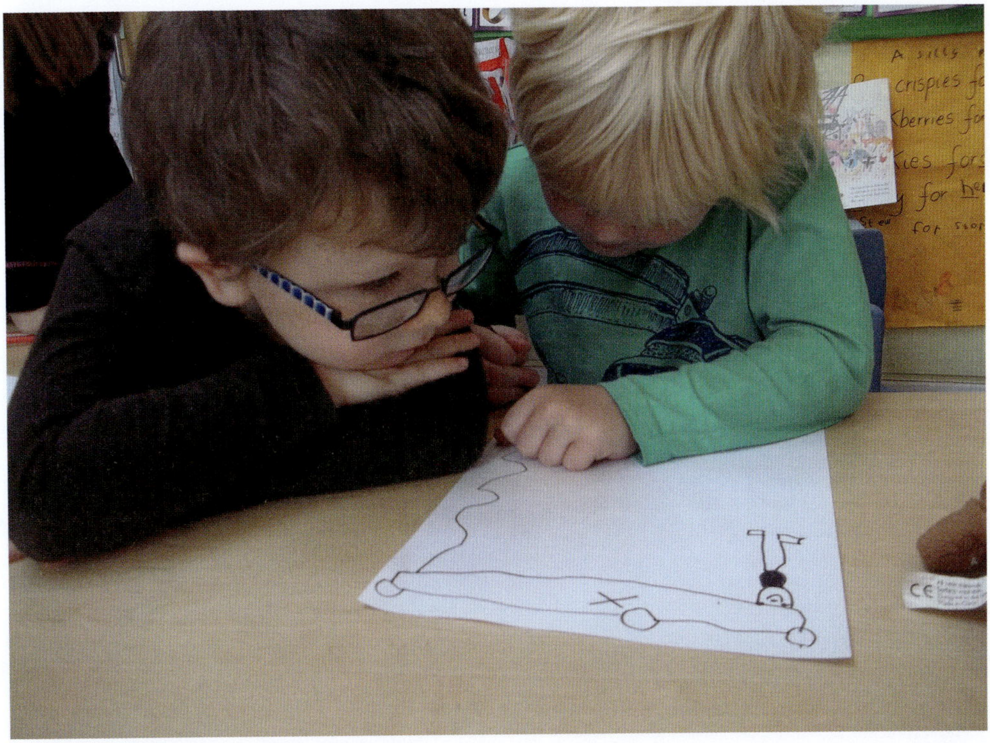

8 Lewis and Freddy's shared drawing venture

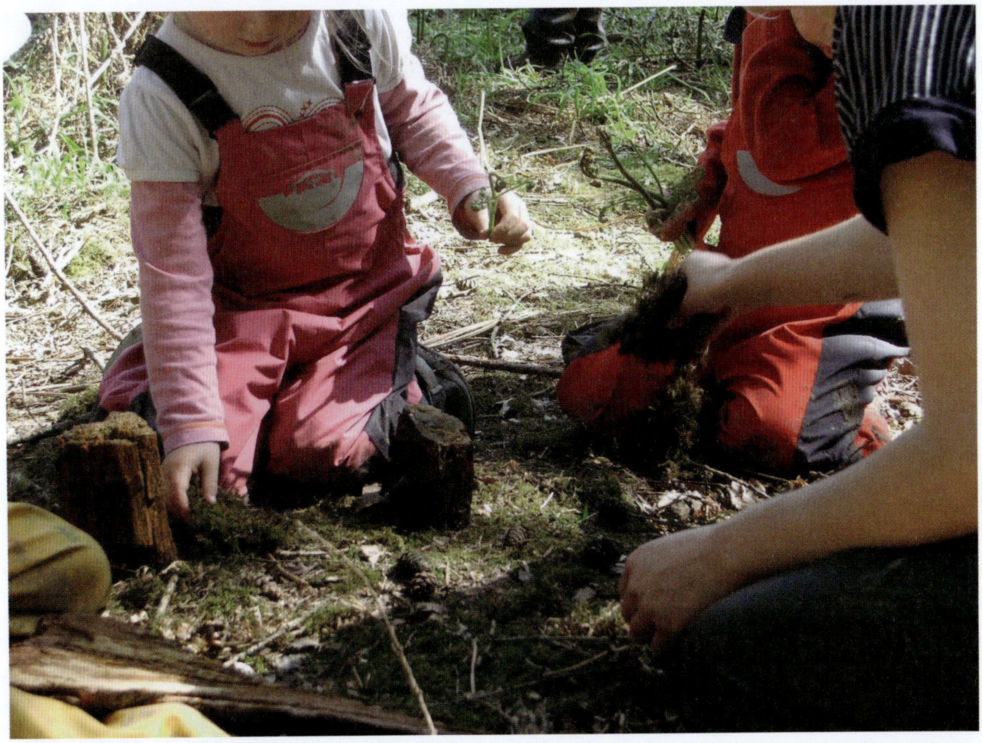

9 Tactile sense-making with moss and plants

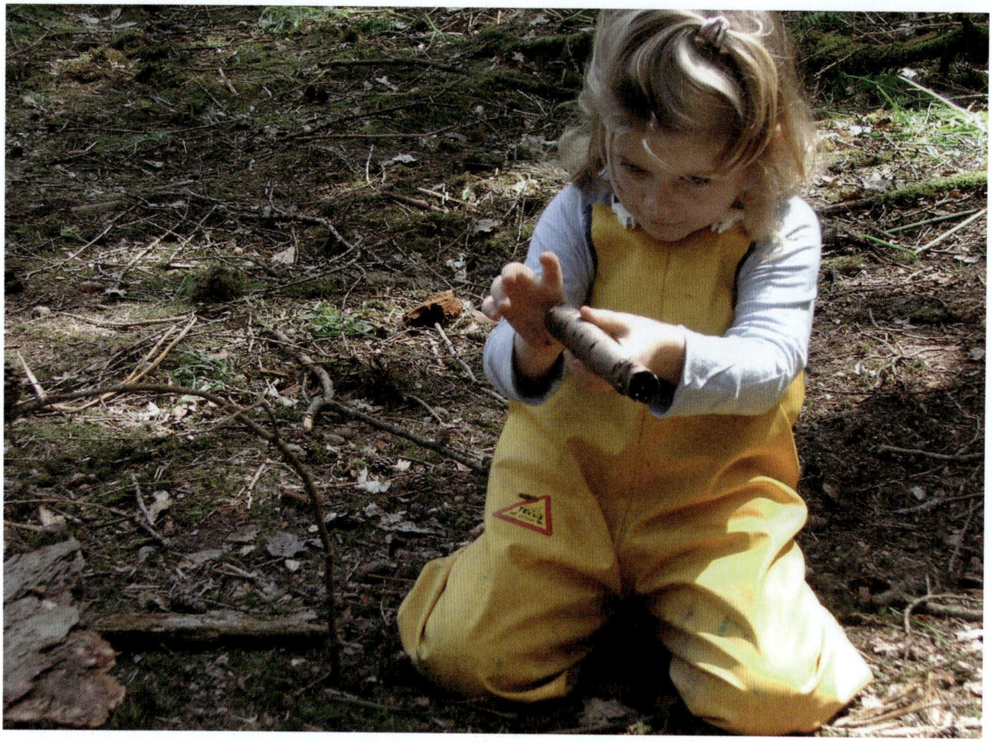

10a Paige experiments with found wood

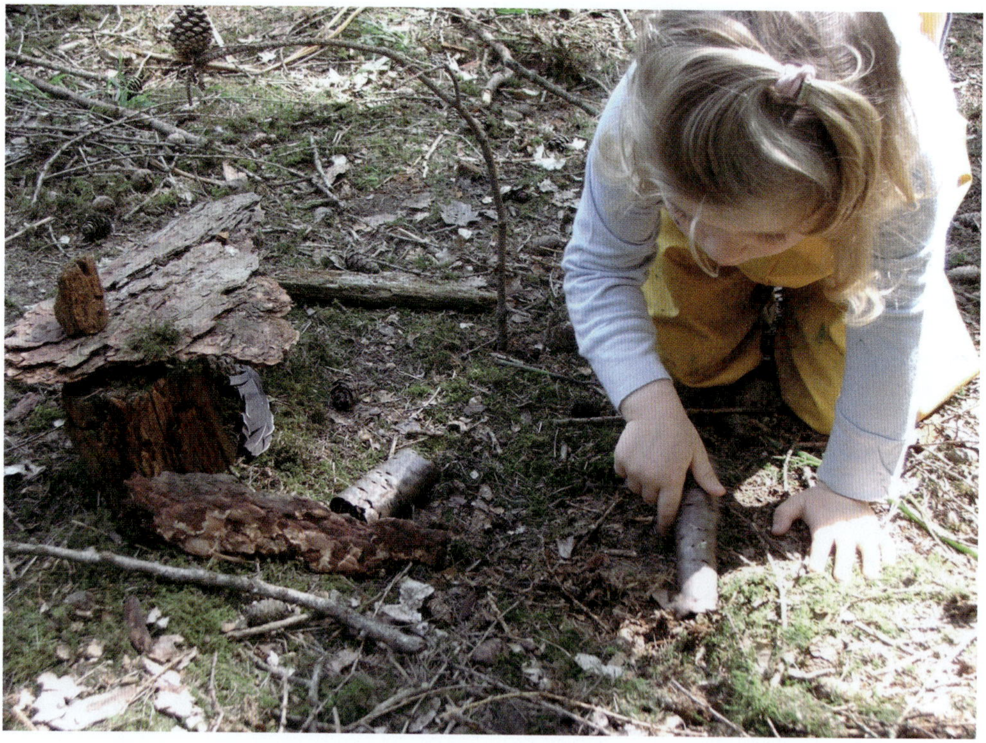

10b Paige explores the forest floor

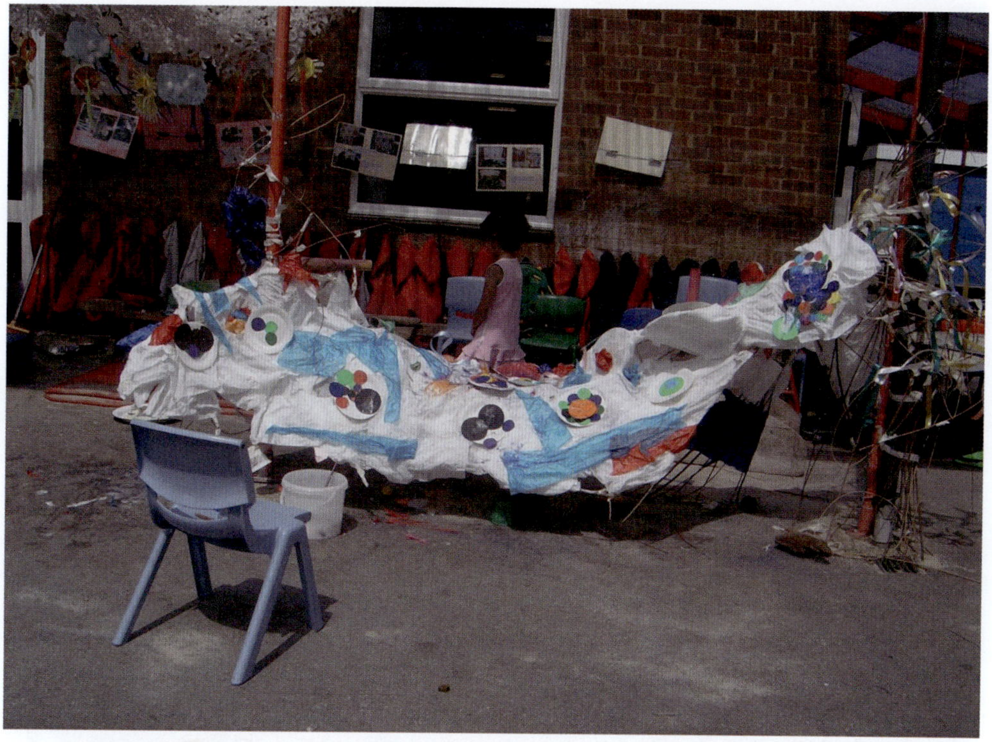

11 Giant dinosaur sculpture

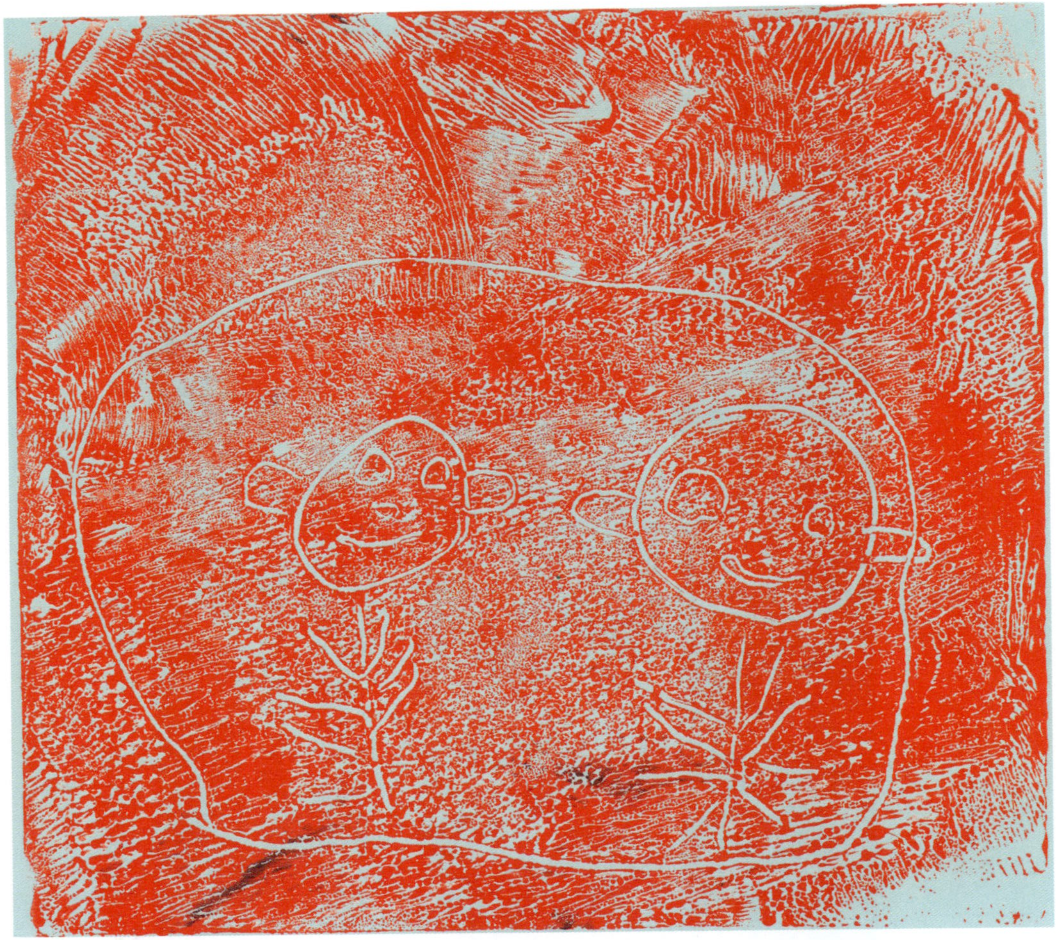

12 Rayaz's house with ears

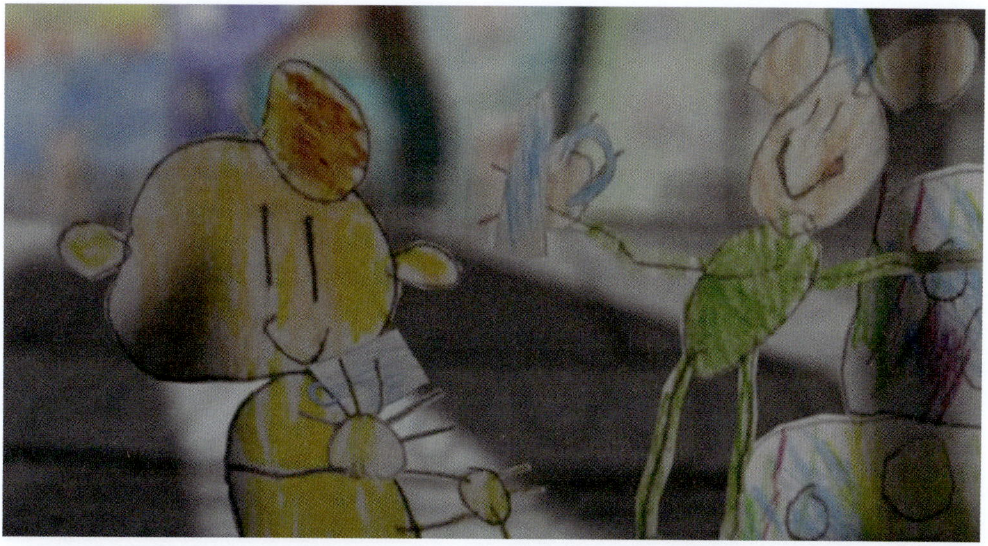

13 Children's drawings for animation 1

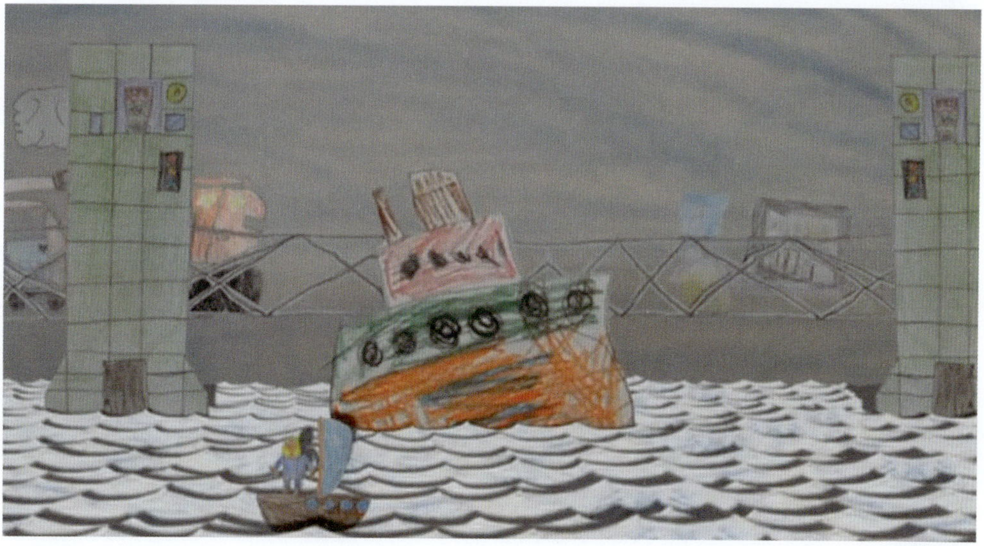

14 Children's drawings for animation 2

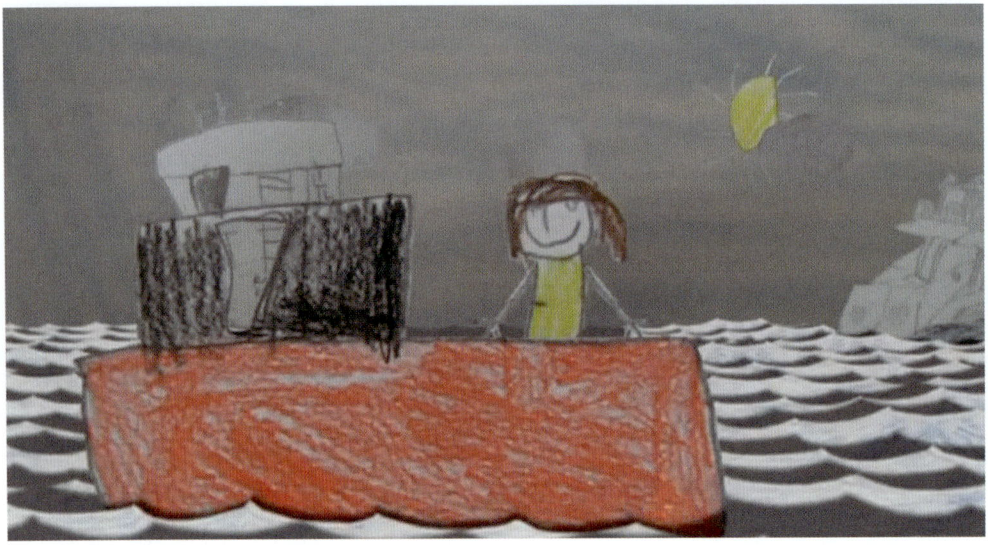

15 Children's drawings for animation 3

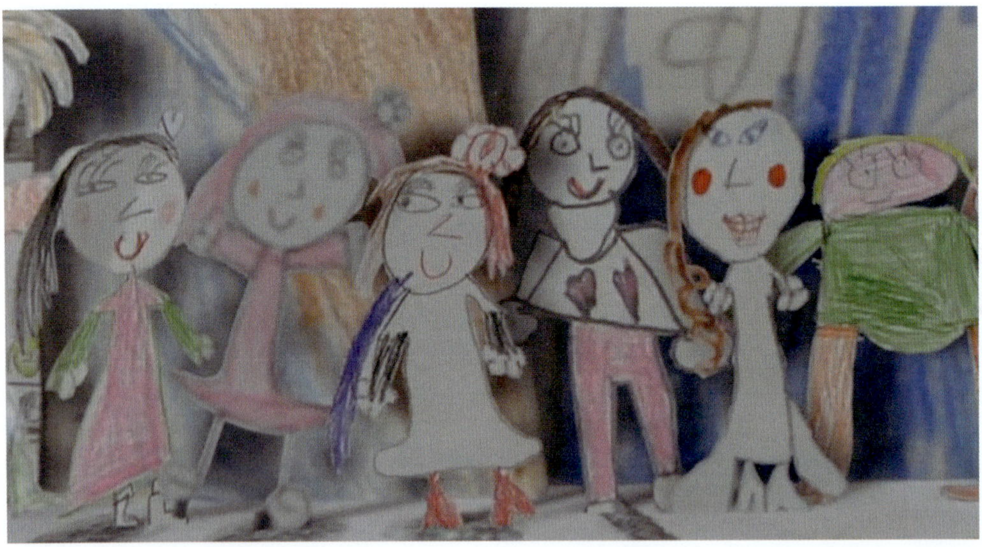

16 Children's drawings for animation 4

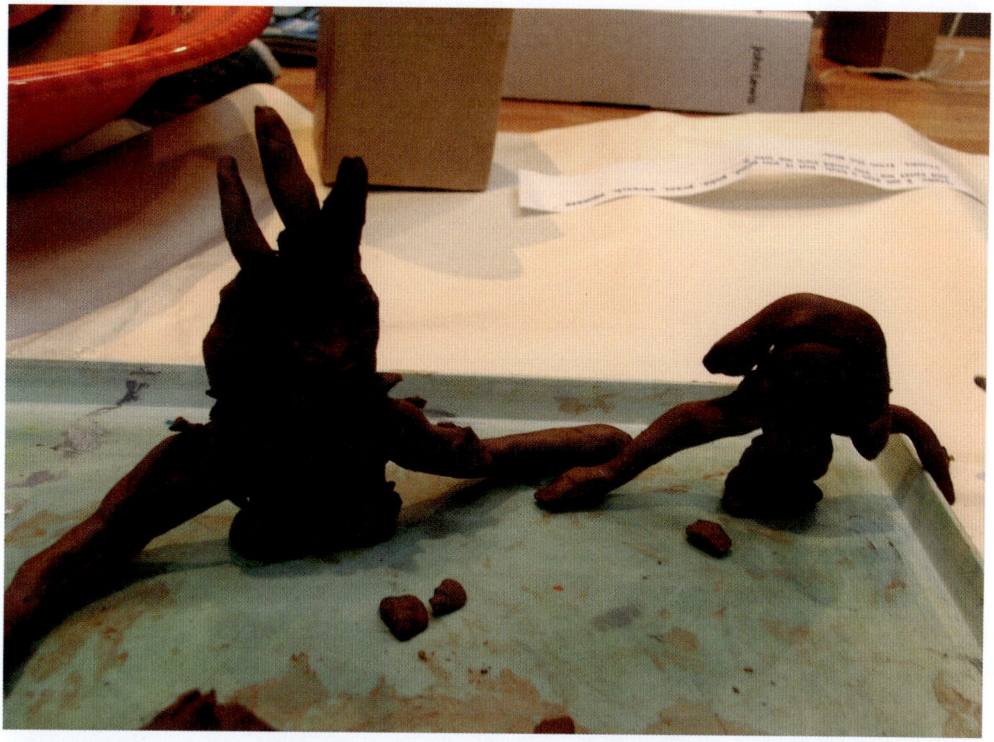

17 Clay family

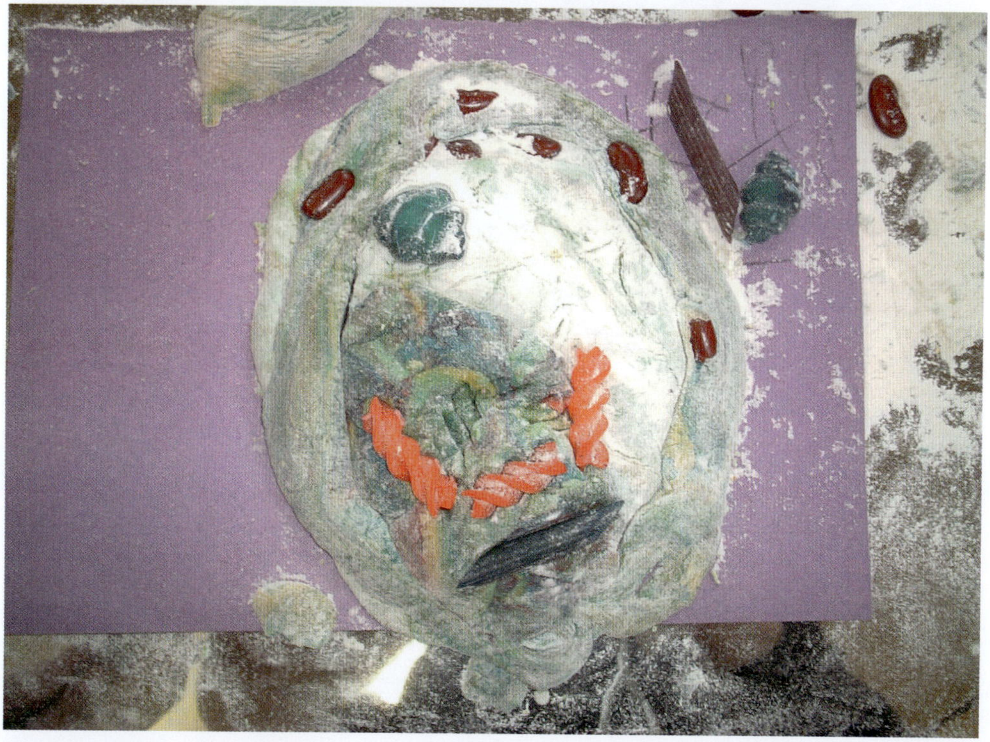

18 A 'happy dad' made from salt

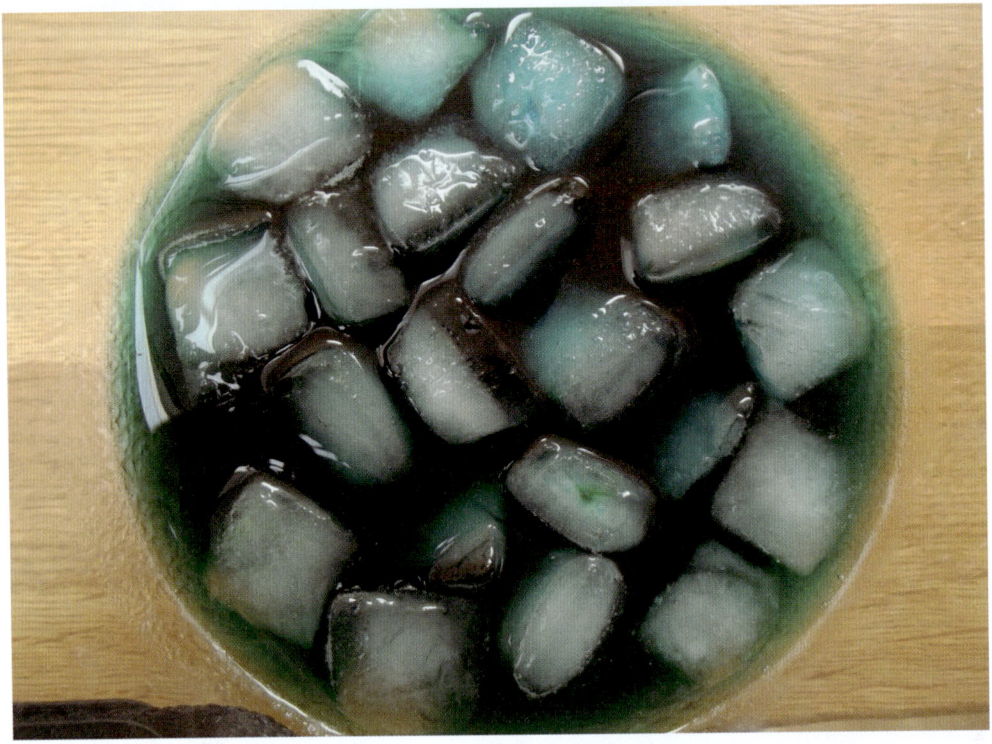

19 Ice-tray colour experiment

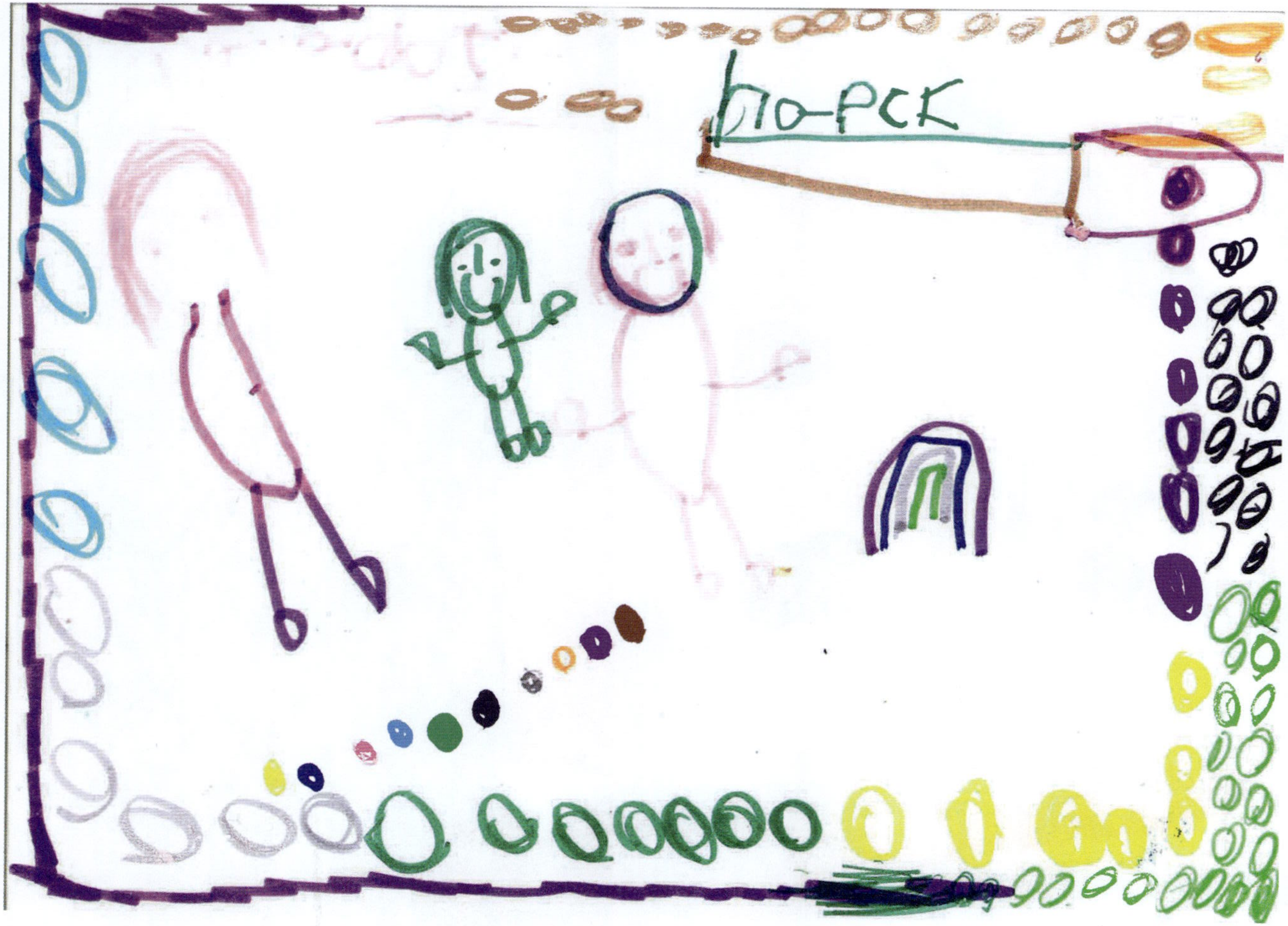

20 Monday picture

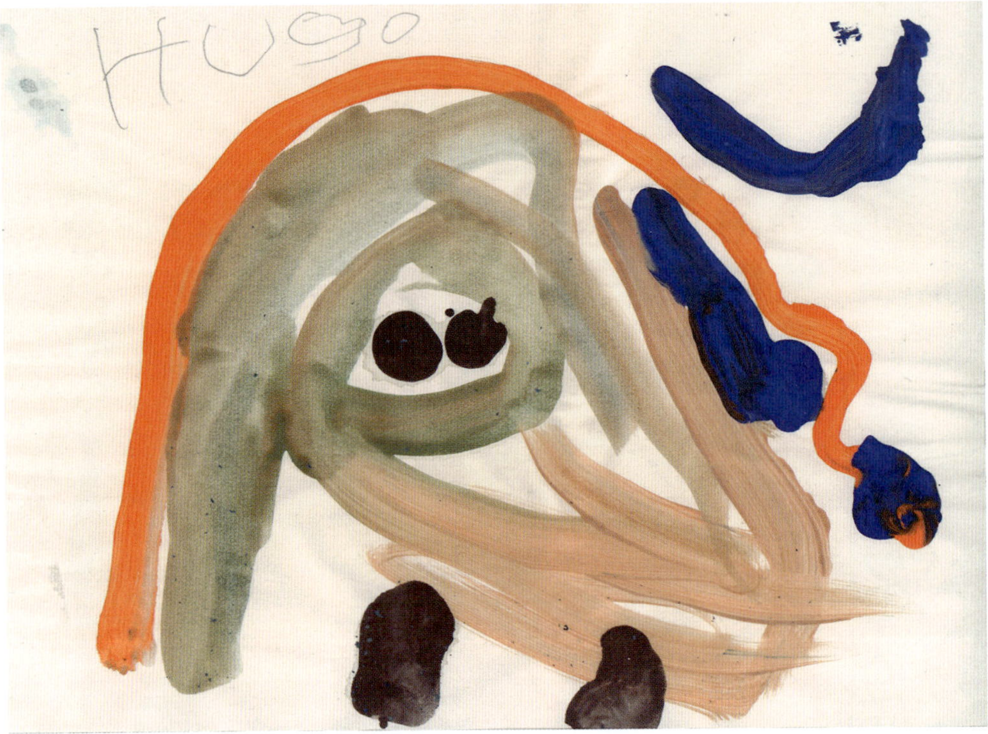

21 Hugo's painting

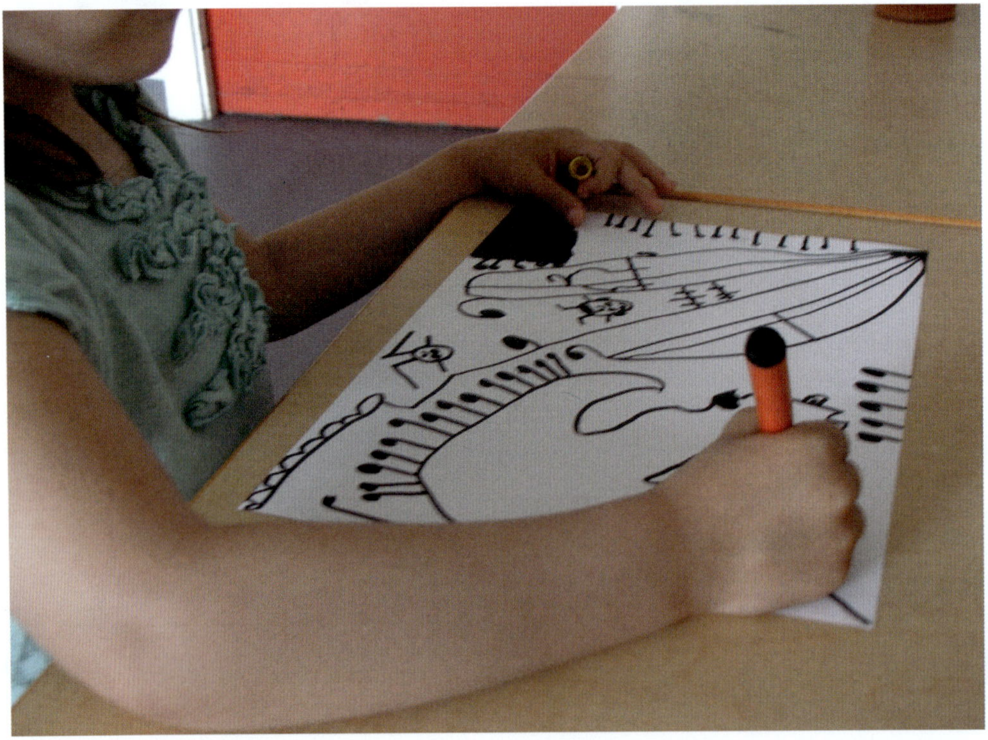

22 Reyna's story

We refer back to Table 5.1, as here is our opportunity to bring in more vocabulary. We are sometimes loath to 'teach' new words which we think may be too complex, but young children thoroughly enjoy getting their mouths, tongues and facial features around a new and complicated word. The vast majority of four-year-olds enjoy the challenge of mastering new 'long' words such as tyrannosaurus and diplodocus – dinosaurs fascinate and so their names are learnt because they are all part of that fascination: grand, long, complex, multi-syllabic names which visually resonate those gigantic and fantastic monsters. With this analogy in mind, consider the plethora of words to be found and created which respond to the art experiences of young children. Most of what a child encounters in their art forms is related, as we have previously discussed, to their sensory modalities and so it follows that their minds link these somatic experiences with corresponding and associative vocabulary and language.

In effect, we are actually praising the *process* of the artwork – we may be looking at the end product when we do this but it is the process that got them there that is key if we want to provide appropriate feedback and encourage young children to reflect on their own artistic processes. Just how much we offer and how much we want to elicit is different with each experience we encounter. The feedback dialogues and conversational exchanges can often occur several times a day with many children, and so the reality is that we cannot sustain long discussions about each and every endeavour. But just as we strive to observe our children individually on a regular basis in all their learning, so we must listen and discuss with them as regularly as time and space permit.

Positive and constructive feedback can significantly enrich and extend the child's artistic experience. This approach undoubtedly helps, when the intervention is appropriate, to direct them further in their studies. Sometimes, however, we need to be cautious not to weigh the balance of thinking towards our own perceptions and perspectives, no matter how much our intention is well meant. It is, on these occasions, simply a case of waiting, pausing and responding using the time and space of the conversation. The gap of silence allows both parties to look together and respond with thought and criticism. Schirrmacher (1986: 5) quite clearly advises:

> The next time children show you what they have created, smile, pause and say nothing at first. This serves two purposes. It gives you time to study the children's art and to reflect on what you want to say before you speak. It gives you time to think of a better response than an impulsive, banal comment like 'that's nice'. Second, and more importantly, it will give children an opportunity to talk first if they so choose.

Valuing contemplation time when responding to an artwork with children also reminds us to be open to what is being presented and what we have seen. By this, we can consider Craft's (2002) words when she warns us not to put 'ceilings' on what children achieve or could achieve. 'Achieve' can also be consigned to the bank of words that can, at times, appear too restrictive – too linear. Achievement is so often associated with badges of merit, attaining a set of goals set by someone else. Achievement is experienced all the time by children on their art journeys, but that achievement is owned by them and described by them. A child who can discuss and critique their artwork is the child who sets their own goals and measures their own achievement.

Role models of skills, application and process

Shared dialogue and discussion are just a part of this understanding and assist with, but do not direct, consequential passages of exploration. In addition, we have to consider, as the accompanying and co-exploring adults, when and if our 'interventionist' approach should include modelling for skills development and design ideas.

Again, we are reminded of the EEL paradigm of adult engagement (Box 5.2). If we follow this with sensitivity it can help guide us in moments when our role is to stimulate. This may come in the form of sharing the experience both physically and mentally but also in imparting an interesting piece of knowledge through modelling practical skills. If the invitation warmly welcomes you, as the practitioner, to model a skill, then you can aid the creative procedure. As the child learns something new through your stimulation and inspiring supportive approach, the child's knowledge is altered. This is what Jerome Bruner termed as scaffolding – it involves a psychological empathy with the child and understanding of what he or she might be moving toward. When it exists, it is a fluid, dynamic and often seemingly effortless dance between adult and child (Matthews, 2003). Modelling skills and showing our own abilities as a part of the process in order to further an interested child is commendable as it co-exists in what should already be a strong and trustful partnership, one where there is mutual respect in art explorations.

An interesting research discussion can be reflected on here and I do not propose a conclusion, merely an interest. This is a discussion prevalent in our education system and one that echoes the discussion of modelling/not modelling in art for young children. Different cultures and classrooms operate in a variety of ways. Research studies have shown that a certain amount of adult direction and modelling of styles results in a particular child art. In opposition to this, an approach firmly rooted in child-initiated art results in a different kind of child art. Many of this book's messages ally with the latter but the following study does offer an interesting situation. Merry *et al.* (2006) present a study where two samples of four-year-old Chinese children were given two drawing tasks: one very familiar task and one novel and challenging task. The first sample was drawn from a nursery that taught art in a similar way to that widely used in the West, with an emphasis on individual expression. The second sample was from a nursery where drawing was taught explicitly and directly in a traditional Chinese way. Some very significant differences were found in both tasks.

In both classes the children were asked to draw characters – they did so and there was not a great difference between the results from both groups of children. The difference that was apparent was that the children in the more formally taught class added external features to their figures such as trees, flowers, clouds and houses. When asked why they had added them, they all gave the same answer: 'to make the picture more beautiful'. Few children in the more 'progressive classroom' had added anything to their figures which, owing to the original and non-stereotypical drawing style they each had, meant that their drawings, in their eyes, were already beautiful. The additions made by the formal class individualised their work; the work in the progressive class was already thus.

This example sets forth our continuing conundrum. Winner (1989: 50) purports that 'unless children are taught the basic techniques they have no means of giving expression to their ideas'. The extreme of this is Lowenfeld's (1957) assertion that the child's expression is sacrosanct and must never be interfered with. Merry *et al.* (2006: 157) conclude:

> Ultimately, each approach has its strengths and weaknesses, and there perhaps needs ideally to be a balance between encouraging individual creativity on the one hand, and directly teaching technical skills on the other hand.

A mindful health warning is attached to the premise of modelling ideas, skills and techniques in order to widen perspectives and possibilities. We must always remind ourselves and our colleagues that modelling must never be the prescription of what to do. This will then fall into the realms of templates and copying; not an ounce of creativity exists for a child in these circumstances.

I strongly believe that art is not about mastering a particular methodology and style which has a standard set of rules to be adhered to. It is about mastering techniques and skills, and combining these with ideas, imagination and inspiration belonging to the artist. Art is about the who of the artist and the journey they take – they will always own this and it remains the responsibility of the maker to define their own outcome, their own artistry and their own idiosyncratic styles. Simpson (2011) concludes this section for us as she redefines our need to retain the 'who' of the child, living with them in their moment as they unfold as creative beings:

> This free unfolding epitomizes the joy of childhood. Each child is unique and it is only by being free to follow their own internal developmental agendas, endowed by nature, that each child can develop and build their own unique individuality . . . their emerging sense of self, more free from unnecessary early conditioning and adult expectations and fears.
>
> (Simpson, 2011: 149)

Conclusion

The concluding thoughts for this chapter are bluntly summarised in the following statement from the Foundation Stage Guidance Curriculum (QCA 2000) for Creative Development. This document is now defunct but the words remain and resonate in our minds as a reminder about our own attitudes and intent in supporting young children's art experiences.

> Creativity is not about pleasing adults or producing adult-determined art, music or dance. While understanding what someone else has done is part of the exploratory process, it is not in itself creative. Creativity occurs when children are able to use that understanding by integrating it into their own work and creating something new. If there is an end product, it needs to be determined by the child and created by the child. Children need access to a wide range of stimuli and ideas. They need opportunities to play with these ideas, incorporating them into their own creations. Practitioners may model and pass on their skills and knowledge, but children must be allowed to make things their own.

Reflection

- How would you describe your view of yourself when engaging in art activity in relation to the approach of interventionists and non-interventionists?
- What can you do to build your own confidence as adult co-explorer in art?
- Track your engagement with one child and their art over a period of time: take note of your conversations, body language and ideas exchanges. Can you plot a layering of knowledge and a development of understanding through your review of the tracking process?
- Take time and space to listen and engage – be mindful of this until it becomes more natural and you are not consciously waiting and listening, it is just something you do.

Further reading

Hallett, E. (2013) *The Reflective Early Years Practitioner*, London: Sage.

Nutbrown, C. (2006) *Threads of Thinking*, third edn, London: Sage.

Pascal, C. and Bertram, T. (2001) *Effective Early Learning, Case Studies in Improvement*, London: Paul Chapman.

Reddy, V. (2010) *How Infants Know Minds*, Harvard: Harvard University Press.

Rinaldi, C. (2006) 'Documentation and research', in *In Dialogue with Reggio Emilia: Listening, Researching and Learning*, Oxon: Routledge.

Siraj-Blatchford, I. (2007) 'Creativity, communication and collaboration: The identification of pedagogic progression in sustained shared thinking', *Asia Pacific Journal of Research in Early Childhood Education*, 1(2): 3–23.

CHAPTER 6

The environment
Spaces and invitations

Our children need to colonise and claim their creative spaces.

(Dr Bernadette Lynch, 2013)

Introduction

We have discussed the young curious child and his or her propensity to sensorially explore art, so now we need, in this chapter, to consider how we physically accommodate these exploratory beings. Thought must be given to the careful and consistent assurance that the spaces they enter are sympathetic and attentive to their multifarious artistic needs and desires.

A potentiating and inspiring environment is a crucial component in the triangular relationship of child–adult–space in our consideration of ever-developing young creative minds. By referring to the environment as the 'third teacher' we designate importance to the status and potential influence it has in young children's developmental learning and creative and critical enquiry. This chapter will attempt to research and present positive and richly inviting environmental approaches that are concurrent, at all times, with alert and eager young occupiers.

Definition of the environment as 'space'

We will continue to refer to the environment as 'space'. A rich plethora of opportunities resonate from the word 'space', as well as responding to potential arenas inside and outside. Space can be defined as the unlimited and incalculably great three-dimensional realm or expanse in which all material objects are located and all events occur. The key words here are 'unlimited' and 'incalculable' as they coexist with, and complement entirely, the young child's unfolding creative self and their ability to think abstractedly, without inhibition and, importantly, without external prescription.

Our discussions purport to recognise space as being both the indoor and the outdoor environment. We will refer neither to the indoor nor to the outdoor *classroom* as this, arguably, confines the environment within a more formal 'school-based' setting. Such a constrictive description diminishes the enthralling vitality contained within the realms of all early years spaces, whether the pack-away pre-school, the childminder's home or a reception unit's garden. There are 'spaces' within classrooms and playgrounds but, more importantly, the classrooms and gardens are spaces themselves. Architectural intelligence urges us to draw on the endless possibilities of what can happen in this space rather than being restricted by building boundaries and hindered by the obstacles of unnecessary furniture. Through flexible organisation and an open mind to young creative potentials, spaces within environments can support and embrace what children can achieve and mastermind.

Non-judgemental spaces

> A non-judgemental space is one in which students can interact with environments, with each other and with us, the facilitators and teachers, without the slightest fear of being judged – of getting it wrong.
>
> (Davies, 2012: 6)

Creating and maintaining spaces where interaction is multi-sensory in exploration and vast in discovery relinquishes the need for and boundaries of conformity. There will be some familiar features and routine procedures, which are necessary for the status quo and social equilibrium. But spaces provided that are open-ended are places where children can flourish in ways that we might not have thought possible. Just as we aim to avoid closed questions that expect a 'right' answer, it is also essential to provide spaces that are flexible and where all questions are journeys and answers individually found. As much as our dialogue responds to this pedagogical approach, so does our organisation of space with regards to furniture, allocation of place, temporary structures, resources, shelves etc. This is a message that we need to keep firmly in our minds as we consider the dynamics of space and all it entails so that non-judgementality is ever-present.

The theatres of space

Dramas of creative discovery take place in what could be viewed as theatres of space. Such dynamic spaces positively encourage successes and failures within explorations and discoveries. Creative dramas are repeated, reviewed, adapted and modified during process-driven moments as discussed in Chapter 4. The spaces also provide dramas that are born out of the physical activities of art – escapades that are akin to the fantasy play of child actors. The art spaces allow children to direct, produce and act out ideas and imaginative wonderings, as we examined in their fantastical drawings in Chapter 4. We are reminded again of the incubation process, illustrated in Chapter 2, as well as the three stages of imaging, imagining and being imaginative, as previously explored in Chapter 1. These dramas and creative episodes exist in the culture of the environment; a culture that opens up possibilities and critical thinking that is at the heart of our spaces. In the book *In the Spirit of the Studio* (Gandini, 2005: 16), Charles Schwall describes and celebrates the art space, the 'atelier' that he was responsible for creating and maintaining within an early years setting at the Reggio Emilia Schools:

> When children live in a space, they own, they feel, and find their place within it. Connections that take place between time and space happen through the rhythms of everyday life, connections to the past events, and new experiences that reach toward the future.

Within theatres of space, our 'expert players', as Pat Broadhead (2012) so rightly describes them, are able to make their own creative stories, full of surprises, unexpected outcomes and winding plot lines. Broadhead defines expert players as children whose capacity to play is highly skilled. She notes that some are more skilled than others in relation to lack of experience, lack of assuredness in involvement, lack of confidence in particular episodes of play. However, with positive encouragement, time to observe and, in particular, the offer of appealing spaces and resources, all children can become expert players. After all, we know they can often reveal far richer intuitive aptitudes and initiatives when it comes to play than adults do. A sinkful of bubbly water is an enticing play invitation to them; to us it means washing up! Their ability to recognise *how* to play, to read a situation and manipulate a space, is directly related to their ability to absorb and conceptualise within that moment. Children can consciously and unconsciously absorb, conceptualise and immerse themselves in the space and creative moment and dream up a whole plethora of possibilities.

Several of John Medina's (2008) recent theories on the 'Brain Rules' can be directly related to the 'space' within which the child works and plays. The theatre they are involved in is rich and alive with the following aspects, according to Medina (2008: 38):

> If you wanted to create an education environment that was directly opposed to what the brain was good at doing, you probably would design something like a classroom. If you wanted to create a business environment that was directly opposed to what the brain was good at doing, you probably would design something like a cubicle. And if you wanted to change things, you might have to tear down both and start over.

If we are committed to opening up space and changing, adapting or retaining aspects depending on the culture of the day, week or month, then we are committed to the infinite possibilities of what children can engage in and make happen. Open systems seek disequilibrium (Wheatley 1999). We need to consider how we manage and maintain this space, which promotes an open creative culture and offers hooks and invitations that support, encourage and promote children as young artists.

Aspects of art spaces

The organisation of space is associated with the shape, size and occupation of that area. The following ingredients (Box 6.1) respond to this and provide a list of changeable possibilities to be reviewed and ruminated on by both adults and children.

Box 6.1 Changeable aspects in art spaces

Light: dark, light, shadows, extra lamps, lightbox

Sound: quiet, purposefully near a particular noise, musical instruments, music player

Furniture: are tables always necessary?

Surface: carpet, floor, window, table, chair, easel, builder's tray

Placement in overall space: corner, middle, side, by a window, near a door

Enclosed or open: purposeful entrance/exit or open-planned

Display and storage: somewhere to leave work, unfinished wall, hanging line (this returns us to the process/end product argument, as perhaps this needs to be thoroughly owned by the child in their moment – they can choose whether to keep, retain for review or leave to the elements – as the process was their endeavour)

Materials: a changing outlook or a familiar feature (or both!)

Accessibility: nurturing independence

In Chapters 2 and 5 we remarked on the need to nurture in ourselves an attitude that meant we 'let go' – we watched, supported and followed without prescription and adult control. We also tempered this within the realms of 'organised chaos'. We know that in order to encourage an epistemic culture of independent learners in our young art spaces, we must gauge children's needs and follow their interests rather than direct, pre-empt and lineate their adventures. The more time we invest in how we organise our spaces and resources, the more time we wisely spend negotiating spaces that are accessible, manageable and visible to children's explorations. If the children know where materials and tools are and they are accessible to their hands and eyes, then both their independence in the journey and our sympathetic organisation work in proactive unison. Making art materials accessible is key if we want to encourage independent thought. It is also key, very importantly, to our own peace of mind when we consider the layout and management of art activities.

I know that, sometimes, the very thought of laying out and clearing up art resources can cause anxiety in many teaching adults. The sheer manageability appears too huge and too unwieldy to contemplate. But this vision is misconstrued as, for the most part, if spaces are regular and habitual, resources are accessible, and systems are recognised and owned by all users, then the experience should be anxiety free. An accessible art space is an easier art space to manage. It encourages independent learners and liberates the adult from the confines of organiser and cleaner. Being in control lends unnecessary fatigue to a process where accessibility designates self-control to the child.

Begin by considering everyday art and the materials that this could include. Everyday art resources can be stored in accessible boxes and containers clearly labelled (pictorially) at child height. You and your children will make the decisions about what appeals, what works in your setting and space. But whatever you use, display and store, ensure they are of a high quality and are accessible, otherwise they will become the 'locked' resources out of reach and never to be used, akin to the locked store cupboards that exist in many primary schools. Resources are there to be used and replenished, not to be left to fester in forgotten exhibition on an inaccessible shelf or box.

Quality and appeal: resources that stimulate

Quality is also paramount as the more enticing a resource, the greater the motivation to use it. In adulthood, stationery and art shops full of coloured paper, sharp pencils, and rainbow packets of felt tips continue to dazzle me and draw me in as would Aladdin's cave. Just consider what we would prefer to use in our adult minds: a chewed pencil or a sharpened pencil with a smooth grip; jam jars of beautiful coloured paint or three-day-old gloopy ready-mixed paint; swathes of different coloured, textured papers or small, neat, pre-cut sticky paper pieces? Take time to consider this, as it resonates with our study of curiosity, motivation and sensory awareness. The quality of materials is not in the newness or the mundane, it is in the variety, the unusual, the aesthetically provoking.

But what do these spaces actually look; how can we visualise and respond as practitioners? There are no hard and fast rules as to how to organise a space – all our settings are different, so are our children and also, just as importantly, are we as practitioners. What is of paramount concern, however, is that there should be a variety of spaces available, where invitational hooks and areas are to be adapted according to the imaginations and explorations of the children. However, perhaps by adopting something similar to the atelier in the Reggio Emilia schools, we are acknowledging a space that is always art-driven and art-focussed, but still open to change in accordance with the children's explorations and research focus.

The art studio

'Atelier' translates from Italian as workshop. It is a space, akin to an art studio, where ideas come to fruition and hypotheses are tested. It is open to all individuals and is owned by both children and adults to change and use within the culture of their interests and endeavours. The atelier is a physical working space where collaboration is fostered alongside individual application.

One of the primary innovations of the Reggio Emilia approach is the atelier, the school studio and laboratory. The atelier is a place for experimentation with separate or combined visual languages, either in isolation or in combination with verbal ones. There are mini-ateliers next to each classroom, which are used for extended projects. These ateliers are equipped with clay, wire, paint, pens, paper, beads, shells and a variety of recycled, natural materials used by the children in short- and long-term projects with the purpose of expressing the 'hundred languages' of children.

> I think the strength of the continuous relationship between atelier and pedagogy is that it has generated a style of thinking that goes beyond the physical nature of the atelier and the classroom and permeates the entire environment.
>
> (Giuidici and Vecchi, 2004: 146)

It is vitally important for us to adapt the 'atelier' model to suit our own practices and settings congruent with our cultural heritage. The countries we live in, the locations we are based in and our own national, political and social culture will also have an influence on how we design and understand the atelier space. So in order for us to adopt our own workshop idea, I shall refer to this space as an art studio rather than an atelier. The art studio has all the same principles as the atelier, except that by renaming it we reconstitute it as a model that we own in our settings and that is steeped in our culture. The principles remain the same, but the actual physical spaces need to be adapted by the proprietors and users in order to evolve in recognition of the setting and all it represents and symbolises.

Box 6.2 An example of an art studio where clay is the focus (following children's interests in sculpture and modelling)

This table is only ever used for claywork, and is never moved. It is both separate from all else in the busy setting but also part of it. It's not unusual for children to spend more than an hour in this space, often for days in a row. As the set-up doesn't change, they know what to expect. It is a space where everyone sees claywork as a serious business. Materials and tools are close at hand in a cupboard accessible to the children, and a nearby display of claywork reminds them of earlier ideas.

(Kolbe, 2001: 114)

Box 6.3 Practical tips for making it work

- A well-lit area.
- Allow for individual and group work.
- What appeals to you. . .
- Certainty and familiarity.
- Materials – good working order:
  - accessible to children;
  - choice.
- Found treasures and artefacts.
- Health and safety.
- Adult and child interaction.
- OHP/angle-poise lamp and white wall space.
- Velcro apron pole.
- Dispensers for glue and paints.
- Systems for next steps.
- Open space.
- Washing line.
- Unfinished board.
- Sketchbooks.
- Art portfolios.
- Marked surfaces.
- Pleasing furniture.

These greatly support young children's learning through:

- familiarity: using the 'root' of knowledge of confidence to explore;
- independence: to create unencumbered by external expectation or direction;
- choice: to develop skills to select and identify materials, tools, resources, intentions;
- continuity: ongoing growth in artistic skills and aptitudes where the progression is steady and visible;
- systems: accessible resources and organisation to ensure independence and frequency;
- reflection and evaluation: time to appraise the longevity and legacy of art-making;
- involvement: affordance in time, space and atmosphere for increased involvement;
- security: a defined space, a micro art world which belongs to the child at art play;
- sharing: collaborative and cooperative opportunities.

The art studio is a space that is constant but can be adapted to the current trends, interests and journeys of the children who use it. It is a physical hub and conceptual space that is a catalyst and container for meaning-making. In Cadwell's (Gandini *et al.* 2005: 145) words:

> We seek to create the most exciting, fertile, safe, irresistible context in which children will take off and clamor to bump their ideas up against each other in thoughts; gestures; words, spoken and written; numbers; drawings; clay; and paint. There are no fixed outcomes. The outcome, we hope, will be beyond our wildest dreams. We know we are shooting for the stars.

'No fixed outcomes' is to be continually repeated in the minds of all adults involved in nurturing and nourishing a studio space. In this affirming message we remind ourselves that we are not creating spaces that foster preconceived outcomes or adult-expected results.

Avi Lubin (2011) describes the essence of a studio space as:

> A type of liminal space that enables detachment from ordinary time and place. It allows the artist to examine fundamental concepts and challenge them. The presentation of works in progress, or groundwork, provides a way to peer into the working methods of the artists including what changes occur, what they choose to leave out, and the evolution of the work. It exposes the subconscious of the finished work.

The art studio exists specifically in its ability to open up possibilities and ideas but within a familiar space. We must not liken the art studio to a 'messy area' or a 'craft table'. These so often have boundaries and limitations where the materials used are considered and provided in advance by an adult. In respect of this, perhaps sometimes the activities assumed and prescribed have a link to a previous exploratory episode in a child's artistic journey. The art studio is a hothouse for process-driven concentration and sustained thinking. It is a space where ideas come to the surface, change, submerge and re-emerge over a period of time. This requires sustained involvement in the process and the confidence to take risks. A space designated for risk-taking makes the action of risk much more tangible and accessible. Security in risk-taking, though contradictory sounding, allows the artist to make critical judgements about what has been made in order to determine what happens next.

The balance of space

In addition to a defined art studio space, there also needs to be a balance of familiar and unfamiliar arenas relating to a setting's provision of learning in art. The familiarity of a space offers a sense of certainty where children return to something and continue to refine. Inversely, areas that stir surprise and offer the challenge of the new also have a very important status. We know that children are keen to explore and veer off in various directions in order to experiment and satisfy curiosity, but we also need to adhere to that which is familiar, comfortable and safe in order to enhance the confidence to indeed 'veer off'. We need to create environments that allow for the unfamiliar but acknowledge the familiar. Both aspects encapsulate a variety of learning stations and it is necessary to examine the benefits that both aspects afford in promoting, developing and inspiring children to be young artists.

There are profits to be enjoyed in the two variants of familiar and unfamiliar spaces, just as there are different characters and learning dispositions in children. One child may find a space that they understand and recognise and therefore feel comfortable with; this is not a dormant comfort, it is very much alive and necessary in their journey of artistic endeavour and layering. Another child may initially be more stimulated by something new and unknown. Both children are dependent on their previous knowledge and understanding to conceive something new but they may go about it inversely to one another. As Wagoner (2008: 470) states: 'The two pathways of creativity are related and opposing processes: the former "makes the unfamiliar *familiar*", whereas the latter "makes the familiar *unfamiliar*".'

In one very creative-thinking nursery school where I once worked as an artist-in-residence, I began to notice that each morning one child, Billy, would, without fail, walk around the nursery and observe, view and absorb what was on offer that day. His routine browsing was a survey of the invitations on offer within spaces and the security bound up in this overview. Without exception, he would always go to a space that he knew and which had not changed too much from previous days. He understood that area; it was familiar to him. In that space, he would exercise his imagination and long-practised interaction. Once he had expertly played in this space, he would confidently visit somewhere else, less familiar, where new and unfamiliar resources and opportunities awaited him.

Familiar → Unfamiliar = Billy's route

Tia, a child who attended the same setting, would grasp the morning's possibilities in a very different way. She actively sought out the unfamiliar. She thrived on the surprise of the unknown and was able to engage immediately with what she found. Her interaction was splendidly chaotic, intertwined with emphatic trepidation. Her eventual discoveries could be linked back to what she already knew and this was the route she would take – the unfamiliar was found first and then traced back to the familiar.

Unfamiliar → Familiar = Tia's route

Unfamiliar Invitations – tactile and visual spaces for surprise and risk-taking

We need to define what we mean by 'unfamiliar'. In this context, we are looking at spaces which offer artistic opportunities and which instil a sense of surprise

Table 6.1 Colour-mixing gel bags

Unfamiliar surprise	*New skills*	*Familiar skills and sensory repertoire*
• Feel of gel	• Unctuous and coagulating consistency • Smells and haptic involvement	• Manipulative abilities: squeezing, squashing
• Pipette drops of colour into gel	• Slow contamination of colour	• Mixing colours and watching changes
• Additional extras	• Choosing a variety of ingredients to add to a new formation: glitter, powder paint, sugar, salt etc.	• Mixing and selecting

and unpredictability. The space may contain resources unseen before and activities unexplored. However unusual and unexpected the contents, it is important to note that there will always be an element of familiarity in response to the unconscious experience and skill set of the child. Tia, the gregarious explorer, knew, unconsciously perhaps, that she could make use of her highly tuned manipulative skills or clear sense of visual discrimination. Sensory awareness and dexterity will always provide a confident base, whether it is a familiar or an unfamiliar adventure.

Unfamiliar experiences will spark and ignite the imagination and then connections will be traced back to an existing known. Table 6.1 suggests an activity that is rich with potential tactile investigations. As the investigation takes shape, the investigator moves between the extremes of knowing and not knowing. This knowledge continuum is a fluctuating process as hands and eyes explore and draw on their sensory expertise and aesthetic experiences.

Surprise and motivation in art experiences

We return again to the premise of 'surprise' as previously examined in Chapter 3 – that very human, inexhaustible resource which children have such a keen and sensitive connection with. To ensure we capture some of the words below and can be assured they exist in our settings, a concerted effort to routinely reflect will help us to evaluate practice:

amazement astonishment astounding bewilderment consternation epiphany incredulity marvel precipitousness revelation shock startling unanticipated unexpected unforeseen wonderment

Reflection

A useful exercise is to think about these states of being and consider a moment in our teaching where we have witnessed this. In our considerations, we need to acknowledge the whole context of:

Who:

- Is this an individual journey?
- Which adults and children were involved?

Why:

- Was there a trigger?
- What was the stimulus?

What:

- Which resources are on offer or being used?
- What is actually happening in the activity?

Where:

- Where was the space designed?
- How was it set up?

When:

- What was the time of day?
- Was the activity repeated, reviewed, re-explored or a one off?

How:

- How was the child interacting: schemas, idiosyncratic gestures and language?
- How long did the moment last and how did it stop or reconvene?

Providing opportunities that incite feelings of surprise, and thus motivational discovery and learning, can only be realised and confirmed if we know the spaces are designed and replenished to house these dramas – familiar and unfamiliar. Table 6.2 suggests ingredients for a contained space in the form of a tray or shallow tub which motivates discovery through its familiar daily existence, but which serves up the unfamiliar in the unknown recipe of the day.

Table 6.2 suggests recipes for the surprise tray, but this list is endless. It is an initiative in operation in many good early years settings, where the intention is to provide something different in a tray each day. The children know that a new material will be lurking but are never sure what exactly it will be until they enter the space. The surprise tray is the subject of anticipation and often the identified recipe of the day may relate to a previous learning activity, a fleeting experience of a child observed by an adult. In Chapter 3 we examined the sensory qualities at play with tactile art experiences and how closely the

Table 6.2 Suggested ingredients for a surprise tray

Grass	Hay	Shredded paper	Jelly	Spaghetti	Pasta shapes
Paperclips	Icing sugar	Shaving foam	Ice	Ice cubes	Cornflour
Marbles	Pebbles and stones	Seaweed	Sand	Salt and glitter	Oil and water
Bubbled water	Flour	Pva glue dribbles	Mud	Earth	Leaves
Coffee	Tea leaves	Powder paint	Buttons	Balls	Petals
Baked beans	Glittered water	Semolina	Eggs shells	Soaked sponges	Netting
Beads and buttons	Crushed biscuits	Shaved wax	Tapioca	Lentils	Rice
Ice cream	Magnets	Mashed potato	Cocoa powder	Clay	Papier mâché
Fur	Felt	Cornflakes	Furry toys	Small world	Cabbage leaves

association of eye, hand and mind are intertwined. This state of being is absolutely key in the experience of the trays of investigation, leading to rich and complex scenarios where children think with body and mind – the embodied sense of art discovery as we have previously encountered.

Spaces that promote exploration of elements in art

Materials, like spaces, are aspects of young children's art-making and creative adventures that need to be reviewed, replenished and adapted with the child. In this case, we are referring to materials as the physical and tangible resources which the child handles and manipulates according to the art experience he or she is wallowing in. The activation of our sensory systems, so crucial in art-making, depends upon our being in an environment that possesses materials and resources of quality to which our senses are responsive.

All settings are different with varying spaces and enclosures. What they all have in common is the capacity to offer open-ended spaces, or as Broadhead (2012) calls them, 'the whatever you want it to be space'. If we view the space in this way, we immediately place the ownership of the space in the hands of the children. Let us relate these owned territories specifically to the young artist. Here we may see spaces which support young children and their ventures into the visual and tactile arts. They have, at their disposal, an empathetic and highly conducive space in which to pursue their ideas and be active in their spirited imaginations. The pursuit reflects, in a variety of images, children's participation in the visual elements we know are at play and also which we have learnt to value.

Flexible, static and reviewed art spaces foster children's growing perception of the basic elements of art. There are discernible elements, conventionally described in the terms below. They serve here as visual and tactile aspects of art, which are useful terms to explore with children to describe aspects of most of the artwork they produce in the early years and beyond.

Lines and marks

Line is the basic element of drawing, a device for describing shape by the use of outlines. A line is essentially a continuous mark, which can be thick, thin, straight, curved or a combination of qualities. Line can be used to tell a story, to express ideas, to report on what is seen, or to make patterns, maps, writing etc. Lines are the bare bones of drawing: bold, thick, fine and spidery. Each child will use line in their own way and become aware that lines can represent things – not only people and objects, but also movements and sounds.

Colour

Colour is something wondrous and uplifting for many of us – it is a visual perceptivity related to the property of something. Colour is a magical and motivational force with young children as they explore and realise that the world reveals an infinite spectrum of colours. With each chromatic existence, further properties can be discovered:

- Primary: cannot be mixed from any other colour.
- Secondary: can be made by mixing two primaries.
- Complementary: colours that contrast and oppose each other on the colour wheel.
- Hue: the property of a colour that allows it be identified as itself.
- Tint: a colour to which white has been added.
- Shade: a colour to which black has been added.
- Tone: indicates a degree of lightness or darkness.
- Intensity: the brightness or saturation of a colour.

Shape

Shape is an area with clear boundaries. It can refer to both geometric and non-geometric shapes. In art, as opposed to form, it often refers to something that is flat and two-dimensional and so is relevant to critique in drawing, painting and printing, for example. Children are eager shape-makers, following the amazing discovery that, as they play with line and join ends, a completed shape emerges.

Form

We can see this as the three-dimensional equivalent of shape. Form is used to describe things in the round, such as sculpture or modelling. Children share and swap all sorts of ideas and vocabulary to describe their investigations with sculptural mass: size, height, weight, texture and shape. They do this with many aspects of their lives from clay playing to climbing frames to construction kits.

Texture

Texture can mean the actual surface qualities of things around us, which can be seen or felt. Among a baby's earliest experiences is the feel of things against skin. As children reach out to touch countless textured surfaces, they learn about their world and can distinguish qualities and properties.

Pattern

Pattern refers to the repetition of shapes in whatever form they may take. Our eyes are drawn to patterns around us and children enjoy, from a young age, arranging and ordering things in their recognition of pattern. Children play with patterns in their artwork, which often encompasses their own set of rules and formulae in the sequences created.

Space

Space is a more complex element to quantify as it relates to the area contained within or surrounding a piece of art. It may be a solid area or an area of atmosphere. It is a concept related to the surface area in which the activity takes place. Shadows and light are played with in the illusory transparency of air; drawings must exist on defined surfaces with varying sizes and measurements. It is, if you like, the outside of a piece of artwork, not directly implied in what is made but essential in how it exists within a defined area.

The visual, tactile and spatial elements, as defined here, are fertile for investigation through the variety of art experiences and media within the early years setting. It is sometimes difficult to encapsulate the actual art practices of young children and name them precisely, as we are mindful to avoid titles of compartmentalisation and, therefore, boundaries. The list in Table 6.3 is absolutely not definitive or exhaustive but simply useful in its value as a starting point. It is to be added to, adapted and redefined commensurate with your children's creative desires and interests.

Photography and lens-based work

In positive response to good observational practice, the use of cameras in settings is far more prevalent now than it was even five years ago. We use photography as a medium to capture wonderful moments of learning and glorious instances of individual endeavour. What we capture is instamatic and perfectly reflects

Table 6.3 Areas of experience and possible materials

Drawing	Chalks Oil pastels Wax crayons Glitter crayons Pencils Pencil crayons Pens Charcoal Graphite sticks Biros Ink Water-based pencils	Brushes Rollers Masking tape Ropes and strings Sand Mud Flour Dough Clay Shaving foam Icing sugar Water	Misters Plastic bottles with nozzles Hoses Torches OHP Paper: variety of size, shape, colour and texture Acetate Tissue Cellophane Watering can Twigs Containers: variety of sizes
Painting	Double primary colours – mixed Double primary colours – powder Coloured ink Brusho – water-based colour Sand Flour Icing sugar Brushes Toothbrushes Nail brushes Scrubbing brushes Toilet brushes (unused!)	Brooms Sweeping brushes Cotton buds Rollers Sticks Twigs Buckets Palettes Trays Jam jars Glass vases Glass bowls	Sponges Spatulas Glue sticks Paper: variety of size, shape, colour and texture Card: variety of size, shape, colour and texture Wood Plastic Natural products: leaves, flowers, petals, branches, stones, pebbles, shells Containers: variety of sizes Dyes Pipettes
Printmaking	Brushes Rollers Trays Slabs Clay Dough Printing ink PVA glue Powder paint Ready-mixed paint Marbled ink Newspaper	Sand Mud Sponges Wooden blocks Polyblocs Sharp pencils Screens Flat surfaces Brushes Twigs Vegetables Natural materials	Plasticine Sticks String Corks Cotton reels Flour Masking tape Bark Crayons Charcoal
Collage	Glue: variety according to need Tape	Made materials: rubber, plastics, glass Fabrics	Plastic Variety of paper Acetate Tissue

continued . . .

Table 6.3 *Continued*

	Natural materials: leaves, soil, shells, twigs, gravel, pebbles, wood shavings, flower petals, seeds Reclaimed materials: plastics, cork, wrappers, paper, packaging, cardboard, wire	Threads Wool Felt Cloths: dusters, wipes, J-cloths Photographs	Crepe Drawings and paintings Graphic materials
Textiles	Range of fabrics: variety of weight, texture, colour, size, sheer, translucent White sheets/cotton Range of threads Twine String Ribbons Cord Rope Glue: variety Food dye	Scissors Loose weave fabric Netting Wooden/metal/ plastic frames Oil pastels Wax crayons Brusho Coloured ink Powder paint Fabric pens Fabric dye	Washing-up liquid Flour and water paste Natural, found and made materials Dressing-up clothes Hats Gloves Buttons Needles Cotton Pipettes Cotton wool
3D/Sculpture	Clay Playdough Plasticine Salt dough Cardboard Tubes Boxes Mod roc Pots and trays Mud Sand Builder's trays	Drainpipes and guttering Containers of different shapes and sizes Mirrors Sticks Twigs Cane Large plastic sheets Muslin Tissue paper Wire (modelling): variety of sizes and weight Natural, found and made materials	Jelly Vegetables Buckets Masking tape Glue: variety Cold glue guns Bamboo Wood: variety of size, weight, length Carpentry tools: child-sized Balloons Newspaper Paper: variety of textures, weight, size, colour

the visible moments that come from a young child exploring and discovering. Digital photography is firmly embedded in our early years settings as a conduit between home and setting where images, shared by children and their parents, illustrate their daily existence away from the family. Images such as these capture the magical art moments that take place at any given opportunity and can be used, as previously examined, to assess individual journeys and personal preferences.

These moments are also captured in photographs by the children themselves. They are experts at taking photos of each other and seeing moments of pictorial worthiness in a way that we adults do not. What they photograph is symptomatic of their existence as children in this world; they see things at their height level not ours; they can venture into small corners and nooks which we are too big to squeeze into. And, very importantly, they will often perform and pose for one another in a way they will not do for an adult photographer. Photography is not simply a medium to observe and record moments of learning and exploration but is also to be valued as a media, an art form, which encourages a particular development of skills from selecting, arranging and focussing, to processing, printing and reviewing.

Video clips are also pertinent to this aspect of art – encouraging children to record film and animate journeys of exploration as well as being used to inspire and stimulate ideas and imaginations in art. As the digital world continues to explode, an increase in materials and tools is at hand to explore possibilities and concepts. As Rachel Levy (2012) commented: 'Children are multi-modal learners from the moment they come out of the womb.' Young children are born into a digital age which I, and perhaps some of the readers of this book, were not. I have to remind myself that this is a fact and a contemporary reality and therefore the children's interest in digital technology as part of the multi-modal approach is vast and powerful. The potentiality of art-based programmes and apps cannot be denied – they often require complex problem-solving and selection skills. They are, however, to be used as part of the materials base, rather than to replace it. A digital art programme where the touch of fingers changes colours on the screen can be exciting and immediately rewarding, but the tactile and visual pleasure of thick cartridge paper, densely fluid paints, spectrums of rainbow colours, dazzling glitter concoctions and squidgy malleable clay *cannot* be matched by a digital alternative. It may symbolise some of the elements within our scrutiny of art, but it will produce a flat and very one-dimensional aspect if used too widely and regularly in the absence of the 'real' art experience.

Art outside

I do not, in any way, propose this section to be a tag-on, a tokenistic acknowledgement of the engagement of art learning and exploration in the outside space. All that has been discussed and considered previously in the chapter responds to both inside and outside environments. Whether image-making, clay sculpting or textile printing, all activities are eligible for both environments. This has been an underlying assumption and, as practitioners, we adapt and rearrange resources and opportunities depending on the space the children work in – interior or exterior.

Our professional and experienced behaviours can tell us that some activities are best suited to an inside space if a sink is needed or a particular temperature. Other endeavours will have a greater impact if experienced outside in appreciation of space, absorbent earth or grass surfaces. The key aspect here, however, is that the spaces *are* different. The outside is not a classroom – it is not a boundary-ridden space that mirrors the classroom. It is an alternative space that importantly exudes different characteristics and qualities in contrast to an inside space. Although activities may happen in both places, the actual engagement and process may be very different because of the 'atmosphere' related to them. Jan White (2010: 5) reminds of this difference:

> Rather than attempting to 'take the indoors out', it is absolutely vital that the play environment captures the special nature of the outdoors to offer children what the indoors cannot. 'Outdoors' is different to 'indoors' and this is exactly why it matters for children.

Perhaps this refers us back to the 'spirituality' of children's endeavours. 'Abstract and awareness' thinking in spaces with ceilings and those which are open to the world affect us very differently and so will have a marked effect on our thought processes.

An outside art space is open – the fresh air, the exposure to the weather of the day, the lack of walls and the infinite expanse of the sky above can increase an exuberance of activity within a human body. A child, in particular, can experience a particular freedom of expression and engagement that is absent in an inside space. The sun's warmth on one's face can shine through to the art being made – it is a feeling that is hard to define but one that is most definitely felt. Puddles on the ground can reflect back colours and images; the expanse of outside brick walls serve as fascinating image-making surfaces. The outside space is a keen supporter of the aspect of surprise which has continued to emerge throughout the book. As we cannot predict the weather, we are unable to plan ahead and this freedom encounters a whole variety of art-based, outside possibilities. 'One of the joys of working outside with young children is that you can never know quite what to expect. Rather like the weather, no two days are the same' (Watts, 2011: 123).

The elemental qualities of space, air, weather and size all create an area where the freedom to play with art is often on a larger scale. It can be less confined and sometimes more collaborative. The ideas in Box 6.4 celebrate some of the wonderful art experiences that the outside makes possible. The weather and climate make these experiences temporary and transitional – another inspiring and motivational qualification.

Box 6.4 Outdoor art experiences

Ink, snow and ice

Squeeze a pipette of coloured ink or food colouring onto snow or icy puddles and watch. The colours will merge in the snow and run through cracks in the ice to create coloured rivulets.

Mud pies and mud kitchens

The sculptural possibilities are endless with this natural supply of material – depending on your location, the soil with water will contain a variety of sensorial qualities from dense and malleable clay-like earth to rough, earthy consistency. The more hands manipulate the soil, the greater the propensity for mud sculpture. Mud kitchens become spaces where tactile adventures are borne out and forms, shapes and textures explored.

Spray textiles – colour-stained grass/tarmac

Use plant misters to spray water coloured with ink or food colouring onto lengths of paper or fabric laid over the outside surface. Depending on the surface, the extension of coloured spray will leave a residue on the surface as well as the intended space. The outside affords an extension of work – a greater length of surface than that inside and so the collaborative quality is inherent in the size and scale.

Big charcoal rubbings

Long and wide lengths of varied paper pieces can be used to rub textures of trees and bark, walls and ground surfaces. Paper can be wrapped around the width of trees or scale long, meandering walls. Individual pieces can join up to create a long line of textured explorations to be walked along, surveyed and compared. The dense velvety quality of the charcoal and its material sympathy with the exterior textures will be experienced.

Weather-bound chalk friezes

Both expansive collaborative and individually mastered chalk images on tarmac or concrete ground spaces will evolve in their transient existence with the elemental force of changing weather. A diary of photographs will record the changing image as it erodes; colours merging, fading and disappearing.

Sky photography

Trajectorial tendencies cause young children to look up – a lot of the world they exist in is higher than them and so they spend much of their time looking up to things. This includes the sky and its ever-changing landscape of colours, clouds and movement. Photography, video clips and bird's-eye-view chalk and pastel sketches record this altering and transitional arena that surrounds us. Capturing daily pictures affords young children a piece of something that is vast, intangible and mighty.

Wild topics – a place for themes

In the preschools of Reggio Emilia, children are encouraged to engage in extended projects. They use their drawings as a 'graphic language' to record ideas, feelings and observations. The projects scale a wide variety of subjects and abstract considerations drawn from the local geographical and demographic landscape. The project titles are a far cry from the bland, commonly used themes often heard in some settings such as 'transport', 'weather' and 'myself'. Granted, within these themes there are many possibilities but the titles themselves are lacking inspiration and magical enticement.

Of course, themes are to be carefully considered in how they are used to instigate ideas and activities. If they have come as a consequence of teacher planning irrelevant of children's journeys and impetus, then they will have little to do with child-invested inspiration. If titles proposed are a direct consequence of watching, listening and illuminating the thoughts and specific interests alive in the world of the children, then they will offer a great many relevant opportunities entirely in relation to the children and their motivational enquiry.

Our spaces, which we have considered throughout this chapter, are dynamic and changeable and so we should be encouraged to adopt a theme of the moment, an interest that pervades children's imaginations and takes them to alternative spheres of thinking. Claxton (2007) refers to these as 'wild topics' and insists that their installation encourages and strengthens a space that challenges and extends the learner.

The key aspects of 'wild topics' or themes are:

- Rich – there is much to be explored.
- Challenging – the topic contains real difficulty.
- Extended – there is time and opportunity to go into it in depth.
- Relevant – the topic connects with children's own interests and concerns.
- Responsibility – children have some genuine control over what, why, how and when they organise their learning.
- Real – solving the problem or making progress genuinely matters to someone.
- Unknown – the practitioner does not already know the 'answer'.
- Collaborative – most children enjoy the opportunity to work together with others on such tasks.

Conclusion

Someone once retorted during a heated discussion about template-driven art in early years setting that classrooms of young children should be alive and scandalous! His impassioned outburst was fuelled by a well-meant, though interesting turn of phrase, in relation to the need to keep our classrooms, our spaces, alive with ideas, risk-taking and challenges. As Eisner (2002: 36) reflects: 'When there is no challenge, when everything is satisfactory, there may be little motivation to stretch one's thinking, to try something new, to experiment, to revise, to appraise, and to start again.'

The spaces we provide for children are not akin to the home, the shops, the cinema – they are particular in their function and they are there to house some brilliant minds where the majesty of creative production is energetic and enthralling. 'When the "atelier" as well as all our school environments are continually developed and used in purposeful ways, they transform our everyday life in school into a living manifestation of the richness of children's potential' (Gandini, 2005: 31).

Reflection

- Take a long evaluative look at your children's learning environment and consider potential adaptation of furniture to allow for a variety of 'free' spaces.
- Experiment with some art resources you have never used yourself so that you remember how it feels to explore and investigate the material properties and the potentialities.
- Have a stocktake of your resources and consider quality, variety, accessibility and aesthetic potential.
- Plan for an art project and space that invites a longevity approach where work is reflected on and returned to: observe and document the process and share this with the whole community to encourage collaboration and reflection.

Further reading

Gandini, L. (ed) (2005) *In the Spirit of the Studio*, New York: Teachers College Press.

Ceppi, G. and Zini, M. (eds) (1998) *Children, Spaces, Relations: Metaproject for an Environment for Young Children*, Reggio Emilia, Italy: Reggio Children Publishers.

Kolbe, U. (2001) *Rapunzel's Supermarket*, Byron Bay, Australia: Peppinot Press.

Vecchi, V. (2010) *Art and Creativity in Reggio Emilia: Exploring the Role and Potential of Ateliers in Early Childhood Education* (Contesting Early Childhood), Oxon: Routledge.

Waite, S. (2011) *Children Learning Outside the Classroom*, London: Sage.

White, J. (2008) *Playing and Learning Outdoors: Making Provision for High-Quality Experiences In Indoor Environments*, Oxon: Routledge.

Reflection

CHAPTER 7

Following their footsteps

Every child is an artist. The problem is how to remain an ***artist*** once we grow up.

(Pablo Picasso)

Introduction

We have reflected on the aspects of high-quality teaching and learning in the lives of young children and we can value and savour these aspects in our early years classrooms. Ideal spaces and real adult engagement help us towards achieving our aspirations for a conducive, proactive environment that relishes and celebrates the individual artist. In this chapter, we now consider the life of the young artist beyond the early years space and into the subsequent phases of primary education. We do not attempt to replicate the early years of art but we reflect on the potential, for this good practice and mindset to continue into the later years of primary school, so that the foundations of the young art career can continue to flourish.

A continuation of understanding and ethos

All this wonderful grounding and encouragement to pursue curiosity and grow as confident, schematically involved artists are roots which, if recognised and built upon in later years, remain solidly reliant for a child. I do not attempt, in the confines of this book, to suggest and advise on a curriculum for art and design that can be adhered to and used to plan with through to Key Stage 2 of a primary school. I simply suggest that the ethos and values relating to teaching and learning discussed in the previous chapters can be retained and embedded with each and every stage of a child's young education. Engaged adults, insightful observations, flexible and accessible environments and positive parent participation are not approaches that exist only in the early years 'art' classrooms. They are pertinent to all age groups and all educational spaces where a child invests time and spiritual endeavour into art-based investigation.

We remind ourselves at this juncture of Bob and Roberta Smith's words in the title of the artwork *Art Makes Children Powerful* (2012), as such a message should serve as a mantra to remind us what this expressive area of learning is capable of. It is, as the painting suggests, a powerful and personally edifying motivator. It is a message that should follow the child throughout their school lives and their art-filled days.

Investigation is visibly and at times absent from many classrooms as children make their journeys through the primary education system. The space and time to explore, peruse, *play* and discover is not something we are guaranteed to witness in a Year 3 or 5 classroom. And yet why is it deemed that at a particular age or key stage, a child's exploration into art learning is no longer of value? I am sure this is not an opinion held by many teachers and practitioners who continue to enjoy and celebrate the many inquisitive children that they work with. It is far more the fault of timetabling and target-setting pressure, which is prevalent in our current education system. Wright (2010: 166) strongly laments the decrease of art experiences in the later years of school: 'The schooling process . . . deprecates the innate abilities of children to use their imaginations and to develop creative thought through art.'

But rather than regretting what is absent, let us consider what is possible in order to alter the mindsets that lead to end-product art experiences and instead see potential in process-driven pursuits. Successful examples of projects, initiatives and committed teaching practices exist in many of our primary schools, so we know that following experiential art practices can happen. In many cases, the commitment to children's art is rooted in an ethos that values children. By this I mean a recognition and commitment to seeing and relishing the child of today and not of the future. When this understanding is in place within a school, the foundations of learning and education – good early years practice and principles – are viewed as simple good practice that can be echoed and adopted throughout the school. Following a child's interest, scaffolding learning and planning for the individual are all rooted in what happens in the first years of school. The importance placed on the individual does not change, their personal values and perceptions are still just as important in Year 6 as they were in a reception class. And so the educational approaches we know to be excellent practice in the early years, which support the individual, are relevant to how we approach learning and individual pursuit of knowing in the later years of school.

Developing aptitudes and understandings

As we continue to consider opportunities for sharing art experiences amongst mixed age groups, we must also examine the differences in approach and mindset which are afforded to children as they develop and grow. The need to play remains and will never fade, but there is most definitely a shift in mindset as children grow, filter and prune skills, and so progress into different realms of

Ages 0–7	Ages 8–11
←——————	——————→
Exploratory experiences	Linking materials, ideas and outcomes
Intense curiosity	Knowing and enjoying
Avid investigation	Meaningful and productive

Figure 7.1 Development in the tactile and visual learner

understanding. A generic view of this progressive experience is shown in the continuum in Figure 7.1.

Whilst considering the development-based journey above, we must be mindful that we do not attempt to adhere to this in our teaching and planning in an exact format. As with all learning, children will oscillate up and down this continuum depending on mood, time, alertness and company, amongst other indicative factors. However, it is a continuum that gives us some insight into the progression that may be visible within whole-school art projects where the playful activities of the very young combine with the intentional and more purposeful art of older children. An older child will be able to model an increasing ability to control a material and, in partnership mode, the younger child will remind them to remain open-minded and exploratory – a very positive working dynamic.

It is important here to focus back on art and creative learning. We will not attempt to rewrite an entire educational approach to learning in the primary school, but by considering some of the initiatives laid out in this chapter, we can feel confident that our schools and classrooms will remain vibrant and exciting places. They should be places where children are creative and critical thinkers and where their ideas and imaginations are still prized as the most important aspect of their learning as they make the transition through primary school. Eisner (2005) speculates that life in the classroom should look more like real life and that we, as teachers, must be committed to raising and nurturing generations of 'imaginative possibilities'.

Research – following lines of enquiry

As we know, children are born researchers. They do not feel the weight of this word as academicians can. They have a natural proclivity to pursue a found interest, to find answers and to follow an initial enquiry. This pursuit, as examined in previous chapters, is what strengthens and elucidates the vision and knowledge of an emerging artist. Children's ability to 'think out of the box' and be imaginative is something adults aspire to in many walks of life. Linear ways of thinking can become a little more familiar to us later in life, as this is often the more straightforward and therefore easier choice. Being creative means being lively and proactive and so requires energy and openness. Children are embodiments of energised states and their minds are open to the puzzling quandaries of life. The puzzles of art paths are ones to be consumed and subsumed as the young artist's research continues. This journey does not suddenly stop in their minds and bodies – it is an internal inspiration to their learning and one that can be externally rewarded and nourished within the classroom, from one year to the next.

Collaborative art: visible layers

Portfolios and sketchbooks are initiatives we have considered in previous chapters when discussing processes in art learning, parental observation and adult observation. We return again to their importance and value as documentation that reflects artwork to be relived and reviewed by artists as they make their way through their young educational lives. An art portfolio that began in nursery and continues through to the end of a primary school offers a rich and valuable picture of a child's artistic journey and progression in art and design. Again, we remind ourselves that the portfolio is owned by the child – it is a device that allows them to review themselves and their artistic character and should be made available for browsing and self-assessment whenever the moment is called for by the child. Portfolios are initiatives that reflect a visible and progressional stratification of learning and unify a child's journey in art. Such portfolios may be historical and autobiographical tomes of kept art but they might also be project-based relating to particular initiatives and events.

Box 7.1 'Take One Picture'

'Take One Picture' is the London National Gallery's countrywide scheme for primary schools. Each year the gallery focuses on one painting from the collection to inspire cross-curricular work in primary classrooms. During a one-day Continuing Professional Development course at the gallery teachers are given a print of a painting. The challenge is then for schools to use the image imaginatively in the classroom, both as a stimulus for artwork, and for work in more unexpected curriculum areas. National Gallery Education then displays a selection of the work in the annual 'Take One Picture' exhibition at the National Gallery. The initiative is one that promotes art across a whole school, combining the ideas and artistic talents of the youngest children in the school through to the oldest. Both process and end product enable teachers and children to be involved in a shared experience, spanning the age ranges and, importantly, enjoyed as a whole school once the artwork is exhibited.

The National Gallery's 'Take One Picture' (see Box 7.1) is a successful initiative that actively engages a whole-school approach. Depending on the level of a school's engagement, the involvement may include the training of all teachers, irrepsective of age group and key stage. All staff members collaborate in their interest and understanding through a focus on painting and art appreciation. The artwork that is produced as a result of the project is an illustrative collation of the whole school's work and reflects all age groups. This unification of ages in relation to children as well as teachers is also reflected in other projects where artists and their work are a focus for the whole school. Graphic collaborative documentation such as this reflects the strong and important cultural heritage and wealth of a school community. The work is a direct result of a combined effort where each child (and teacher) owns the investigation and creation.

Artists in schools

Initiatives regarding artists-in-residence will be examined in more detail in Chapter 9 but here our focus relates to the importance of continuation through the school. When an artist works with a whole school, whether with a particular key stage or a set of classes, there will be a natural transitional characteristic attached to the format, process and production. The reflective time spent with such an initiative is valuable for both children and teachers in the comparison and contrast of experiences.

An artist-in-residency encourages a multitude of dialogues owned by the various parties involved, and therefore discussion on visual and tactile elements will inevitably form part of the conversational exchange. The vocabulary and language used to describe, understand and interpret in an early years classroom will differ and yet correspond to that of an older classroom. The same artist is being worked with but with different-aged children whose trained eyes and minds will interpret according to understanding and experience.

In Reggio Emilia, children's shared experiences with artists are an everyday occurrence. The influence and inspiration of an atelierista – an artist – is firmly at the root of the creativity umbrella that presides over the early years and toddler centres. As a result of their detailed and historically rich documentation process, they also clarify the underlying importance of transition and collaboration of age-related interception and interaction. During one particular episode where children worked with an exhibition and artists' work, the 'pedagogue' of a nursery commented on the interplay and interrelation of the micro-generational strata involved in the initiative:

> In bringing materials together, the children experimented with subtle relationships by overlapping, fitting together, tying; strategies discovered and invented in getting to know the qualities and characteristics of each material in the encounter with their hands – competent and imaginative hands that appropriated the material in this way

> and reinvented it with unusual combinations . . . Children had analogous strategies but based on different criteria:
>
> - Contrasts
> - Symmetries
> - Overlapping and stratification
> - Multiplication of form
> - Chance
> - Logic relationships
> - Sensory correlations
> - Sonorous quality
> - Beauty
>
> (Giuidici and Vecchi, 2004: 39–40)

The experience, though perceived and conceived in different ways depending on age, had the generic quality of tactile investigation. As the various ages of children – in this case aged between three and seven – worked collaboratively, they explored together contemporaneously with hands and minds. Individual investigations belonged to the specific age of the child but they were, at the same time, being shared and exposed as a part of the collaborative activity. Response and review firmly layered this rich experience as all views, interplay and combinations of possibilities were played out in a public, homogeneous art arena.

A whole-school initiative – documenting a joint venture

Case study 1 presents a collaborative piece of artwork which in itself documents a whole-school initiative. The art journeys involved in the project were experienced by all the children and the end product was a testament to all the minds and hands that participated in the instalments of making. The case study has been related here by the headteacher, Maria Vinney.

Whole school – homogeneous art communities

Transitionally rich projects draw on the intergenerational aspect as discussed in Chapter 8. Within our specific focus on children and teachers' experience of collaborative art, we are able to consider the intergenerational significance of whole-school projects. Younger children influence older children through their investigative natures and the older child influences the younger with their intent and purposeful pursuit. We see this when we consider siblings at play: the older child focuses on a 'theme' and 'plot' for the play, and the younger child follows with enthusiasm and respect but with an added ingredient of playful tangents – they offer a variety of directions and possibilities that the focussed mind of the older child may have missed.

Case study 1: Exploring opportunities for engaging whole school communities in art and design

This we know: art and design can be such an engaging and exciting process for all members of a school community – children, staff, parents and governors. The positive impact on both children and adults can be significant and lifechanging. Schools that come together in this way appear closer and more cohesive and it is with this in mind that we need to create and explore opportunities to share a rich tapestry of memorable experiences, with art and design at their heart.

The following case study took place in a first school in the centre of a coastal town, with its own nursery and an adjacent Children's Centre. The school has a long established history and is very much a vibrant community school, supporting approximately 300 children between the ages of three and eight, and their families, just over a quarter of whom speak English as an additional language. This mixture of different cultures and faiths provides a rich layer of character to the school community. In excess of 20 different languages are spoken. Staff have worked hard to involve and engage parents and the wider community in the life of the school. The following project is a typical example of how this has been achieved in recent years.

Beside the sea: making a very special film about where we live

We knew we wanted to do something different: a project involving all the children and the adults in our whole school community, which would not only challenge us to work in a different way, but where we could show people a bit about this quite unique and special place where we live and work.

We considered our initial ideas for the project and successfully bid for a small grant from Creative Partnerships. They then put us in touch with a digital artist and film-maker

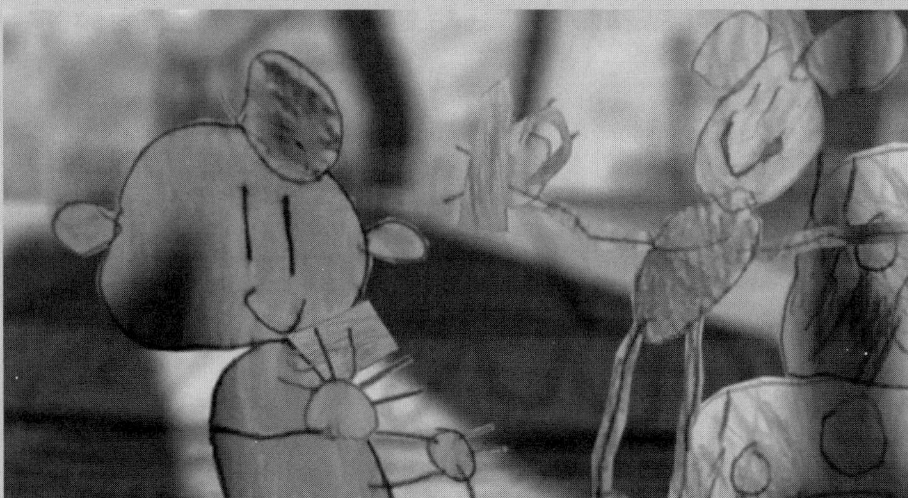

Figure 7.2 Children's drawings for the animation 1

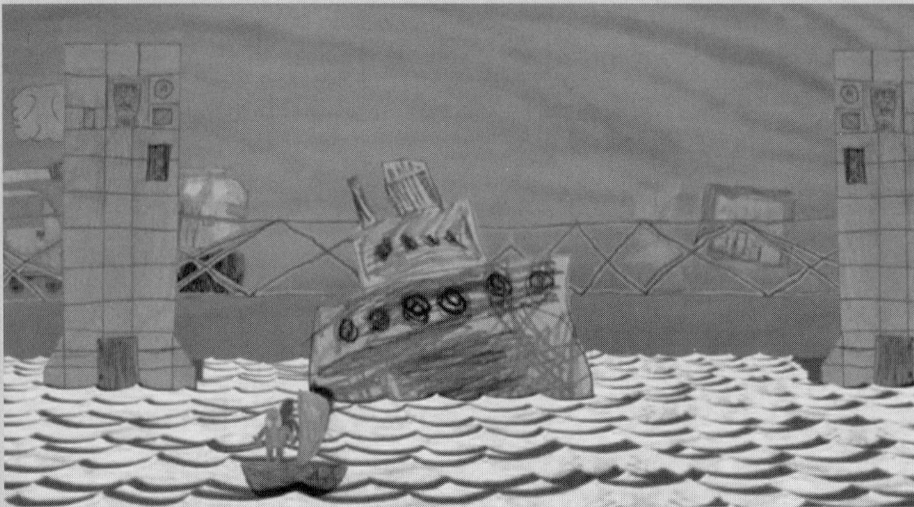

Figure 7.3 Children's drawings for the animation 2

who had some experience of working with children, although not as young as ours, who come into the nursery at the age of three. This was important to us. Previous experience had taught us just how important it was for the artists and practitioners we worked with to feel comfortable and confident in supporting our children, who are at the centre of the process.

The planning meeting at the start of the autumn term went very well; it was clear that this would be a different way of working for the artist, as well as for us. Previously, he had always gone in and worked with small groups of children in schools, never before had he tackled something with the whole school community and worked with such young children. His enthusiasm for the project was evident and we were confident that his positive problem-solving approach and sense of humour would go down well with the children. He very quickly became one of the team.

We began by planning a focus week, which we launched with a staff inset day at the start of the spring term, for teaching assistants as well as teachers. We felt it was important to go through the same process and journey that we would, later in the week, take the children through. There was a tangible feeling of anticipation and excitement in the room and, to some extent, nervousness and a sense of trepidation. For some people, this was quite an unnerving process, particularly because there was a significant aspect of creative technology involved. The artist's enthusiasm and reassurance was, however, confidence boosting and he soon put us at ease.

Small groups of staff set out by foot to photograph and draw different parts of the town that we could get to from our school. Back at base, the artist showed us how the software he planned to use would enable us to begin converting the drawings we had made into film. It was a really positive and exhilarating day and staff looked forward to using their new skills with the children the following morning. How would the children engage and respond? Only time would tell. As with any creative process, the excitement of not quite knowing how it is going to go or what is going to happen is all part of the motivation and enjoyment.

The next day, after a whole-school assembly to introduce and explain the project, each year group, from reception through to Year 3, set off, with great excitement, to explore a different part of the town: the park, the waterfront, the shopping centre and further afield. The nursery children enjoyed spending the morning investigating the school itself and the grounds, which were now absent of any other children. The freedom of an uncrowded space allowed the youngest children to intrepidly discover corners and cupboards they had never ventured into before.

Equipped with sketchbooks, cameras, camcorders and clipboards, the 4–8 cohort of children eagerly collected images, thoughts and sounds from the places they visited around the town. As always, the children noticed and observed things that so often, as adults, pass us by. Of course, they recorded the usual landmarks from their town but they also spotted the details; things that may otherwise go unnoticed or remain hidden: a crack in the pavement, a spider, a dripping drainpipe. To the children, these were important and all were recorded with enthusiasm.

There was a happy encounter with a family of ducks as they waddled noisily across the path in front of the reception children, and great excitement for Year 1 when a train whizzed by in the distance, and when the lifeboat was spotted amongst the boats bobbing up and down on the water. The children chatted happily about the things they knew about their town: what time the ferry arrived from France every morning, the kind of sweets you could get in the shop on the quay. The things they liked and did not like about their town; the way that, if you weren't careful, a hungry seagull would swoop down and nick one of your chips! (This experience was included in the final film!) And did you know, there's a mermaid who lives in the water?! They were thrilled at the prospect of potentially sharing it all with a worldwide audience on the web.

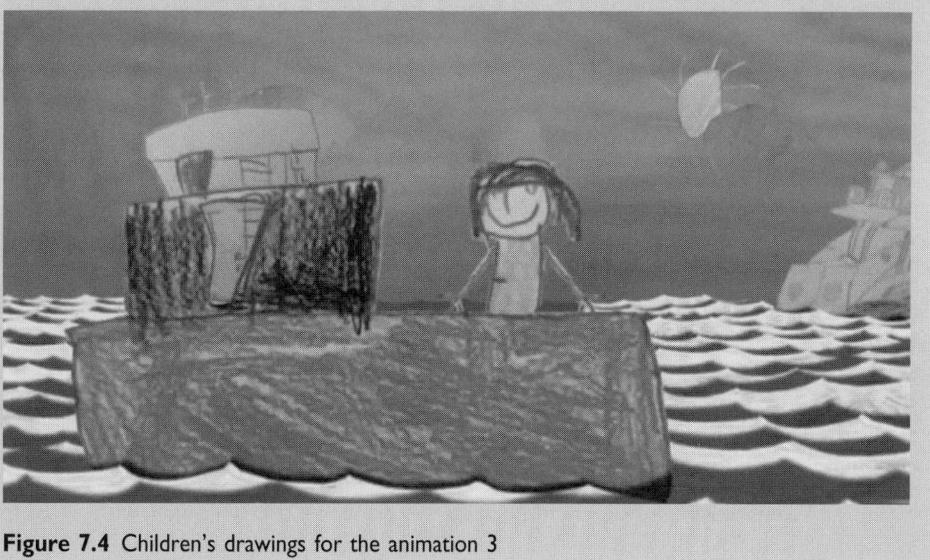

Figure 7.4 Children's drawings for the animation 3

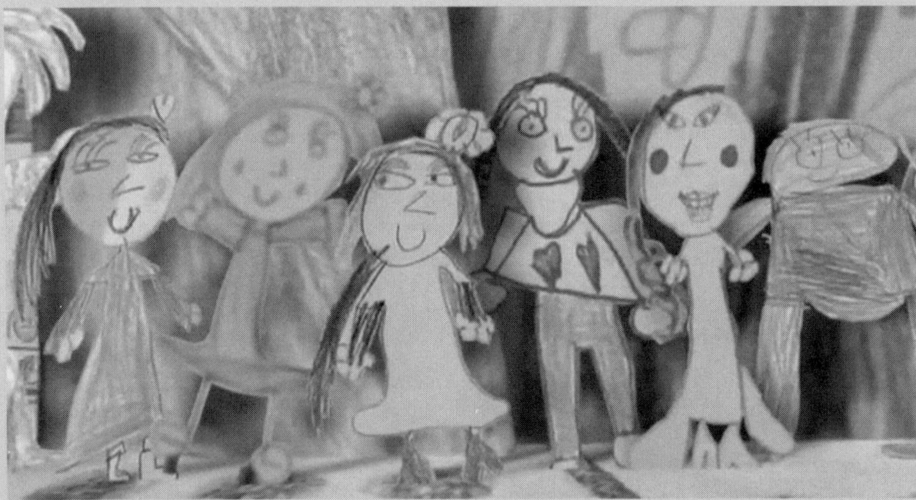

Figure 7.5 Children's drawings for the animation 4

As always, the children's ideas constantly surprised and delighted us. A group said they felt it was important to include something about keeping safe when you are near the water. With their collection of drawings and photographs, recordings and experiences, thoughts and ideas, they gathered back at school.

The rest of the week was spent working with the artist: drawing from the sketches they had made and the photographs they had taken, adding detail and colour, refining and embellishing, working independently and in collaboration. Under the artist's guidance and expertise, we began to create our animation, made entirely from the children's drawings. Every child's contribution was interwoven into work-in-progress, linked by the thoughts and words of Year 3, who had the additional task of writing the script for the film. The nursery children created the sound effects and listened to themselves on the backing track. At the end of the week, the film was taken away and pieced together, and we waited, with great anticipation, for our first viewing.

I contacted our local Arts Centre, explained the project and asked if they would be willing to host the 'premier' of this rather special film so that we could watch it, all together, children, staff and parents, on their huge screen. They were more than happy to help and we set the date. We invited our whole school community and asked them to dress in their best outfits. Although we couldn't quite manage the red carpet, we did arrange for a group of 'paparazzi' (staff with cameras) to be waiting for the children outside the theatre and I was there, with my pretend microphone, getting interviews with the 'stars' as they arrived. Despite it being a somewhat soggy morning, there was such a buzz of excitement. No one other than the artist had seen the final film, and he had only viewed it, of course, on a small computer screen.

It was an exhilarating and highly memorable experience that will stay with all of us for a long time. The film itself is only about four minutes long but it is, quite simply, magical. We watched it through at least three times because each time we saw different things, subtle details that perhaps we had missed first time around. All the children were, of course, ecstatic and extremely proud of their achievements. When the film first came up on the enormous screen there were gasps of amazement from the audience and then excited whispers of 'There's the girl I drew!', 'There's my dog!', as each child spotted their contribution.

The artist was as awestruck with the end result as we all were. The film achieves not only what we set out to do, which was to promote our town, but so much more. It also reflects the warmth and sense of fun in our school community. We were so pleased with our little film that we decided to contact our local tourist board to see if they would like to use it on their website and share it with a wider audience and, to our delight, they leaped at the chance.

Feedback from the children, parents and staff about the experience was extremely positive, as it was also from the artist, who felt he had really been welcomed and become part of our community in helping us with the project. We all reflected on the fact that we had learned a great deal from the process and from each other. We had said that we wanted the film to be true to the children and, certainly, we feel we achieved this. It was important to all of us that the film reflected the children's perspectives, not ours. We love the fact that it is unique and probably not what you would get in the usual tourist promotion film. It is fantastic to think that our little film is out there now, for everyone to see and enjoy, promoting the town and all it has to offer, but from all the children's points of view, from nursery age through to Year 3.

See the film at: www.youtube.com/watch?v=OY435x4Q328&feature=youtu.be

Such intergenerational or cross-phase artwork will impact on learning for all children. They respond to one another's creativity and there is a powerful reciprocity to their collaborative work. This is very evident during 'art weeks' or 'art days' – a popular initiative in primary schools. A health warning attached to this is the fact that we must ensure this is not symptomatic of a decrease in the older child's ventures in art. The themed day/week must not replace regular visits to art learning and art exploration for any class in a primary school. An art day or week will add to and enrich what is already a lively and animated subject area of learning, but not solely represent it.

Positive and highly successful art-themed days/weeks are richly rewarding with regards to the homogeneity of a school and the cross-phase sharing of ideas. One primary school I visited embarked on a wonderfully creative and ambitious whole-school project related to the theme of the Fire of London. A living street was created by the school with each class making a house representative of one from Pudding Lane in the 1600s. The school then collectively gathered to witness the street catching fire and the buildings burning down. This re-enactment of history was powerful in its ability to affect each child. The children knew, in advance, that this was going to happen so the destruction was not as shocking as it may have been if warning had been absent.

The process of planning, building and display as a collective whole, and then setting fire and witnessing the aftermath, was a dynamic re-enactment of both sculpture and history. As all the school was involved, the post-discussions varied depending on the age of the children but all views and voices were shared and therefore respected as a part of the art history experience.

Altering knowledge with shared thinking

As we have previously acknowledged, Craft (2002) discusses the aspect of possibility thinking in creative development and creativity-based learning. She comments, in particular, on the generative sense of possibility thinking and its continued growth through the nurture and encouragement of teaching and environmentally conducive circumstances. In consideration of this, we can be assured that the initiatives under review in this chapter will result in divergent thinking as minds and bodies converge in thought and creative processes. Children sharing moments generate immense possibilities; children of *varying ages* sharing moments is even more productive for the potential of thinking paths and the surprising and unpredictable cognitive wanderings. Initiatives such as mixed-age art projects, exhibitions, themed weeks, artist-in-residencies and shared buddying activities will encourage a discussion between children. Talk between children produces a very different dialogue to talk between an adult and child. Quite often, inhibitions are allayed in child-based conversational exchanges as there exists an equal platform of contribution. Even within a group of mixed age groups the very fact that they are all still working as 'thinking children' offers a safe and secure base to contemplate and discuss equally. Such bases, however, are vibrant laboratories of thought and decision-making where children alter knowledge paths in response to their young partner's enquiries. Buddying in art activities will see these enquiring communities in a very real way and their existence serves and benefits all age groups.

Karmiloff-Smith (2013) talks of the deceleration in older children's creative learning abilities. She claims that at around the age of seven children can experience a period of learning where the unpacking of knowledge takes precedence over the finding out. They stall the process for a while and in doing so, errors and frustration can be experienced. During, and as a result of, the pruning process they become more aware of others especially, as in the case of art-making, awareness directly related to the expectations of teachers and influential adults. At these times, we see furious rubbing out of pencil drawings and tiny frail sketches that are too afraid to be bold.

This is a stage that, if it is to be experienced in all areas of a mid-primary school life, can be one that will be enlightened and reinvigorated by that of a younger child. We are reminded again of our siblings and their 'play-based' relationships; a partnership that liberates the older child to experiment again, as they did in earlier years, as personified by the younger child.

In a school where art-based experiences were firmly rooted in whole-school approaches to learning, the upper KS2 classes spent a consecutive run of Wednesdays in with the reception and Year 1 children, predominantly supporting and developing skills in 3D projects around a variety of themes. The project was sold to the older children in the guise of supporting and 'helping' the younger children; senior guidance such as this is often a motivational factor. Of course, in practice the support was in fact a two-way dynamic. In our dialogic example below, the older child, Lexie, became, often unconsciously, enamoured by the monologue accompanying the young child, Lucia's physically creative endeavours. The body language alone of the older child reflected interested engagement and enjoyable humour as the young child's choice of language and words transported her senior partner back to the infant-endorsed world 'where anything is possible'. The words in Box 7.2 are testament to a lucrative sharing process.

Collaborations

The EPPE findings (Sylva *et al.* 2003) show that children's future successes are greater if they have social confidence and we have examined a great number of initiatives in many of the chapters, including this one, where collaboration, social interaction and shared cooperation play a very important part.

Collaboration may come in the form of parallel art play, working alongside each other but not necessarily converging, or group work as a team to produce a joint art piece where each component is recognised and visible in recognition of all the individuals who actively participated. What we also know during these and many other indicators of collaboration and sharing art-based moments is that children respond to each other's ideas and imitate their creative applications. As they learn to respond to new sensations and aesthetic experiences in relation to one another, they will become increasingly aware that their perceptions and responses to the same sensory phenomena may differ greatly, adding an extra dimension to one particular experience and their developing repertoire (Tutchell, 1998). Intergenerational projects certainly present imitational visual endeavours in which children help and 'copy' one another because they respond to a 'good idea' and wish to take it for themselves, adapt and regurgitate a new 'original'.

> One child may copy or imitate another; others will take up a particular vista, idea or symbol and use it in their own way. Themes, techniques, approaches and ideas are exchanged and assimilated into their visual approaches and vocabularies.
>
> (Gentle, 1985: 85)

Box 7.2 Lucia's monologue as she creates her own family out of clay

I'm going to make me bigger than Bella – this time she is the baby and I'm the older one. I'm up to here *(indicates against the model of her father).*

I am older and bigger than her.

Look and mummy is going 'oooooo' – look at her mouth. I tell you why, because she's learning to read – and the first sound is 'ooo' – look *(she mimics the phonic shape with his own mouth).*

Daddy's got hair gel in *(laughs, looking up at Lexie)* – his hair is all sticky-uppy!

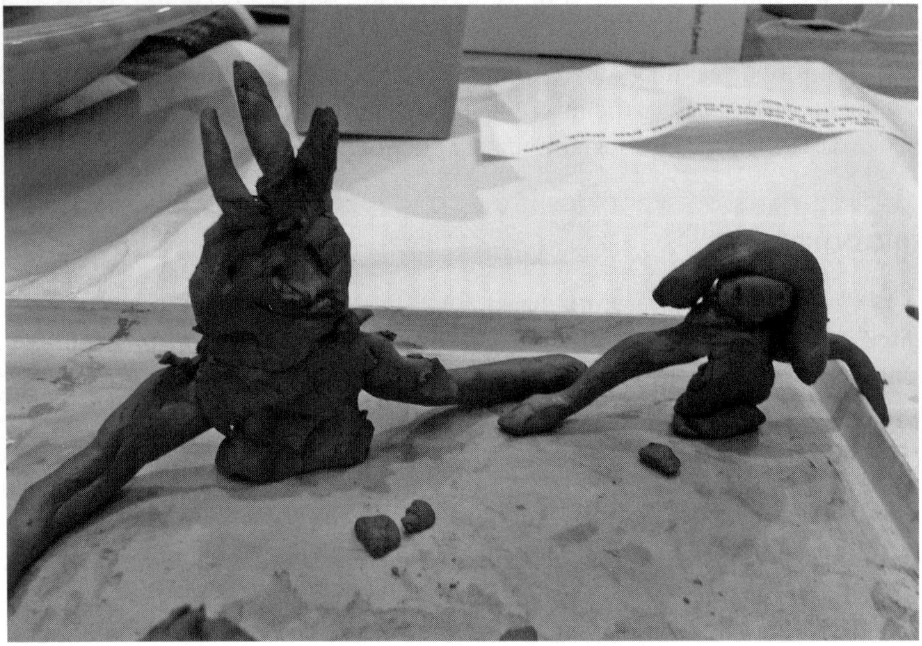

Figure 7.6 Clay family

Transition is about the journey of the individual as they adapt to change. But intrinsic to this personal journey are the many people and situations that influence certain paths and decisions. Transition will always have about it a 'collaborative' element in educational terms as the child is helped and assisted through the process. We know transitions take place from birth, as babies learn to go from milk to solids, from crawling to walking, from home to school, from EYFS to KS1 and from KS1 to KS2. We expect much from our children and so we need to reciprocate with efficient, accessible and enjoyable approaches so that the 'change' is exciting and, at times, seamless.

Art projects, as discussed, serve well in the transitional process. This is not just in their intrinsic value as art in its continuation as an expressive dynamic discipline as children continue in their primary school life, but also as vehicles to assist transition in general. An example of such a project is 'Advisories', books written and collated by six- and seven-year-olds at the Diana Preschool in Reggio Emilia. These are presented to the youngest and newest children on arrival at the preschool and contain pictures, stickers, diagrams and words aimed at easing the transitional process. In this example, we have a transitional initiative where the older, more experienced child helps to advise the younger child using visual images and therefore an inevitable 'child speak' will occur.

Another initiative similar to this is the buddying portraiture project in an art-active primary school in West London. Near to the beginning of the academic year, Year 3 and 6 children draw each other's portraits and exhibit them in their classes. The same process takes place with reception and Year 2 children. Their collaborative humour is what drives this project as well as a mutual understanding of and respect for the resulting portrait. In both scenarios, the younger child is delighted with the sophistication of the older child's impression and the older child is happily humoured by the infant interpretation of their face.

Conclusion

I think it is fair to say that early years still suffers from the ignorance and misunderstandings afforded it by teachers and adults inexperienced in this phase of education. The 'they just play' comment can still sometimes be heard, though perhaps, we would hope, less than in previous years. It is not always intended as disrespect but rather it represents a misconception and misconstrued vision of what an early years setting looks like. We cannot reach everybody and inject them with the same excitement and irresistibility of teaching this age group as we might have, but we can invite them in to be part of the community. This is true of all early years settings, whether a pre-school, nursery or reception class. Our initiatives and projects, which exceed the number we have examined in this chapter, all seek to nurture a positive and proactive transitional attitude in which children of all ages and the adults who work with them have an understanding and interest in each other. Art projects are strong contenders in this transition as their production is visible and tangible to all participants. They are projects and initiatives that are owned by all involved and seek a mutually respectful attitude from all collaborators.

Jerome Bruner's passionate words underline this way of thinking:

> The most profound way in which respect between human beings shows itself is by taking to heart, taking seriously the meanings that each of us seeks to create from our experience of the world: the world of things and the world of people alike . . . The truest courtesy in human interaction and in pedagogy (which after all is just an extension of such interaction) is to help others discover what their

> experiences mean in their minds and hearts. And then helping them find richer, fuller, more communicable meanings . . . schools are communities, mutual communities of learners/doers/imaginers, all engaged in exploring the world of the possible, constructing new experiences . . . It is a community of mutual respect.
>
> (quoted in Filippini and Vecchi, 1996: 117)

Reflection

- Can you remember your early experiences in art and how your own journey developed and changed as you moved through the education system?
- Were there particular projects you can recall which retained your early enthusiasm for art?
- How does your setting promote visual and tactile art experiences across all age groups effectively?

Further reading

Bloomfield, A. and Childs, J. (2000) *Teaching Integrated Arts in the Primary School: Dance, Drama, Music and Visual Arts*, London: Fulton.

Cox, S. and Watts, R. (eds) (2007) *Teaching Art and Design 3–11*, London: Continuum.

Craft, A. (2005) 'Changes in the landscape for creativity in education', in Wilson, A. (ed.) *Creativity in Primary Education*, Exeter: Learning Matters.

Eisner, E. W. (2005) 'Reimaging Schools', *The Selected Works of Elliot. W. Eisner*, Oxon: Routledge

Fisher, J. (2010) *Moving on to Key Stage 1*, Maidenhead: Open University Press.

Key, P. and Stillman, J. (2009) *Teaching Primary Art and Design*, Exeter: Learning Matters.

Strozzi, P. and Vecchi, V. (eds) (2002) *Advisories*, Reggio Emilia, Italy: Reggio Children Publishers.

CHAPTER 8

A shared understanding

> We've made a gallery now at home, with all his pictures from nursery – just as good as the Tate!
>
> (Lucy, parent)

Introduction

Having examined the engagement of the 'teaching' adults, our attention turns to the 'home/family' adults. We now need to consider more closely the very important aspect of home as a branch of their developing artistic natures. An early years setting connects with this in order to promote and enjoy significant family partnerships and parent/carer relations where the primary carers are fully involved in their young artist's development.

A child's artistic journey is a testament to the many contributing factors that enter their young lives. The family home, a visit to a friend's, a walk with the dog, the climbing wall in the school garden or a drop of rain on the nose are all to be credited as part of life's experiences which infuse the child with ideas, creative thought and imaginative concepts. The incidents and events that fill a young child's life occur in all their various surroundings and daily existence. The social construct of their first few years is strongly reliant on who and what they come into contact with and how they pursue and develop that contact.

> Responsive and loving adults are crucial to all aspects of infant development. And you cannot overdose young infants with attention. Every time a baby receives a response to something she appears to need, the better.
>
> (Dowling, 2005: 22)

Significant others

Much of what we have discussed in the previous chapters is related, predominantly, to children's time spent within a setting and in relation to other human beings they reside and explore with during their shared hours in this space. What we also know, and are very sure of, is the fact that, as the brain develops, the influence of the engaged adults who surround young children can inspire and stimulate significant, lively, animated and puzzling opportunities. Such positive sociointeractivity aids the busy and ongoing connections in children's developing cognitive maps of thinking. These 'people' – significant adults, siblings, younger/older friends – come into contact with the young child in all their walks of life from birth. At this young age, their walks of life are overseen by those who watch over them. Outside of shopping trips, the cinema, theatre, granny's house, the park or a friend's garden, the two places where a young child spends the majority of their days are the home and the setting.

Learning to see what they see – parents' understanding of their children's art

We will, for good reason, consider a scenario that is negative as it may resonate with many a practitioner and is often the reason supplied to defend the existence of prescribed, tempered and controlled creative activities within settings. I have often visited settings where what I am shown as evidence of children's creative expression is actually evidence of the artistic capabilities of the practitioner. A wall display of 30 identical collaged fish; a portfolio of 'artwork' where colouring in photocopied images dominates, as well as role-play areas where scenery, masks, puppets, and other creative props have been beautifully constructed by the adults, *not* the children, are all examples of this. The latter role-play example not only excludes the involvement of the children but also creates a sense of territorial ownership on the part of the adult creator. Impeccably designed and window-dressed role-play areas are not child-friendly as they indicate the message: do not disturb!

This all sounds terribly negative and, of course, it is, but we need to face these realities if we want to dig deep and nurture a more honest approach to what constitutes children's creative and artistic spirits and how we value and nourish them. When those working in settings are asked why templates are produced, why the Mother's Day cards all need to be identically constructed, more often than not the answer is based in the idea of parents' expectations. Such expectations relate to what a parent understands art and creative expression to be in the early years. We are, of course, not talking about all parents and all practitioners. In fact, what we need to respect is that there are plenty of families out there who we work with who fully understand, enjoy and celebrate their child's creative endeavours. Duffy (1998: 134) reminds us: 'If parents feel confident that we are clear about what we are doing with their children and why we are doing it they will be reassured.'

Misunderstandings of an area of learning and stages of development are symptomatic of simply 'not knowing' and lack of experience. If we take time to explain, discuss and, importantly, share the artistic endeavours of young children with the family they live with, both home and setting can work together in the nourishment of the young artist. The connection of home–child–setting creates a supportive and encouraging triadic network where dialogue occurs, actions are observed and image-making is recognised. A triangular laboratory aids the adventures of the emerging artist and remains continuous and connected. The combination of the involved adults acknowledges and increases a child's self-esteem, offering positive and encouraging assurances to keep painting, drawing, sculpting. The support network also views the child as a holistic being who learns at home and away. Within such a secure but lively scenario, both experiences impinge on the other.

Sharing the results

As examined in Chapters 3 and 5 in particular, the development of art appreciation and aesthetic understanding can extend to the family. The role of the 'setting' adult engineers and extends discussion relating to the visual and tactile merits of a piece of artwork with a child, and this can also be mirrored with the 'home' adult. Previous dialogue with the child at the setting about their art will be followed through in the home environment and affords credence to a conversation between child and parent about the child's work. The words and vocabulary drawn out from a piece of artwork keeps it 'alive' in its aesthetic existence in the minds and eyes of both child and parent.

Pick-up time is not always conducive to a parent giving full attention – there are often many other things and issues to discuss and consider at this busy time, so we often see artwork gathered, folded and ignored. This is not always done with intentional negativity, but is a consequence of life's busyness. The often prolific production of artwork by a young child may also undermine the successes of what they produce in the eye of the parent, as there is always something to collect from the drying rack and the home box. The regularity of such prolific art-making can deprecate the recognition of significant pieces of work.

This commonly seen occurrence refers us back to the point of discussion in Chapter 4, when we looked at the need to retain artwork and display it on work-in-progress or child-initiated boards, shelves and washing lines. The artwork can be stored in portfolios or sketchbooks and then taken home at a later date with an annotated inscription to further inform the parent what it signifies.

By sharing artwork at appropriate moments, and enthusing, explaining and reflecting on the art, the parent can begin to appreciate the process and therefore understand the true nature of young children's art.

Understanding 'Expressive Arts and Design'

Discussion and practical shared enjoyment of a piece of artwork enhances parental appreciation. Encouraging parental participation offers the 'home' adults the opportunity to experience art and therefore gain a much more personal and involved insight and understanding about what expressive arts actually mean in the development of a young child. It is important to share with parents the 'experiential' nature of this area of learning so that the process becomes key in their understanding of how children explore and develop. The revised EYFS (2012) sets out key paths towards learning in a creative and critical way, where children explore, play and make choices. This exploratory path can also be experienced by the parent through activity sessions, sharing events, art-based projects and home–school initiatives. Sharing practical experience emphasises the multi-faceted 'process' of art and clarifies the reasons for a less structured approach which is sometimes alien to an adult way of thinking.

Intergenerational dialogue and enjoyment

For some parents, school will seem like a long and distant memory and for others their vague recollection of art might be that of a secondary art classroom where the omnipresent atmosphere was that of prescription and expected 'ways of doing'. The haptically rich experiences expended through printing experiments, clay investigation and woodcarving may not have featured in their own art education, so their knowledge can only be based on the experiences they had. Of course, as many of us know, our former childhood experiences can colour our interpretations of learning as adults and the premise of art is undeniably contained within this uncomfortable conundrum. Not only is it an area of learning where we will have had a variety of experiences, it is one that expects us, in its 'expressive' nature, to expose ourselves with more than usual candour. Baring soul and spirit is something, as we have acknowledged, that young children are able to do happily, easily, willingly and, importantly, often unconsciously.

This last consideration is what can stall parents, because, as adults, we become much more conscious of our acts. To engage in an art activity is not something we all feel inclined towards nor comfortable with. Included in this personally emotive tangle is the end product discussion once again. The tangle can be unpicked and offered up as exciting, tangible and enticing if it is seen as play and exploratory adventure. Playing with the art is something we can all do and our participation with this play will diffuse the heavy, burdensome and anxiety-ridden 'end product' preconceptions based on previous experiences. The more we play in this manner, the more we understand the process.

We can now consider some examples of what is possible in order to develop successful and positive family partnerships in young children's journeys as artists. The examples are all tried and tested and, importantly, they include the potential participation of all family members.

Shared moments: connecting home to school

To consider the child as a very young infant in the home environment is beneficial to our study here. The baby who learnt to become part of the world we live in did so through interaction with the human beings around him or her. Learned gestures, expressions and mannerisms are idiosyncratically owned but their existence came about as much through nurture as nature.

> Within a very short period of time babies are 'reading' eye contacts, facial and body gestures and the tone of voice of those significant people who care for them . . . My experience tells me that these are the small individuals who have already had their early attempts at conversation valued; they quickly learn that what they do and the sounds they make are of interest to adults, and they want more of this affirming experience.
>
> (Dowling, 2005: 23)

Consider the mother and child who 'tune into each other' (Anning and Ring, 2004). As they exchange facial expressions and participate in interactive rituals and movement games, the child and parent learn something more about each other. Their interaction is saturated with multiple examples of sensory exploration, particularly the tactile modality that began as part of pre-natal existence. Goddard-Blythe (2004: 194) discusses the very powerful role of the maternal parent within the security of the domain and through the communication of touch: 'at the beginning of post-natal life, touch begins with the mother – nature's universal teacher'.

With each encounter they have their rituals but they find a few other elements to add in. Each interpersonal 'melody exchange' (Matthews, 2003) ensures another layer of shared understanding. This dyadic experience is very much in existence within the secure home environment, where rituals and routines abound, as does the familiarity of continuities and commonalities associated with objects, spaces and activities. The transitional journey of home to school requires the young child to familiarise themselves with a whole *new* set of continuities and commonalities which are accommodated within the domain of the setting. They will need to use what they have learnt and experienced at home and transfer these skills into a different environment but without the physical presence of the familiar parent to tune into.

We know, as examined in Chapter 4, how important the engagement of the adult in the setting is to the learning journey of our young artists. If the appropriate skills are applied, as discussed, we can be assured that the transitional bridge between home and setting will be acknowledged and scaffolded carefully and consistently. But what we also want to ensure is that the presence of the parent and the very important early intersubjective existence that the child experiences is somehow retained and reflected within the setting. Creating opportunities for the parent to be involved in the setting and encouraging moments when 'tuning in' happens within this more public space are key to transitional bridge-building.

The parent and child's shared moments in the setting allow for an atmosphere that fosters security and focussed engagement. If we now specifically consider this within the domain of paired art-making, we can also grant the additional aspect of emotion within our understanding. As child and parent undertake a shared art moment, they tune in with an unspoken but very present emotional security. An intergenerational exchange where attention to a set of materials within an art-based exploration is a two-way process can provide a source of emotional security, which enhances further motivation for learning. The tuning in that happens so crucially at home and from birth is now continuing into the educational environment. With appropriate engagement, a 'teaching' adult can effect a security for the child as they imagine, make and create, but the emotional security cannot match that of the engaged 'parent' adult.

Matthews (1999: 161) says of such rich joint journeys:

> Both infant and mother share a field of view which is also a field of action. This consists not only of the physical surface of the paper, the pots of paint and brushes and so on, it is also a window opening onto a variety of potential but unknown futures – neither mother nor child has any idea where the painting will go.

We are reminded here of the wonderful sense of surprise that lies at the heart of art exploration (Eisner, 2005) – the astounding anticipation of the journey is now also being experienced by the parent.

Joint reflections and perspectives

Joint adventures will help to inform and transform the reflections of the 'home' adult on their child's art. The setting is helping to provide a space 'where children feel confident that people will take their drawings seriously, and where it would be unheard of for a child's drawing to be dismissed as mere scribbling' (Matthews, 1994: 24). 'Seriously' is an important word here, as a joint quest is one where both parties – parent and child – are responsible for what they do and see. Their analysis will reflect both their endeavours, and so the actual effort in performance can be proudly felt by the adult as well as the child – a resounding acknowledgement that there is nothing 'mere' about it at all.

Consider the following shared dialogue in Box 8.1 as Madison (4 years and 8 months) and her mother discuss issues whilst they make a dinosaur out of clay. Their thoughts turn to shape, form and proportional hypotheses in relation to the sculptural features.

Important hierarchical affectations can emerge from the child's perspective during active engagement with their parent during an art-based exploration. Sharing creative moments such as these happens in a space that is far more familiar to the child than their parent. From a territorial perspective, these settings belong to the children, not to the parents, for the former are the frequenters and protagonists of these spaces. The encounters that take place in these spaces are shared, but there will be a tip in the balance of the child's familiar reconnaissance as they 'know' where the art materials are; where a particular object

Box 8.1 Madison and her mum sculpt a dinosaur

Madison: Is your tummy the main part of your body?

Mum: Well, it's kind of the middle of your body, isn't it?

Madison: *(Looking down at her own body and then the body of the emerging dinosaur.)* Yes, it's here. *(She moves her hands up and down to show the central space of her torso.)*

Mum: Yes, I suppose because it's the middle part, most things come off it don't they?

Madison: No, not everything, look my head comes off my neck, not my tummy. *(Laughs as she gestures to her body parts.)*

Box 8.2 Some shared activities to offer moments of interactivity between parent and child

These experiences are inviting, accessible and very sensorially explorative in their nature so as to encourage dialogue and shared discoveries:

- Modelling with playdough/clay.
- Adding to playdough: glitter, beads, rice etc.
- Cutting and folding paper structures.
- Drawing and narrating to one another.
- Threading and weaving; inside and outside.
- Printing shapes and patterns.

is; where best to sit and such acts of accustomed understanding. The knowledge of the setting is interpreted by them to their parent, and such a shift of power affords a further arm of security and allows self-esteem to grow. The art-based joint involvement episodes see the child taking the lead. As the child presides in this role, their own knowledge deepens. Informing and guiding the adult reaffirms what they already know and roots itself well and truly in their repertoire of understanding.

Intergenerational projects

An approach embracing family inclusivity will see the participation of grandparents, who are often among the child's main caregivers. The rich intergenerational dialogue grandparents have with their grandchildren enables both age groups to share experiences from the past and the present.

A memorable feature of the excellent creative early years settings in Reggio Emilia is the presence of the grandparent. In these settings, the grandparent is often the family member who drops the child off at the setting in the morning and picks him or her up at the end of the day. These older members of the family are extraordinarily involved in this particular and unique educational system. But we have also seen a shift in our own culture where reports (e.g. Statham, 2011) reveal how grandparents play a prominent role in providing childcare and supporting maternal employment, especially for low-income families. Their role and involvement in childcare is key in the early development of their young grandchildren. Within our early years settings we have the opportunity to invest value, interest in and respect for these senior members of the family in an intergenerational context. Invitations to participate in their grandchildren's development in the settings may include offering opportunities to experience art-making and artistic adventure. It is an avenue that, as we well know, includes play as this is actually something grandparents have often come round to enjoying again later in their life. A return to understanding the special and magical moments in life can re-emerge as they watch and experience life through their young grandchildren. My own children's grandparents are visibly rejuvenated in the presence of their grandchildren, as they enjoy their playful and innocent adventures.

Case study 1: The paper room

Baker *et al.* describe an inspirational grandparent–child project in the edited book *In the Spirit of the Studio* (Gandini, 2005). The 'paper room' is a space-related activity that was designed to be enjoyed and explored by both the older and the younger generation. A room in this particular setting had been filled with a variety of white paper; rolls of wallpaper and frieze paper, tissue, crepe, thick and thin, smooth and rough sheets of all varying sizes, had been found and laid out horizontally and vertically so that the entire space was a zone of paper structure. Joint participation and adventure was experienced during the session and many comments and observations were made. The following comment clearly captures the rich influences of these shared and unusual moments:

> Grandparents watched as the children played with the paper, and a few of the braver grandparents ventured into the paper room to play with their grandchildren. Later, a grandmother told us that for most of her life she had always found pleasure in writing handwritten notes and letters to her family and friends, but after her experience in the paper room that morning, she would never write another letter without feeling the paper's texture and observing the way the ink seeps into its fibres. Her experience with the children had taught her . . . to appreciate the small, beautiful things in life.
>
> (Baker *et al.*, cited in Gandini, 2005: 18)

Case study 2: My street

In this particular setting, there was a very strong presence of the 'grandparent'. The numbers who dropped the children off and picked up at the end of the session were high. The setting was keen to celebrate their involvement and also draw on their long and various experiences. The children had been discussing their local area and had been on study walks to sketch features of interest that they found in the local streets. They had specifically been drawing and image-making large-scale pieces with charcoal and chalk for a few days, both inside and outside the setting. They had also been making use of the photographic images they had collected.

Grandparents were then invited to join in with the charcoal investigations and, with the children, created big friezes of the streets they lived in. The invitation and session planning led to a consideration of space, furniture and resources as mobility and physical implications came into play. Mindful that the floor work that the children had been involved in may not be appropriate for their more elderly carers, a variety of creative spaces was established to cater for all physical needs.

The outcome of the shared session was a rich reflection of both generations' input, combining the physical ability and somatic adventures of the children and the historical and geographical knowledge of the grandparents. This image-making activity allowed reciprocal participation in a meaningful experience that led to engagement in self-discovery through experimentation with materials and a chance to build a bridge of relationships across the age span. Their magnificent street scenes were testament to both parties' involvement. Their pride and enjoyment in this shared moment continued way beyond the realms of the actual activity. The outcome was to be celebrated and referred to in the successive weeks as displays were erected inside and outside the setting, parents were shown the work and the dialogue continued.

These case studies reflect richly historical and culturally bound opportunities where settings have acknowledged the role of the grandparent in the developing understanding and experiences of their grandchildren's creative time outside of the home.

Sketchbooks: home/school

A further initiative in our commitment to sharing the art experience with families and strengthening the transitional bridge between home and setting is the use of sketchbooks. The naming of such an initiative will come in many shapes and forms, but we will refer to it as 'sketchbook' here in order to evoke its rich significance. The sketchbook, as examined in Chapter 4, is a secure 'place' for thinking through ideas. It is also a 'scrapbook' where imagination is viewed, in both process-driven evidence and end product. Whatever the title adopted or the contents of this sketchbook, it is a visually rich tool which houses the ideas and workings of the young artist. As such it is a very personal and historical possession.

A sketchbook can be shared between home and school so that the child's continuing ideas can be included from these two domains. The sketchbook may contain drawings, collages, photographs of collections, models and scenes captured. The components are considered for inclusion by the owner of the sketchbook, and these take many shapes and forms. The content will be a combination of moments encountered in both places – home and setting – and, therefore, will emphasise a strong connectivity where borders have been crossed and, importantly, merged. Acknowledgement by adults in both domains will give rise to dialogue stimulated by the contents and so the discussions will also draw on this important connectivity. A child at home may be very different to the child they are in a setting and so, too, may their imagination and art explorations. The sketchbook of art will help us in some way to understand and appreciate these two different personas.

An additional aspect of sketchbook sharing is the potential involvement of the sibling. A brother or sister's own interest and input may somehow feature within the work collected within 'the sketchbook at home'. Siblings are, of course, highly influential in the young life of a young artist and so this may well have some bearing on the content whilst the sketchbook is in use in the home environment.

We witness in Box 8.3 a snapshot of such a sibling dialogue. Amongst the many battles of status and equality common to sibling relationships, familiar to us all, there also exists an amazingly powerful communicative reciprocation. At times, such dialogue excludes the adult and the language used is evidence of a relationship closer than any other in a young child's life as it represents the other child they live and breathe their experiences alongside. As Sophie (aged ten) and Jake (aged four) draw a large-scale picture of 'the world' – the incentive

Box 8.3 Sophie and Jake discuss who holds the world

Sophie: When I was little, I thought England was really small because it all looks small if you look at the map. But it isn't small and the world is really big – it's just the picture is small.

Jake: (*Thinking about this for a long time.*) But is there someone who holds up the world?

Sophie: Well, do you think anyone would be strong enough and big enough?

Jake: No . . . well apart from Captain America . . . he is really, really big and really strong too, and his mates.

Sophie: Yes, but is he real?

Jake: Yes because he is Captain America, he is the captain of America. Him and his mates are really strong.

coming from the older child's school-based investigations in a geography topic – understandings and perceptions of the enormity of the world enter their dialogue.

Photo diaries

In keeping with our theme of home–setting connectivity in art exploration, a photo diary can also be considered as a conduit of this. Diaries are begun at the setting, continue in the home environment and are returned to the setting. This journey reveals a richly visual and holistic documentation of a child's imaginative life along with those other influential beings that feature within the framework. The different places and experiences graphically featured in the diary sequentially present episodes in the life of the whole child. The photography itself offers a form of art that requires choice, selection and decisiveness in its execution and so moments are captured by the child and serve as narratives to be discussed in the triangulation of parent–child–practitioner.

These pictorial and personally produced diaries will always remain as historical evidence of the world captured through the child's eyes. Sharing such photographs allows us, the adults, to see the magical moments of life and existence as perceived by the children. This again reminds us of sharing the pleasures of seeing again with refreshed eyes and revisiting those rich sensory experiences of which we talked earlier in the book.

Portfolios and exhibitions

We consider here the following statement written by an art therapist when in dialogue about how we respond to children's artwork:

> Remarks made by a parent can have an impact on children's desire and motivation to make art; even the most well-meaning parent has, on occasion, misinterpreted the content of a child's drawing, perhaps unknowingly discouraging the child from continuing to draw.
>
> (Anning and Ring, 2004: 22)

We have examined the issue of response and 'praise' from the position of a supportive adult within the setting in Chapter 4. This also needs to be related to how parents respond to their child's artwork and art adventures. Banal statements and perfunctory praise is recognised as such by the child who offers their art to a parent. Encouraging responses that look deeper into the experience itself, and that serve as audience appreciation of the artistic elements involved in the spectacle, is what we can aid parents to do. Positive dialogue such as this can be aided in specific events such as art exhibitions, but also on a more regular basis through the sharing of portfolios of work.

Art exhibition

The invitation of an exhibition alone serves an important purpose. It raises art-making to a public level of appreciation where people are invited to browse, muse over and celebrate the development of young artists. Spaces exhibiting work become the gallery where visual and tactile elements are taken seriously by the adults in the room as the children lead tours of their work, entering into dialogue about the how, why, what and when of their artwork. Some settings have gone so far as to sell the work to the parents (a perfectly valid fundraiser!) and so the exchange gives credibility to the magnificence of the artwork being purchased. It is a lovely role-play in which both adults and children can participate. Inclusion of video excerpts at such events reveals to the parents a bird's-eye view of their child engaged in art play at a time when they would not normally be present. It is an opportunity to witness their child existing creatively and securely in an environment. Such footage is often welcomed by the parent in order to 'know' the child at the setting as opposed to the child at home.

Sharing portfolios

In Chapter 4, we gave some consideration to the experience of children's self-assessment and self-awareness of their own progression in art, through sketchbooks, displays, collaborative discussion and dialogue. We are reminded of this once more in relation to the involvement of parents in the assessment process. I am not suggesting in any shape or form that parents make decisions about what stage of development their child is at, and in doing so become restricted by notions of progress and developmental expectations. Their involvement is represented by the joint dialogic analysis that takes place between child and parent when they discuss the various pieces of evidence stored and collated by the child in their portfolios. The portfolios may contain any sort of evidence related to a child's art journey:

- paintings;
- drawings;
- photographs of sculptural explorations;
- rubbings;
- designs;
- textile art;
- prints;
- collages.

What is important here is that the portfolio contains the child's learning moments and interests and is therefore the property of the child. If it is owned by them, it must always be accessible to them. During a visit to a kindergarten in southern Sweden, I observed a very special moment between a parent and a child as they sat together in a big armchair and shared the child's portfolio, which had been started a few weeks prior to this occasion. The interlude was made even more pertinent as the family had arrived from Turkey a couple of months previously. Neither the child nor the mother had spoken any Swedish prior to their arrival in the country. Their shared dialogue whilst looking through the book was conducted in their mother tongue, but the portfolio gave them a reason to sit together and share the art experience that had taken place in the Swedish nursery. The portfolio offered a link between parent and setting and the connection created an opportunity for the child and her mother to contemplate and appreciate the child's recent art endeavours. The dialogue involved much body language – pointing, gesturing in acknowledgement – as well as moments of appreciative silence as they perused the content.

Such shared moments present real opportunities for parental understanding of their child's art development and, crucially, within the context of their age. They provide visual access to who the young artist is at this moment in their childhood. Such celebration of the 'present-day child' is to be valued and encouraged for as long as possible so that we, as collective adults, enjoy the child and their art for who they are *today*.

Continual work in progress: small moments of sharing

Successful partnerships can be encouraged through small, regular snapshots of sharing. These take many shapes and forms but it is the regularity and accessibility of the initiative that is key. If the activity is inviting as it continues to develop, the progress will be both influenced and witnessed by child and parent. Living and growing artworks are exciting and stimulating ventures that are fascinating in their evolving form to all involved. They offer opportunities for ongoing visual and tactile projects that invite all to join in on a regular basis.

Some examples of these are as follows:

Box 8.4 Wishing tree

A place where ideas and dreams are written or drawn and then hung on a tree (real or created by children and adults). The contributions are made by everyone at the setting: staff, children and families. Additions can be made in response to any particular occasion or are made on a regular basis. From time to time the contributions are shared as a group to form a rich dialogue around parent–child aspirations.

Box 8.5 Wall of colour – mood histories

This is a wall designated to patches of colour extending over time as children and parents create their own favourite colour of the day. The colour may be inspired by mood, emotions or shared experiences. The patch can be coloured with a chosen material: pastels, inks, paints, pencil marks – all are welcome. The wall can be returned to on a regular basis or just as a one-off experience, depending on the choices of child and parent. It will be a wall that changes from day to day as it grows in size, colour and shades. It will visually tell a hundred stories about its makers. It is a wall steeped in their families' emotional and cultural heritages that exist in the setting.

Box 8.6 Living sculptures – growing, collaborative endeavours

A living sculpture is an aesthetically pleasing and growing sculpture which is the investment of each and every child and a member of their family. The sculpture is made of bricks with holes and inside the holes are planted seeds. The seeds are regularly watered and the plants start to grow out of the brick holes. The living bricks sit side by side or on top of one another in a variety of chosen sculptural configurations. The growth and development of the living sculpture not only depends on the nurturing of the child/parent gardener but also has a collegiate dependency as each brick forms a collaborative whole.

Box 8.7 Expanding mosaics – collections and connections

A project that extends over a period of time is the expanding mosaic. The mosaic may be flat or covering a piece of furniture. The essence of the mosaic is that all its components have been collected and brought in by child and parent. The components can be anything collected from home: beads, buttons, tiles, badges, material pieces, old toothbrushes, pebbles, pens – a whole weird and wonderful myriad of found objects. The mosaic's evolving design depends on what is brought in and it will be the choice of the whole setting and all those involved as to when the mosaic collection is complete and the making can take place. Continually adding to the mosaic once it has been constructed will not 'spoil' the final effect as finality is not necessarily a feature. It is an aesthetically dynamic art piece, the installation of which is ongoing and develops with the different generations of children who enter the setting. It is a culturally rich masterpiece that tells a historical story of the connection between setting and home and of all its past and present occupants.

Box 8.8 Artwork shared – home and school

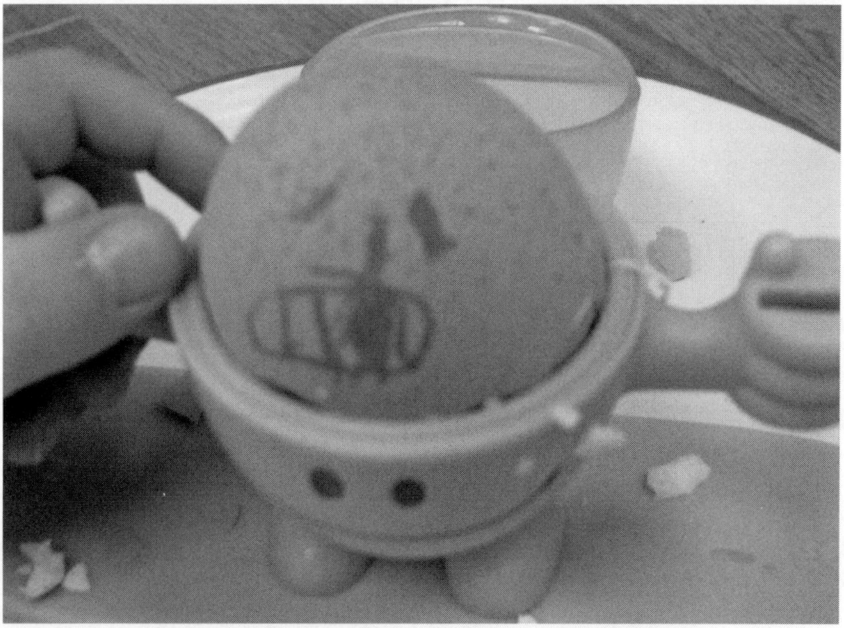

Figure 8.1 Mark-making at home

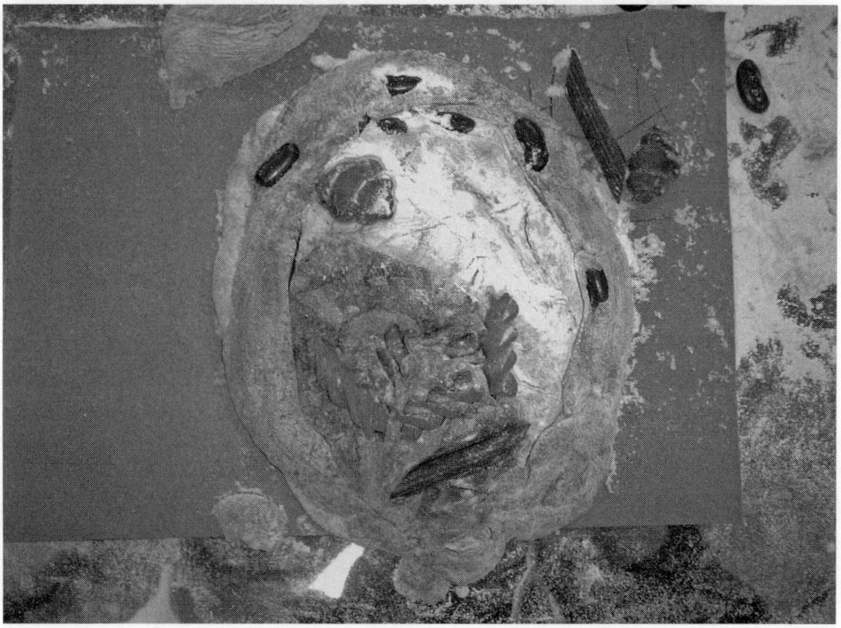

Figure 8.2 A 'happy dad' made from salt

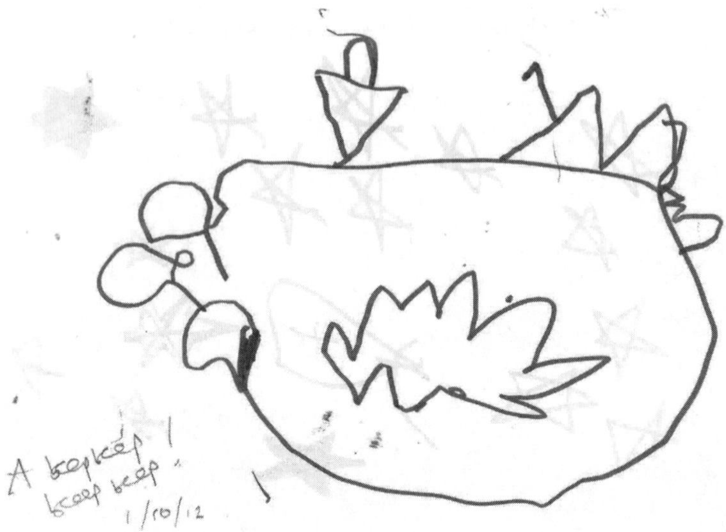

Figure 8.3 A beep beep beep beep

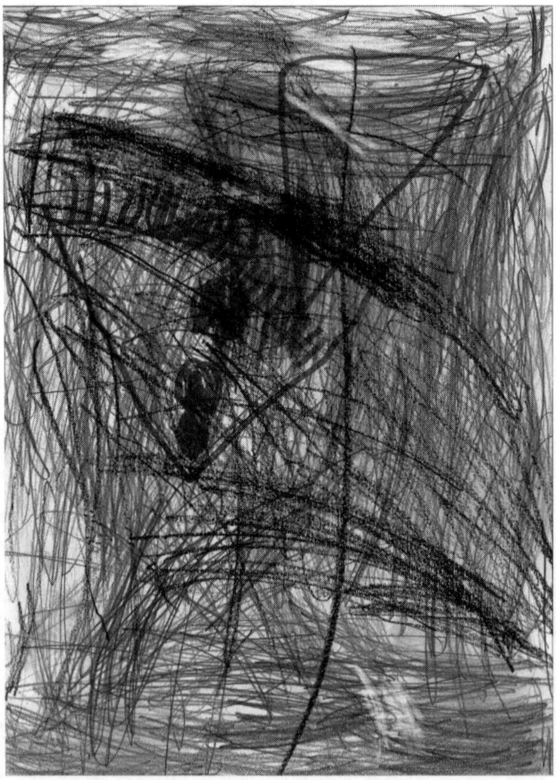

Figure 8.4 Angry sky

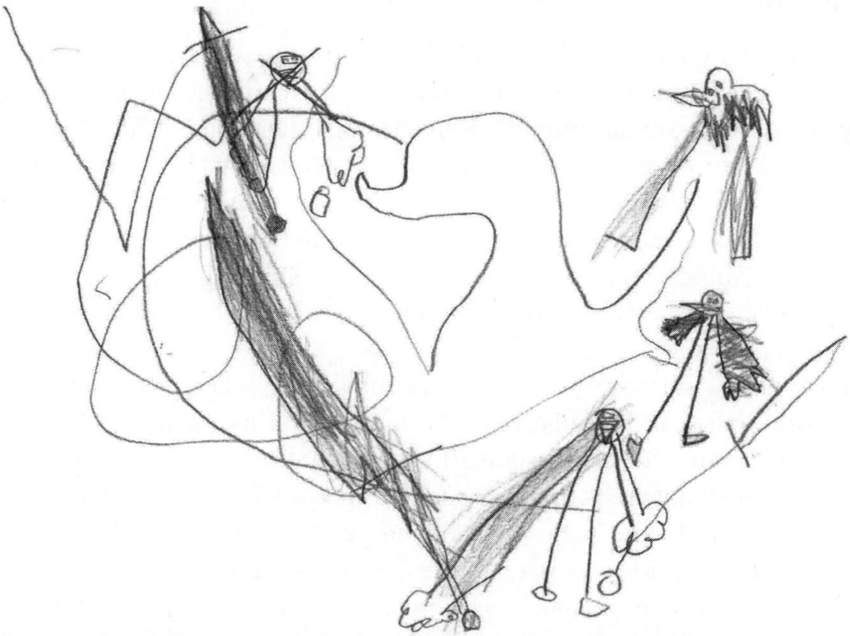

Figure 8.5 Fighting

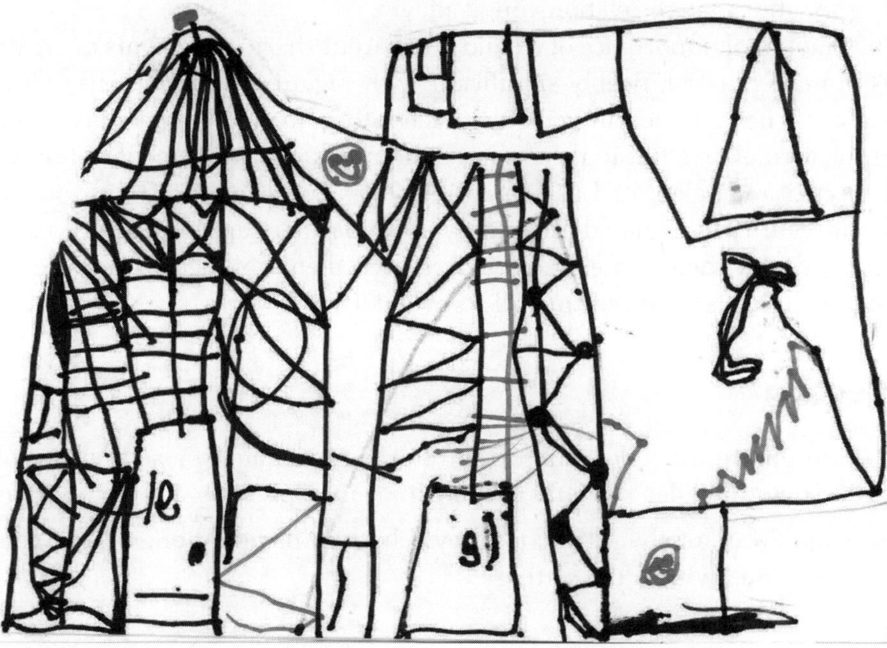

Figure 8.6 Scaffolding and stairs

Conclusion

We conclude this chapter with a reminder of abstract and awareness sensing, as discussed previously in the chapter. This very personalised sense is a quality we all possess – it is about our relationship with the moment, the experience of who we are in that given time span. If we consider this 'felt' sense existing alongside the rich engagement of an adult, we can surmise that a deep and at times elaborate conjoining will be taking place. The heightened sense of awareness – the two minds and bodies thinking and feeling together – will further enhance the development and understanding of the given moments and the discoveries that ensue.

We have also considered the issue of 'intersubjectivity' (Trevarthen and Aitken, 2001) as both bodies and minds share the motive of a moment's exploration in art-making. The joint sharing episode affords a joint understanding and requires a level of interpersonal skills that has been at play since the relationship started – presumably from birth, in the case of the parent. Such a rich interpersonal ability is further enhanced if opportunities are recognised and offered within a setting for the family and child. It is a joint journey that began at the child's point of entry into the world and one that can be welcomed and continued with vigour and enthusiasm to connect art experience in the setting and art experiences at home. The intersubjectivity of these moments allows for both collaborators to have an intimate understanding of one another's minds – an empowering feeling for the creative relationship at play.

The emotional importance of a child and parent sharing moments of creativity is, as aforementioned, deeply significant with regards to attachment and independence. They are learning about each other in a different environment from their usual one. But in these shared moments, the attachment to the parent is respected and celebrated as something that allows for a soft and nurturing sense of security in a shared art activity. Both partners are feeding off a mutual attachment and their shared experiences give them courage to venture on in search of the delights of art and all its wonders.

Reflection

- What opportunities do you currently orchestrate at your setting to ensure positive and regular parental participation in expressive arts and design?
- Are you aware of the artistic journeys children have at home but which are not discussed within the setting?

Further reading

Clarke, M. (2007) *Involving Parents in their Children's Learning*, London: Sage.
Gopnik, A., Meltzoff, A. and Kuhl, P. (2001) *The Scientist in the Crib*, New York: HarperCollins.
Malloch, S. and Trevarthen, C. (2010) *Communicative Musicality: Exploring the Basis of Human Companionship*, Oxford: Oxford University Press.
Matthews, J. (1994) *Helping Young Children to Paint and Draw: Children and Visual Representation*, London: Hodder and Stoughton.
Ring, K. (2006) 'What mothers do: Everyday routines and rituals and their impact upon young children's use of drawing for meaning making', *International Journal of Early Years Education*, 14(1): 63–84.

CHAPTER 9

Artists
An external dynamic

I think the strength of the continuous relationship between atelierista [artist working in the setting] and the children is that it has generated a style of thinking that goes beyond the sociological nature of the classroom and permeates the entire environment . . .

(Vea Vecchi, Crossing Borders conference, 2004)

Introduction

In this chapter we consider some of the benefits to be had from inviting artists into settings by focussing on two case studies in particular. The purpose of inclusion of these projects is to provide an insight into the legacy of outreach art, where the expert works within the community of the setting, influencing and opening up alternative possibilities in art-thinking that may not have come to fruition otherwise. We can reflect individually in respect of our various settings and communities as we consider the many aspects that will arise in reading the case studies, but presented is a generic set of issues that relate to all the examples critiqued:

- artists working with children;
- artists working with practitioners;
- the legacy of the work.

An artist-in-residence

Artists-in-residency is not a new innovation only just discovered. Successful projects have been in existence for many years, involving professional artists who work with children in a variety of educational settings. Artists, musicians, dancers and actors, to name but a few, engage with children, teachers/practitioners and families to lend a professional and expert knowledge to expressive disciplines.

However, such practice has, in the last ten years or so, grown in popularity within early years settings, perhaps as a result of the good practice we have come to know from Reggio Emilia nurseries, and perhaps additionally because educationalists' overall awareness of early years as a deserved beneficiary of such creative outreach has increased. Whatever the reason, initiatives have been introduced to raise the profile of art in early years through the employment of professional artists in many early years settings up and down the country. Innovative projects, often funded by Creative Partnerships and programmes initiated with Arts Council money, for example, have aided this very worthy and positive move.

The role of the artist

First, we have to consider why we want to invite artists into our setting. If we feel confident that we are operating in a positive, productive and dynamic forum of art on a regular basis, what would be the benefits of adding another string to this already rich bow and what role would an artist have within our spaces and activities for young artists? We have, throughout the book, been very clear about the confident, child-initiated direction of embryonic art-making. Accessible spaces to encourage independent creative thinkers, the appropriate engagement of the interested adult and the appreciation and longevity of process are to name but a few. The inclusion of a professional artist must work concurrently with what we have set up in line with all our ongoing considerations.

An artist is not invited in to direct, to model or to be copied, or to undermine the inspiration of the adults who work within the setting. Their presence invites a 'something else' which can only be defined by the practice and character of the particular professional. Their provocative engagement with the children potentiates others ways of thinking and challenges some of the norms that we accidentally, through time and habit, become too comfortable with and accustomed to.

> Artists offer children provocations and challenges to create interventions that playfully expand and add dimension to the focus of interest. The emphasis is on children initiating ideas with the artist. This approach develops observant systems that prioritise children's engagement, curiosity, communication, theories, exchanges and learning dispositions.
>
> (Fawcett and Hay, 2004: 239)

The artist provides a set of new opportunities for the children, and different ways of seeing and interacting for the adults. His or her presence lends an air of confidence to art-making in the very fact that he or she is a professional artist whose self-recognition of being such suggests the status of the role within this discipline. Working with an artist can highlight different skills in the children that may not have been seen before. An artist can, importantly, challenge assumptions and this is dynamic, exciting and rewarding; live art in the making at the setting ensures vibrancy in the art of the here and now.

A further dynamic is the important contribution an artist can make towards young children's developing understanding of cultural enquiry and critical reflection. Bloomfield and Childs (2000) refer to this as the cultural context of the visual art mode. Opportunities within this construct include the invitation of artists into schools and settings, work produced by practising artists displayed in the environment, and also the importance of art gallery visits outside of the educational establishment.

> The vibrancy of children's own art work is enhanced when they become sensitively aware and appreciative of other works of art that somehow relate to their own work and will be linked to what is known about selected historical, social, cultural, philosophical, or aesthetic aspects of painting, sculpture, architecture, industrial design or photography.
>
> (Bloomfield and Childs, 2000: 94)

A fluid environment

In striving for success in an artist-in-setting project, consideration of time is essential to build up a relationship between the artist and the staff. Recognition and appreciation of mutual understanding, trust, collaboration and support are vital aspects of this dynamic. Both artist and practitioners have separate skills, knowledge and abilities which when merged and combined can lead to surprising and innovative outcomes. We often have the opportunity to celebrate and explore the enquiring minds of children, but we do not spend adequate time in consideration of our adult enquiring minds. A practitioner who is infused with ideas, inspiration and incentive as a result of partnered investigation and discussion is one who continues to invest dynamic and creative professionalism into their practice. We are reminded of our own need to be refreshed, reinvigorated and 'disturbed' out of a linear equilibrium and not only do we benefit from this, but so do our children.

In the Open Sesame project (Box 9.1), both artists and practitioners discussed the refreshing reward of 'going with the flow' and seeing how things turned out. A supportive environment was seen to be helpful in having a more responsive and less structured approach. It is important to establish a 'safe' environment where staff and children feel comfortable and free to express themselves in a range of ways.

The art-making sessions entrenched within a residency are often fluid and responsive, where the relationships of all involved are based on respect and reciprocity. As sessions are organised and discussed, suggestions, re-shaping ideas, joining different ideas together and coming up with variations of the original ideas combine within a collaboratively responsive atmosphere.

Box 9.1 Open Sesame

> It opened doors for the staff and children . . . it liberated us to take more risks.
>
> It was brilliant being in such a process-led environment so that you didn't always feel under pressure.
>
> (Early years practitioner)

In 2010–11, a project called 'Open Sesame' ran in Sussex where artists worked with early years practitioners in their settings, supported by a series of creative 'masterclasses' where new creative practice was modelled and explored. The programme was evaluated and it was found that the project broke through 'inhibitions' towards expression of 'self' and ideas in creative activities.

Six artists worked with one or two nurseries each, visiting them on a weekly basis over a four-month period. The artists all had different skills and the nurseries explored music, dance, stories, shadows and light, links between inside and outside and making 3D spaces. The longevity of the project afforded time for the artist and

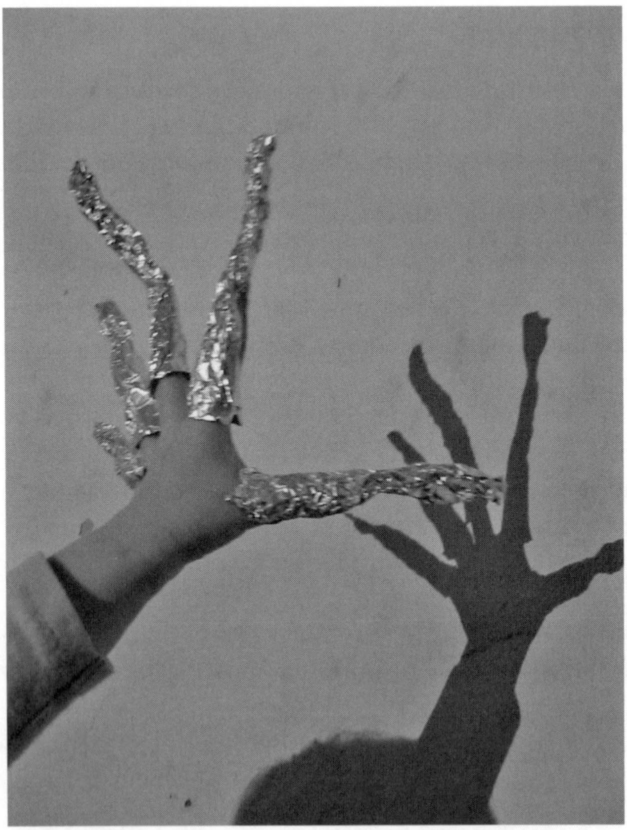

Figure 9.1 Exploring shadows and light in Open Sesame

early years practitioner to form a supportive, positive relationship. This was felt to be key in creating a supportive environment, where children and practitioners could build their confidence in being creative, and feel safe enough to try things at which they may fail.

The following aspects of the project were recognised as successes:

- There was evidence of shared sustained thinking in the dialogic approach and spiritual development in the expressive and sensory nature of arts and creativity.
- Self-esteem was raised for artists, early years practitioners and the children.
- Positive relationships developed between children, staff and artists, as emotions were shared and acknowledged, which enabled everyone to have a sense of freedom, which is necessary for problem-solving skills to develop.
- The artists going into the settings, the ongoing relationships of the artists in the settings and the creation of a community of learning that supported experiential learning which promoted a 'playful pedagogy'.
- The early years practitioners were supported and took creative risks which, in turn, supported children's own risk-taking and their ability to learn from doing so.
- The value of cross-professional working and opportunities for early years practitioners, settings and wider family/community to make contact with the creative and cultural sector.

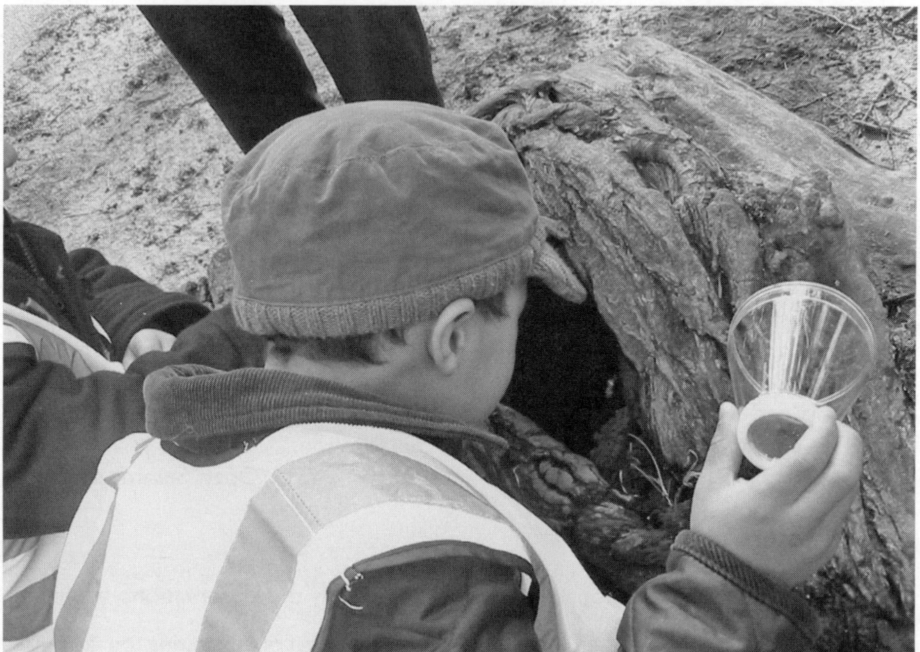

Figure 9.2 Bug hunting

- The benefits of using simple materials and the possibilities for learning, creativity and play offered by them.
- Observations of children during the project are evidence of holistic learning and show that (in child development terms) they were given a high level of opportunity for exploration and manipulation with a variety of resources: they engaged for long periods of time (giving greater opportunity for learning/cognitive development); they were learning by observing others; they were being supported in their schemas; they were learning through listening and socialising.

Impact on the practitioners

Staff in the early years settings felt that working with an artist helped them to become more confident in trying things out. They became more open in not knowing what the outcomes would be, as well as accruing more playful approaches to use with the children, not only as activities but for warm-ups with the staff and children.

In some of the nurseries members of staff were observed to be distracted by other children who were not participating and also to feel underconfident in 'letting go' of learned disciplines. Staff training sessions before the workshops aided an increased confidence in their willingness to get involved in creative activities. In order for the school and nurseries to benefit on a long-term basis, it was recognised that the staff could learn new techniques and skills alongside the artist, which could then be utilised and revisited in the future. Staff and settings acknowledged the need to ensure adequate time was set aside for practitioners to join in freely with the activities, unencumbered by their routines and duties.

> I need time to play myself and time for conversations.
>
> (Early years practitioner)

Impact on the artists

Artists in this project have found it to be an incredibly enriching experience working with early years children.

> It is hard to predict how young children will react to different things, and I think this is part of the learning journey for me. I love to find out what children are interested in, what they enjoy doing and what they think about. My creative journey is to work alongside early years children using a range of tools and skills to help them explore and examine the world around them and to create new things based on their exploration.
>
> (Open Sesame artist)

Impact on the children

There were many key developmental advantages from the observations made:

- The length of time that children were engaged or concentrating on activities was increased; this was also intrinsic or self-motivated.
- Development of schemas was evident as children were encouraged to develop their imaginations through stories and positive relationships.

- Fantasy and imaginative worlds were encouraged and psychologically this is a positive developmental need.
- Social skills were observably increased. The whole project revolved around all participants developing confidence in 'self' and sharing their experiences. This interconnectedness of self and others was holistic in nature and increased an atmosphere of 'innovative' people.

The children have more confidence to work on a larger scale and working collaboratively on their own ideas such as building dens together. They developed fine motor skills in cutting, rolling etc. They explored new materials and different kinds of spaces. They worked with a wide range of materials – clay, sticks, boxes, charcoal, paper structures, found objects from the woods such as conkers and other natural materials – and this extended their knowledge greatly, as did making and building a fire, which helped develop their imaginative skills, e.g. the fire became a dragon – one child said, 'Look, my friends, it is the dragon's fire!'

(Early years practitioner)

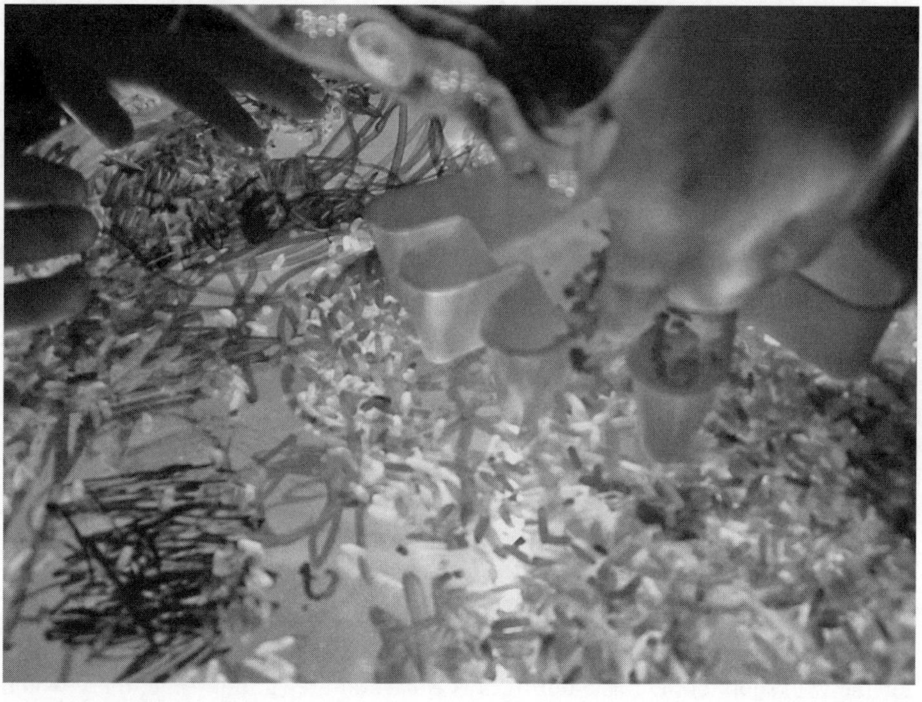

Figure 9.3 Exploring materials

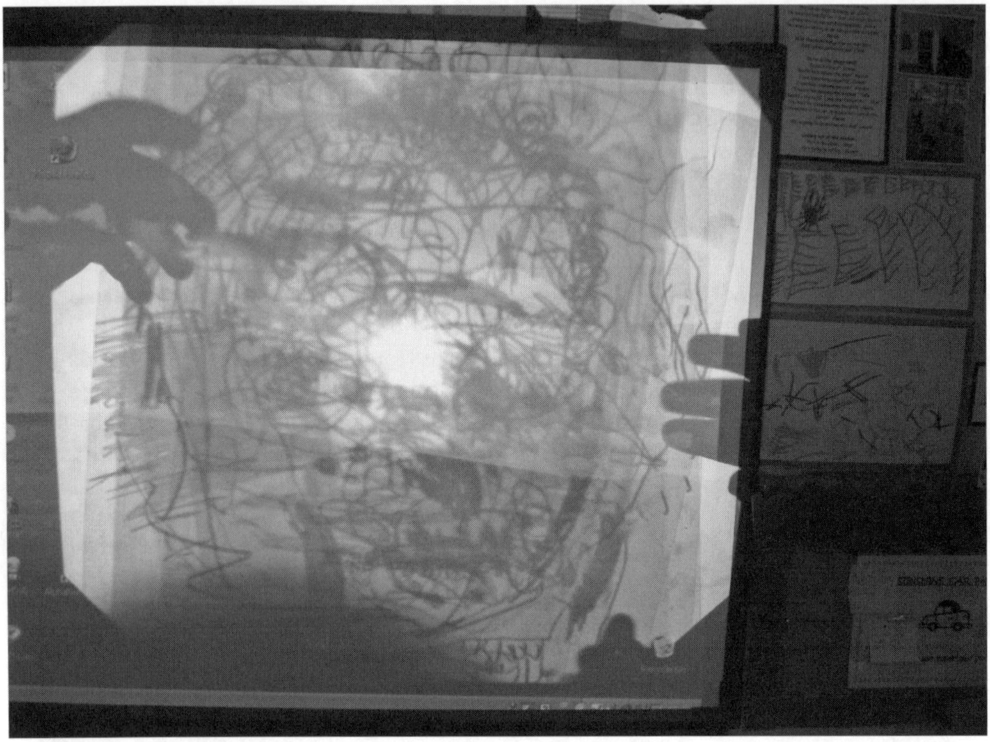

Figure 9.4 Projecting images

During a Creative Partnership-funded artist-in-residency project, Echo, one artist commented on the professional and respectful reciprocal exchange between herself and the practitioner she was working with during a residency:

> I can safely say that the ideas that we came up with together (and through reflecting on the children's ideas and interests) were far more interesting and stimulating than ideas that we had separately. Of course, developing ideas in this way took time; we spent time before the session to recap on what we were about to do, and followed up at the end, reflecting on what had worked, how the children had responded and where we might take the activities the following time. In between, I developed the ideas for the session and between us we collected the materials or equipment for the workshop. Sometimes, during this collection/preparation time, there would be changes due to new ideas, or a shortage or abundance of a particular material. It was very important to have the time before the session to establish what was actually going to happen, compared to what had been planned at the end of the last session. If there were big changes, I discussed these with the nurseries during the week and we came up with alternatives to the original idea.
>
> There was a large degree of experimentation in the workshops, and this became more so throughout the workshops. I think that as we worked together, we built up

trust and knowledge of how each of us worked, which allowed us to take more risks, to ask more questions about 'What would happen if . . .?' This made it exciting for me; finding out with the children and the teachers/staff about what they found interesting and exciting was a fascinating journey.

The legacy

The following case study (Box 9.2) examines the importance of 'legacy' – what is left as a lasting impression and influence on art practice for all involved once the residency and outreach project has finished. The busy and vibrant energy of workshops, dialogues, exchanges of ideas must not just be contained within the days of the artist's physical presence – this is akin to art days in school that supposedly represent the art curriculum for a whole term's work. The legacy must grow out of the artist-based project and evolve with time, long after its visible completion.

All projects will differ in process, results and longevity of impression. What they all have in common is the child, the practitioner and the artist. If the project is embracing of the entire community, families can also participate and reflect upon experiences outside of the everyday. Experiences will always be subjective

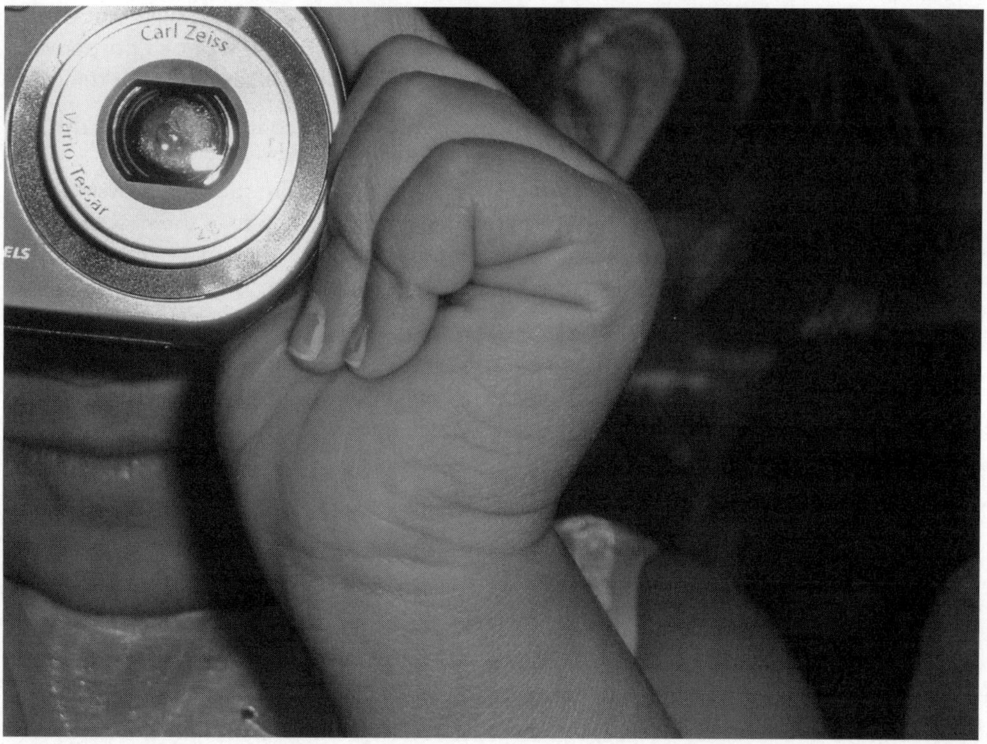

Figure 9.5 Taking photographs

Box 9.2 London Children's Museum and Comet Nursery – creating different worlds

By Vicky Cave, artist

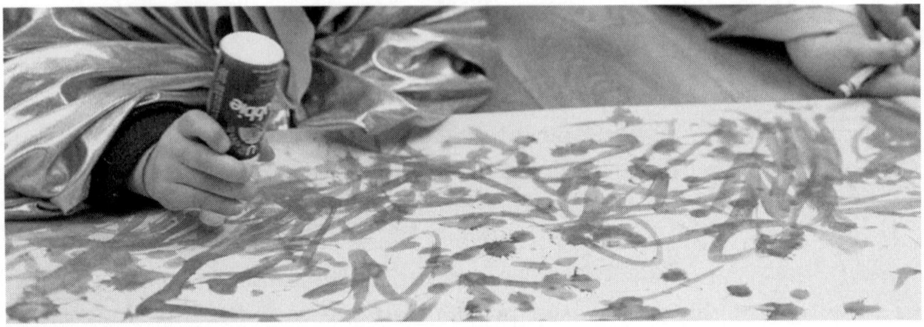

Figure 9.6 Work on one part of a giant floor painting

At Comet Nursery in Hackney a study had arisen for the adults to explore the different types of experiences that children enjoyed, and to find out how they responded to different sensory explorations. The children collaborated to make a giant floor painting, and then used masking tape and newspaper to create a whole environment in which they could play. I showed them some simple skills, such as how to stick one end of the tape to the wall and another to the wall or floor; how to stick on the newspaper; different ways to tear the paper to create different things.

It became apparent, early on, that the children loved taking control of building their own environment – they stretched masking tape across the room, fastening it on to different pieces of furniture or walls. They could then easily stick the newspaper on and create walls, doorways, windows and letterboxes. They tore the newspaper into strips so that they could make things to push through. They made 'fringes' by tearing strips into the sheets of paper and hanging them from the tape.

Masking tape makes a great sticking material, as it can be torn. The children loved experimenting with the masking tape and learning to tear it instead of cutting it. They used it in many different ways; stretching from the wall to the floor and sticking crayons onto it; wrapping toys and attaching them to the structure; putting it over their mouths and on their faces!

The giant floor painting underneath the structure encouraged the children to lie down, wriggle and crawl through. They gained different perspectives on the sculpture, the surrounding environment and the adults as they peeped up through the newspaper layers. One boy who was wriggling along roared like a lion, another hissed like a snake. They let the physicality of the space dictate their movements, which, in turn, informed the roles that they took on and the stories that they began to construct. As well as encouraging imaginative play, the workshop prompted lively, descriptive and analytical language. The practitioners I worked with on the project noticed the following:

It definitely helped M to achieve his Speech and Language therapy target (which was to ask for help when he was stuck, instead of becoming frustrated and upset), as he was so motivated to participate that I think he said 'help me' about 20 times without any prompting!

I thought that some children were able to speak quite eloquently about what they had made, and it was really interesting to see some of their more abstract ideas in a physical form (I especially liked the indoor flower carpet and the room that was made of four-poster beds for horses).

Having created a large world which the children could inhabit, the following week, they focused on making small environments which could be a place for their favourite toy or animal to live. After reading *Cave Baby* by Emily Gravett, the children were then tasked with creating their own world in a box. Each child was given a box and there was a range of different materials for them to choose from: fur of different lengths, colours and textures, shiny fabric, gold material, feathers, pompoms, patterned paper, as well as a range of fixing methods (clothes pegs, masking tape, glue). The children sat on the floor to make their creations and as they created

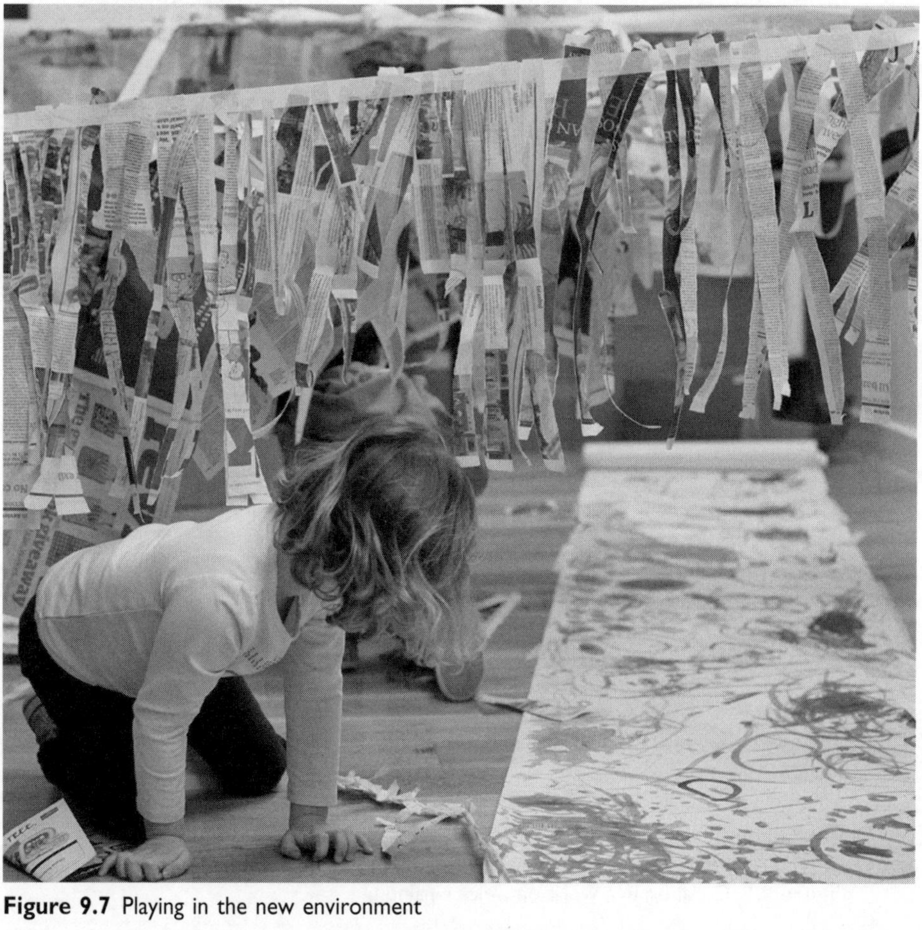

Figure 9.7 Playing in the new environment

they developed their ideas and talked about who lived there, what was in the space and what they did there. The adults helped them with some cutting and talked to them about what they were making and their ideas. As each child finished their world, they started to play with it. The children found small-world-play characters and vehicles and added these into their play. These familiar items seemed to enrich, extend and deepen their play.

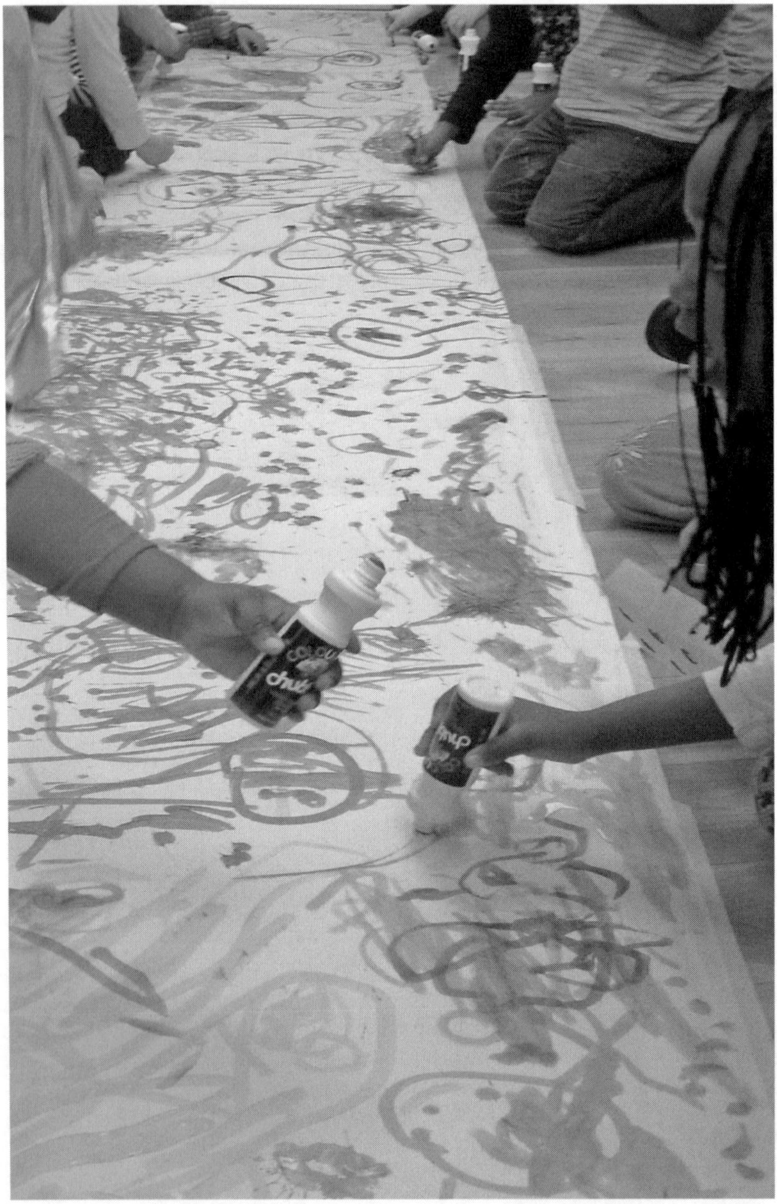

Figure 9.8 Collaborative work on a floor painting

The legacy of these worlds

The boxes that the children transformed into rooms and a building remained in the nursery for weeks after:

> Every day it would generate lots of discussion as the children came into school (we stapled it onto a noticeboard by the entrance to make a multi-room building).
>
> It definitely inspired lots of ideas for creative work in the studio – one boy involved in the sessions went on to make an amazing bat cave, with 3D Batman, Batmobile etc. all cut out of card and stuck in place – even with stalactites and bats dangling from the ceiling.
>
> (Vicky Colbourne, Comet Nursery, Hackney)

Building on the experiences that had taken place

The nursery staff was involved in the sessions and saw how the children became excited and engaged. Based on the level of enthusiasm for the work that had taken place, the nursery incorporated ideas from the sessions in its planning and focussed its work around 'homes' for a couple of weeks afterwards. They used similar techniques as used in the sessions, carrying on using the boxes and fabrics to create a range of different homes for different characters. They also had enjoyed the range of materials brought in such as the furs and silky fabrics and spent more time getting more fabrics, such as fur, animal prints, camouflage netting, psychedelic patterns and day-glo colours which they used to create small spaces and dens or change small areas, and then used these spaces as places to play in or relax.

> The paper cave eventually moved outside and we hung it from the trees and plants in the garden where it was turned into a jungle by the children!
>
> (Early years practitioner)

in their dynamics, though responding to a generically visible impetus. The intersubjectivity, as discussed in Chapter 5 when we examined the role of the adult, is a key aspect of artists and their relationships with all the members of the setting's community. Through practical involvement, shared dialogues, collaborative reflection and agreed continuation, there will exist a reciprocal flow of human thought, critical and creative in its nature and grace.

The longevity derives from a collaborative commitment to continue with the successful features of an artist-based project, and, of course, a part of this collaboration lies with the involvement of parents, carers and the family that surrounds the child participants. A family dynamic in a project ensures continuity between art in the setting and art at home, as examined in Chapter 8. When collaborative artists-in-residence embrace parent participation, there will exist a sense of excitement and pride for the entire community of a setting and a legacy will result from such cooperative exhilaration where participants wish to prolong and extend that positive involvement. Artist Jane Gordon of one of the 'Open Sesame' workshops reflected on this aspect in her evaluation of the project:

> The nursery staff were really good at raising awareness of the project with the parents, and the children had been sharing what they had been doing over the weeks. They put up images and information on display boards throughout. Many parents made cakes which were then sold at the open day, raising money for the nursery.
>
> We opened up the garden and had a few examples of things that we had been exploring through the project. The trees that were made were on display in the garden and I was able to chat with the parents about what their children had been involved with . . . The families hung out and the children played and it was a very sociable event. The parents that came were really interested in the creative journeys their children had been on and many commented on how their children had been talking about the project outside the nursery.

Throughout many artist-in-residency projects, there also remains a relational parallel with regards to the 'artist'. A project will define the various artists involved, from the children as artists, to the professional as artist and the practitioners supporting the overarching artistic journey of the setting as a whole. All these dynamics will converge, diverge, poke and prod at each other throughout the course of a project. It is this at times haphazard and creatively chaotic character of an artist-based project which produces such richly varied and vicarious processes and outcomes.

Conclusion

The longevity of an artist-driven initiative represents, importantly, the ownership of the child and the gems and momentary treasures that remain with them and infect and affect their growing repertoire of skills and knowledge as young artists. If a child is exposed only once to the thoughts, skills and perspectives of one artist in their school life, this alone will enhance their capabilities to be critical agents. Engagement with an artist 'in the flesh' brings to life a cultural perspective where the child can explore parameters of an art form and point of view as an active participant, not a passive consumer (Lynch, 2013).

Reflection

- Research your wider setting community for potential visitors who can visit and offer cultural and artist-led projects.
- Consider opportunities that would benefit from the inclusion of a visiting artist.
- Ensure you discuss as a team of staff how to retain and utilise the outcomes and findings of artist-based projects and visits in order to hold onto the legacy.

Further reading

Early Arts: www.EarlyArts.co.uk

Fawcett, M. and Hay, P. (2004) 5x5x5 Creativity in the Early Years, *International Journal of Art and Design Education*, 23(3): 234–45.

Open Sesame: Early Years Creativity Toolkit (2012) West Sussex County Council.

Rinaldi, C. (2006) 'Documentation and research', in *In Dialogue with Reggio Emilia: Listening, Researching and Learning*, Oxon: Routledge.

Further reading

Bibliography

Abbs, P. (1994) *The Educational Imperative: A Defence of Socratic and Aesthetic Learning*, Brighton: Falmer Press.

Abbs, P. (2003) *Against the Flow: Education, the Arts and Postmodern Culture*, London: Routledge.

Adams, E. (2003a) *Drawing Inspiration 1, 2, and 3*, Drawing Power, London: Central Books.

Adams, E. (2003b) *Power Drawing*, Drawing Power, London: Central Books.

Adams, E. (2003c) *Start Drawing*, Drawing Power, London: Central Books.

Adams, E. and Chisholm, T. (1999) 'Art, design and environment: A programme for teacher education', *Journal of Art and Design Education*, 18(3): 337–44.

Adams, K., Hyde, B. and Woolley, R. (2008) *The Spiritual Dimension of Childhood*, London: Jessica Kingsley.

Allen-Harris, J. (2008) *Street Art: Joshua Allen Harris' Inflatable Bag Monsters, New York Magazine*, retrieved from www.youtube.com/watch?v=PH6xCT2aTSo&list=TLRsWX2QQpLhRFMuBu6BXgyTMpI76CZTZI

Anning, A. (2002) 'Conversations around young children's drawings: The impact of the beliefs of significant others at home and school', *Journal of Art and Design Education*, 21(3): 197–208.

Anning, A. and Ring, K. (2004) *Making Sense of Children's Drawings*, Maidenhead: Open University Press.

Arnold, C. (2010) *Understanding Schemas and Emotion in Early Education*, London: Sage.

Athey, C. (2007) *Extending Thought in Young Children*, second edn, London: Paul Chapman.

Barnes, R. (2006) *Teaching Art to Young Children 4–9*, second edn, Oxon: Routledge Falmer.

Beckley, P., Elvidge, K. and Hendry, H. (2009) *Implementing the Early Years Foundation Stage: A Handbook*, Maidenhead: Open University Press.

Bendon, A. and Tydeman, K. (eds) (2007) *Art in the Early Years*, Suffolk: Suffolk County Council Publications.

Bibliography

Bloomfield, A. and Childs, J. (2000) *Teaching Integrated Arts in the Primary School: Dance, Drama, Music and Visual Arts*, London: David Fulton.

Bowden, J. (2006) *The Primary Art and Design Subject Leaders' Handbook*, Wilts: NSEAD.

British Association for Early Education (2012) *Development Matters in the EYFS*, London: Early Education.

Broadhead, P. (2004) *Early Years Play and Learning*, London: RoutledgeFalmer.

Broadhead, P. (2006) 'Developing an understanding of young children's learning through play: The place of observation, interaction and reflection', *British Educational Research Journal*, 32(2), April: 191–207.

Broadhead. P (2012) Address at 'How children learn: Exploring the importance of creativity throughout the early years' conference, September, Aston University, Birmingham.

Brockes, E. (2013) 'Carl Andre: "I'm a hopeless drawer – and a terrible painter"', *Guardian*, 23 January, retrieved from www.theguardian.com/artanddesign/2013/jan/23/carl-andre-turner-contemporary.

Bruce, T. (2001) *Learning Through Play*, London: Hodder and Stoughton.

Bruner, J. (1986) *Actual Minds, Possible Words*, Cambridge, MA: Harvard University Press.

Bruner, J. (2004) Video address at opening session of Crossing Boundaries International Conference, February, Reggio Emilia.

Brunton, P. and Thornton, L. (2009) *Understanding the Reggio Approach*, second edn, Oxon: Routledge.

Brunton, P. and Thornton, L. (2010) *Science in the Early Years*, London: Sage.

Bryce-Clegg, A. (2012) *From Vacant To Engaged: Putting Child-led Learning at the Heart of Your Planning*, London: Featherstone Education.

Buckler, L. (2009) *The Inspired Child*, Hereford: Berrington Press.

Callaway, G. and Kear, M. (1999) *Teaching Art and Design in the Primary School*, London: David Fulton.

Cavazzoni, P. (2012) 'What is a Child?' Paper presented at University of Winchester, November 2012.

Ceppi, G. and Zini, M. (eds) (1998) *Children, Spaces, Relations: Metaproject for an Environment for Young Children*, Reggio Emilia, Italy: Reggio Children Publishers.

Chilvers, D. (2012) 'What does "creating and thinking critically" mean?', *Early Years Update*, 9: 5–7.

Clarke, M. (2007) *Involving Parents in their Children's Learning*, London: Sage.

Claxton, G. (2002) 'What's the Big Idea?', *The Observer*, 22 September.

Claxton, G. (2005) 'Mindfulness, Learning and the Brain', *Journal of Rational-Emotive and Cognitive Behaviour Therapy*, 23: 301–14.

Claxton, G. (2006a) 'Nirvana and neuroscience: The self-liberating brain', in Nauriyal, D. K., Drummond, M. S. and Lal, S. B. (eds), *Buddhist Thought and Applied Psychological Research*, London: Routledge, pp. 93–111.

Claxton, G. (2006b) 'Thinking at the edge: Developing soft creativity', *Cambridge Journal of Education*, 3: 351–62.

Claxton, G. (2007) 'Expanding young people's capacity to learn', *British Journal of Educational Studies*, 55: 1–20.

Clement, R. (1993) *The Art Teacher's Handbook*, Cheltenham: Stanley Thornes.

Clough, P. (2007a) *Clay in the Primary School*, London: A&C Black.

Clough, P. (2007b) *Sculptural Materials in the Classroom*, London: A&C Black.

Coates, E. (2002) '"I forgot the sky!" Children's stories contained within their drawings', *International Journal of Early Years Education*, 10(1): 21–35.

Coates, E. and Coates, A. (2006) 'Young children talking and drawing', *International Journal of Early Years Education*, 14(3): 221–41.

Cote, C. and Golbeck, S. (2007) 'Pre-schoolers' feature placement on own and others' person drawings', *International Journal of Early Years Education*, 15(3): 231–43.

Cox, M. (1992) *Children's Drawings*, London: Penguin.

Cox, S. (2005) 'Intention and meaning in young children's drawing', *International Journal of Art and Design Education*, 24(2): 115–25.

Cox, S. and Watts, R. (eds) (2007) *Teaching Art and Design 3–11*, London: Continuum.

Craft, A. (2002) *Creativity and Early Years Education*, London: Continuum.

Craft, A. (2005) 'Changes in the landscape for creativity in education', in Wilson, A. (ed.) *Creativity in Primary Education*, Exeter: Learning Matters.

Craft, A., Jeffrey, B. and Leibling, M. (2001) *Creativity in Education*, London: Continuum.

Curiger, B. (2010) Interview with Rachel Whiteread, 'The process of drawing is like writing a diary: It's a nice way of thinking about time passing', *Tate etc.*, 1 September.

Dahlberg, G. and Moss, P. (2005) *Ethics and Politics in Early Childhood Education*, London: Routledge Falmer.

Davies, C. (2012) *Creating Multi-sensory Environments*, Oxon: Routledge.

DCSF (2008) *Early Years Foundation Stage Statutory Framework*, Nottingham: DCSF Publications.

Department for Education (DfE) (2012) *Statutory Framework for the Early Years Foundation Stage*, London: DfE.

Dewey, J. (1934) *Art as Experience*, New York: Penguin Group (USA).

DfEE (1999) *The National Curriculum*, London: HMSO.

Dixon, P. (2004) *Let Me Be*, Slough: Peche Luna Publishers.

Dowling, M. (2005) *Young Children's Personal, Social and Emotional Development*, London: Paul Chapman.

Drake, J. (2009) *Planning for Children's Play and Learning*, Oxon: Routledge.

Duffy, B. (1998) *Supporting Creativity and Imagination in the Early Years*, Maidenhead: Open University Press.

Duffy, B. (2006) *Supporting Creativity and Imagination in the Early Years*, second edn, Maidenhead: Open University Press.

Eglinton, K. A. (2003) *Art in the Early Years*, Oxon: Routledge.

Bibliography

Eisner, E. W. (2002) *The Arts and the Creation of Mind*, Yale: Yale University Press.

Eisner, E. W. (2005) 'Reimaging Schools', *The Selected Works of Elliot. W. Eisner*, Oxon: Routledge.

Fawcett, M. and Hay, P. (2004) '5x5x5 Creativity in the Early Years', *International Journal of Art and Design Education*, 23(3): 234–45.

Filippini, T. and Vecchi, V. (eds) (1996) *The Hundred Languages of Children*, Reggio Emilia, Italy: Reggio Children Publishers.

Fisher, J. (2010) *Moving on to Key Stage 1*, Maidenhead: Open University Press.

Gandini, L. (ed.) (2005) *In the Spirit of the Studio*, New York: Teachers' College Press.

Gardner, H. (1980) *Artful Scribbles*, New York: Basic Books.

Gendlin, E. T. (2004) Introduction to 'Thinking at the edge', *The Folio: A Journal for Focusing and Experiential Therapy*, 19: 1–8.

Gentle, K. (1985) *Children and Art Teaching*, Kent: Croom Helm.

Gentle, K. (1993) *Teaching Painting in the Primary School*, London: Cassell.

Giuidici, C. and Vecchi, V. (2004) *Children, Art, Artists*, Reggio Emilia, Italy: Reggio Children Publishers.

Goddard-Blythe, S. (2004) *Well Balanced Child*, Stroud: Hawthorn Press.

Goldsworthy, A. (2001) Andy Goldsworthy in conversation with Conrad Bodman, curator at the Barbican Arts Centre. Interview produced by the Barbican to mark Goldsworthy's 'Snowballs in Summer' project. Copyright Andy Goldsworthy 2000. Retrieved from http://lindaweintraub.com/andy-goldsworthy-anthropocentriceco centric-beauty

Gopnik, A., Meltzoff, A. and Kuhl, P. (1999) *How Babies Think*, London: Orion Books.

Gopnik, A., Meltzoff, A. and Kuhl, P. (2001) *The Scientist in the Crib*, New York: HarperCollins.

Gormley, A. (2012) 'From Hare to Hytner: Leading cultural figures oppose the EBacc', *The Guardian*, 15 December.

Gussin Paley, V. (2004) *A Child's Work*, Chicago: University of Chicago Press.

Hall, E. (2009) 'Mixed messages: The role and value of drawing in early education', *International Journal of Early Years Education*, 17(3): 179–90.

Hallett, E. (2013) *The Reflective Early Years Practitioner*, London: Sage.

Hart, T. (2003) *The Secret Spiritual World of Children*, Novato, CA: New World Library.

Herne, S., Cox, S. and Watts, R. (eds) (2009) *Readings in Primary Art Education*, Bristol: Intellect Books.

Hickman, R. (2005) *Why We Make Art and Why it is Taught*, Bristol: Intellect Books.

Hopperstad, M. (2008) 'Relationships between children's drawing and accompanying peer interaction in teacher-initiated drawing sessions', *International Journal of Early Years Education*, 16(2): 133–50.

House, R. (ed.) (2011) *Too Much, Too Soon*, Stroud: Hawthorn Press.

Hoyuelos, A. (2004) Address at Crossing Boundaries International Conference, February, Reggio Emilia, Italy.

Karmiloff-Smith, A. (2013) 'The Life Scientific', BBC Radio 4, 22 January.

Kelly, D., D. (2004) *Uncovering the History of Children's Drawings and Art.* Westport: Prager.

Kendrick, M. and McKay, R. (2004) 'Drawings as an alternative way of understanding young children's constructions of literacy', *Journal of Early Childhood Literacy,* 4(1): 109–28.

Key, P. and Stillman, J. (2009) *Teaching Primary Art and Design,* Exeter: Learning Matters.

Kimes-Myers, B. (1997) *Young Children and Spirituality,* New York: Routledge.

Kolbe, U. (2001) *Rapunzel's Supermarket,* Byron Bay, Australia: Peppinot Press.

Kolbe, U. (2005) *It's Not a Bird, Yet,* Byron Bay, Australia: Peppinot Press.

Kress, G. (1977) *Before Writing: Rethinking the Paths to Literacy,* London: Routledge.

Kudryavtsev. V. (2011) 'The phenomenon of child creativity', *International Journal of Early Years Education,* 19(1): 45–53.

Lambert, E. (2005) 'Children's drawing and painting from a cognitive perspective: A longitudinal study', *Early Years Journal of International Research and Development,* 25(3): 249–69.

Lancaster, J. (1990) *Art in the Primary School,* London: Routledge.

Levy, R. (2012). Address at 'How Children Learn: exploring the importance of creativity throughout the Early Years' conference. September 2012. Birmingham: Aston University.

Lewis, C. S. (1998) *The Lion, The Witch and the Wardrobe,* London: HarperCollins.

Lindqvist, G. (2001) 'When small children play: How adults dramatise and children create meaning', *Early Years,* 21(1): 7–14.

Litman, J. and Spielberger, C. D. (2003) 'Measuring epistemic curiosity and its diversive and specific components', *Journal of Personality Assessment,* 80: 175–86.

Litman, J., Hutchins, T. and Russon, R. (2005) 'Epistemic curiosity, feeling-of-knowing, and exploratory behaviour', *Cognition and Emotion,* 19(4): 559–82.

Lowenfeld, V. (1957) *Creative and Mental Growth,* third edn, London: Macmillan.

Lubin, A. (2011) Exhibition text (22 December) by Curator of 'Gideon Gechtman and Tomer Sapir' exhibition, Sommer Art Gallery, Tel Aviv.

Lynch, B. (2013) 'Whose cake is it anyway?', Keynote address at Artsaward regional conference, Cornerstone Arts Centre, Didcot, May 2013.

McInally, M. (2003) *Children's Art,* Devon: Southgate Publishers.

Macintyre, C. (2012) *Enhancing Learning Through Play,* Oxon: Routledge.

Mairs, K. (2013) *Young Children Learning through Schema,* Oxon: Routledge.

Malaguzzi, L. (1998) 'History, ideas and basic philosophy', in Edwards, C., Gandini, L. and Forman, G. (eds) *The Hundred Languages of Children: The Reggio Emilia Approach – Advanced Reflections,* second edn, Stamford, CT: Albex, pp. 49–97.

Malloch, S. and Trevarthen, C. (2010) *Communicative Musicality: Exploring the Basis of Human Companionship,* Oxford: Oxford University Press.

Martindale, C. (1995) 'Creativity and connectionism', in Smith, S. M., Ward, T. B. and Finke, R. A. (eds) *The Creative Cognition Approach,* Cambridge, MA: MIT Press.

Matthews, J. (1994) *Helping Young Children to Paint and Draw: Children and Visual Representation*, London: Hodder and Stoughton.

Matthews, J. (1999) *The Art of Childhood and Adolescence*, London: Falmer Press.

Matthews, J. (2003) *Drawing and Painting: Children and Visual Representation*, London: Paul Chapman.

Matthews, J. and Seow, P. (2007) 'Electronic paint: Understanding children's representation through their Interactions with digital paint', *International Journal of Art and Design Education*, 26(3): 251–62.

May, P., Ashford, E. and Bottle, G. (2006) *Sound Beginnings, Learning and Development in the Early Years*, London: David Fulton.

Meager, N. (1993) *Teaching Art at Key Stage 1*, Wiltshire: NSEAD.

Medina, J. (2008) *Brain Rules*, Seattle: Pear Press.

Merry, R., Wei, Z. and Rogers, J. (2006) 'What's got two heads and no nose? Young British and Chinese children's representations of unreality', *Early Years Journal of International Research and Development*, 26(2): 143–58.

Mindham, C. (2005) 'Creativity and the young child', *Early Years – Journal of International Research and Development*, 25(1): 81–4.

Montessori, M. (1995) *The Absorbent Mind*, Carlsbad, CA: Holt, Rinehart and Winston.

Moore, C. (2013) Address at Artsaward regional conference, Cornerstone Arts Centre, Didcot, May 2013.

Morgan, M. and Robinson, G. (1997) *Developing the Art Experience*, Oxford: Nash Pollock Publishing.

Moss, P. (2004) Address at Crossing Boundaries International Conference, February, Reggio Emilia, Italy.

Moss, P. (2012) *Early Childhood and Compulsory Education: Reconceptualising the Relationship (Contesting Early Childhood)*, London: Routledge.

Moyles, J. (1994) *The Excellence of Play*, Buckingham: Open University Press.

Moyles, J. (2008) 'Empowering children and adults: Play and child-initiated learning', in *Like Bees not Butterflies*, London: A&C Black.

Neill, A. and Ridley, A. (2002) *Arguing About Art*, London: Routledge.

North Lincolnshire Council (2007) *The Atelier . . . An Invitation to Explore Young Children's Thinking and Creativity*, Lutterworth: Featherstone Education.

Nutbrown, C. (2006) *Threads of Thinking*, third edn, London: Sage.

Ofili, C. (2009) 'A Door to Freedom', *The Observer*, 20 September, retrieved from www.theguardian.com/artanddesign/2009/sep/20/chris-ofili-guide-to-painting

Oldfield, L. (2011) 'The Steiner Waldorf Foundation Stage: "To Everything there is a Season"', in House, R. (ed.) *Too Much, Too Soon*, Stroud: Hawthorn Press.

Palmer, S. (2008) 'An Inconvenient Truth', in Featherstone, S. and Featherstone, P. (eds) *Like Bees not Butterflies*, London: A & C Black.

Pascal, C. and Bertram, T. (2001) *Effective Early Learning, Case Studies in Improvement*, London: Paul Chapman.

Pascal, C. and Bertram, T. (2003) 'The quality of adult engagement in early childhood settings in the UK', in Laevers, F. and Heylen, L. (eds) *Involvement of Children and Teacher Style*, Leuven: Leuven University Press.

Pavlou, V. (2009) 'Understanding young children's three-dimensional creative potential in art making', *International Journal of Art and Design Education*, 28(2): 139–50.

Penny, S., Ford, R., Price, L. and Young, S. (2002) *Achieving QTS: Teaching Arts in Primary Schools*, Exeter: Learning Matters.

Phillips, A. (2009) *Imagine – Art is Child's Play*, BBC1, 22 June 2012.

Piaget, J. (2001 [1950]) *The Psychology of Intelligence*, London: Routledge.

Picchio, M., Giovannini, D., Mayer, S. and Musatti, T. (2012) 'Documentation and analysis of children's experience: An ongoing collegial activity for early childhood professionals in Early Years', *An International Journal of Research and Development*, 32(2): 159–70.

Prentice, R. (1994) 'Experiential learning in play and art', in Moyles, J. (ed.) *The Excellence of Play*, Bucks: Open University Press.

Prentice, R. (ed.) (1995) *Teaching Art and Design*, London: Cassell.

Prentice, R. (1999) 'Art: Visual thinking' in Riley, J. and Prentice, R. (eds) *The Curriculum for 7–11-Year Olds*, London: Paul Chapman, pp. 146–64.

Qualifications and Curriculum Authority (QCA) (2000). *Curriculum Guidance for the Foundation Stage*. QCA/00/587. London: QCA.

Reddy, V. (2010) *How Infants Know Minds*, Cambridge, MA: Harvard University Press.

Rinaldi, C. (2006) 'Documentation and research', in *In Dialogue with Reggio Emilia: Listening, Researching and Learning*, Oxon: Routledge.

Ring, K. (2006) 'What mothers do: Everyday routines and rituals and their impact upon young children's use of drawing for meaning making', *International Journal of Early Years Education*, 14(1): 63–84.

Robinson, K. (1999) *All Our Futures: Creativity, Culture and Education*, London: DfEE.

Robinson, K. (2001) *Out of Our Minds: Learning to Be Creative*, Chichester: Capstone Publishing.

Robinson, K. (2006) 'How schools kill creativity', TED talk, February 2006, retrieved from www.ted.com/talks/ken_robinson_says_schools_kill_creativity.html

Robson, S. (2006) *Developing Thinking and Understanding in Young Children*, London: Routledge.

Robson, S. (2012) *Developing Thinking and Understanding in Young Children*, Oxon: Routledge.

Rutanen, N. (2012) 'Socio-spatial practices in a Finnish daycare group for one-to-three-year-olds in Early Years', *An International Journal of Research and Development*, 32(2): 201–14.

Salaman, A. and Tutchell, S. (2005) *Planning Educational Visits for the Early Years*, London: Sage.

Salmon, P. (1995) *Psychology in the Classroom*, London: Cassell.

Schirrmacher, R. (1986) 'Talking with young children about their art', in *Young Children*, 4(5): 3–7.

Sedgwick, D. and Sedgwick, F. (1993) *Drawing to Learn*, London: Hodder and Stoughton.

Sedgwick, F. (2002) *Enabling Children's Learning Through Drawing*, London: David Fulton.

Shahn, B. (1967) *The Shape of Content*, Cambridge, MA: Harvard University Press.

Sharan, S. and Sharan, Y. (1992) *Expanding Cooperative Learning through Group Investigation*, New York: Teachers' College Press.

Sharp, C. (2004) 'Developing young children's creativity: What can we learn from research?', Topic, *NFER Journal*, 32: 5–12.

Siegesmund, R. (1998) 'Why do we teach art today?', *Studies in Art Education, A Journal of Issues and Research*, 39(3): 197–214, Washington: National Art Education Association.

Simpson, K. (2011) 'The unfolding self: The essence of personality', in House, R. (ed.) *Too Much, Too Soon*, Stroud: Hawthorn Press.

Siraj-Blatchford, I. (2007) 'Creativity, communication and collaboration: The identification of pedagogic progression in sustained shared thinking', *Asia-Pacific Journal of Research in Early Childhood Education*, 1(2): 3–23.

Siraj-Blatchford, I. (2009) 'Conceptualising progression in the pedagogy of play and sustained shared thinking in early childhood education: A Vygotskian perspective', *Educational and Child Psychology*, 26(2): 77–89.

Siraj-Blatchford, I. and Manni, L. (2008) '"Would you like to tidy up now?" An analysis of adult questioning in the English Foundation Stage', *Early Years: An International Journal of Research and Development*, 28(1): 5–22.

Siraj-Blatchford, I., Sylva, K., Muttock, S., Gilden, R., and Bell, D. (2002). *Researching Effective Pedagogy in the Early Years (REPEY): DfES Research Report 356*, London: DfES, HMSO.

Skinner, S. (2007) *Creative Activities for the Early Years*, London: Sage.

Statham, J. (2011) *Grandparents Providing Child Care: Briefing Paper*. London: Childhood Wellbeing Research Centre.

Stephen, C. (2010) 'Pedagogy: The silent partner in early years learning', *Early Years: An International Research Journal*, 30(1): 15–28.

Strozzi, P. and Vecchi, V. (eds) (2002) *Advisories*, Reggio Emilia, Italy: Reggio Children Publishers.

Sylva, K., Melhuish, E., Sammons, P., Siraj-Blatchford, I. and Taggart, B. (2003) *Effective Provision of Pre-School Education (EPPE) Project*, London: DfES Publications.

Thornton, L. and Brunton, P. (2009a) *Making the Most of Light and Mirrors*, London: A&C Black.

Thornton, L. and Brunton, P. (2009b) *Understanding the Reggio Approach*, Oxon: David Fulton.

Trevarthen, C. and Aitken, K. J. (2001) 'Infant intersubjectivity: Research, theory, and clinical applications', *Journal of Child Psychology and Psychiatry*, 42(1): 3–48.

Tutchell, S. (1998) *Collaboration in Art – Young Children Working Together*, MA dissertation, Institute of Education, University of London.

Vecchi, V. (2010) *Art and Creativity in Reggio Emilia: Exploring the Role and Potential of Ateliers in Early Childhood Education (Contesting Early Childhood)*, Oxon: Routledge.

Vygotsky, L. (1962) *Thought and Language*, Cambridge, MA: MIT Press.

Vygotsky, L. (1978) *Mind in Society*, Cambridge, MA: Harvard University Press.

Wagoner, B. (2008) 'Making the familiar unfamiliar', *Journal of Culture and Psychology*, 14: 467–74.

Waite, S. (2011) *Children Learning Outside the Classroom*, London: Sage.

Waters, S. (1994) *Living Without Boundaries*, Bath: BCHE Press.

Watkins, M. (1998) *Artworks*, London: LBTH Learning Design.

Watts, A. (2011) *Every Nursery Needs a Garden*, Oxon: Routledge.

Watts, R. (2005) 'Attitudes to making art in the primary school', *International Journal of Art and Design Education*, 24(3): 243–53.

Wheatley, M. J. (1999) *Leadership and the New Science: Discovering Order in a Chaotic World*, San Francisco, CA: Berrett-Koehler.

White, J. (2008) *Playing and Learning Outdoors: Making Provision for High-Quality Experiences in Indoor Environments*, Oxon: Routledge.

White, J. (2010) 'Gardens of delight', *Early Years Educator Magazine*, 11(10): 5.

Williams-Siegfredsen, J. (2012) *Understanding the Danish Forest School Approach*, Oxon: Routledge.

Wilson, B. and Wilson, M. (1977) 'An iconoclastic view of the imagery sources in the drawings of young people', *Art Education*, 30: 4–12.

Winner, E. (1989) 'How can Chinese children draw so well?', *Journal of Aesthetic Education*, 23(1): 41–63.

Wright, S. (2010) *Understanding Creativity in Early Childhood*, London: Sage.

Wroe, N. (2012) 'Thomas Heatherwick: The new Leonardo of design', *Guardian*, 12 May, retrieved from www.theguardian.com/artanddesign/2012/may/18/thomas-heatherwick-da-vinci-design

Index

Note: figures and tables are referenced in **bold**.

Index